International Perspectives on Early Childhood Education and Development

Volume 24

Early childhood education in many countries has been built upon a strong tradition of a materially rich and active play-based pedagogy and environment. Yet what has become visible within the profession, is essentially a Western view of childhood preschool education and school education.

It is timely that a series of books be published which present a broader view of early childhood education. This series seeks to provide an international perspective on early childhood education. In particular, the books published in this series will:

- Examine how learning is organized across a range of cultures, particularly Indigenous communities
- Make visible a range of ways in which early childhood pedagogy is framed and enacted across countries, including the majority poor countries
- Critique how particular forms of knowledge are constructed in curriculum within and across countries
- Explore policy imperatives which shape and have shaped how early childhood education is enacted across countries
- Examine how early childhood education is researched locally and globally
- Examine the theoretical informants driving pedagogy and practice, and seek to find alternative perspectives from those that dominate many Western heritage countries
- Critique assessment practices and consider a broader set of ways of measuring children's learning
- Examine concept formation from within the context of country-specific pedagogy and learning outcomes

The series covers theoretical works, evidence-based pedagogical research, and international research studies. The series will also cover a broad range of countries, including poor majority countries. Classical areas of interest, such as play, the images of childhood, and family studies will also be examined. However the focus is critical and international (not Western-centric).

More information about this series at http://www.springer.com/series/7601

Linda Mitchell

Democratic Policies and Practices in Early Childhood Education

An Aotearoa New Zealand Case Study

 Springer

Linda Mitchell
Faculty of Education
The University of Waikato
Hamilton, Waikato, New Zealand

ISSN 2468-8746   ISSN 2468-8754   (electronic)
International Perspectives on Early Childhood Education and Development
ISBN 978-981-13-1791-0   ISBN 978-981-13-1793-4   (eBook)
https://doi.org/10.1007/978-981-13-1793-4

Library of Congress Control Number: 2018957464

This Springer imprint is published by the registered company Springer Nature Singapore Pte Ltd.
The registered company address is: 152 Beach Road, #21-01/04 Gateway East, Singapore 189721, Singapore

Foreword

Towards New Political Times

This book makes a fresh contribution to international early childhood policy discourses. Early childhood policy and pedagogy in Aotearoa New Zealand has, over several decades, created interest in international arenas, and aspects of the story have been selectively documented. Linda Mitchell's book is timely, presenting a comprehensive case study analysis, illustrative of wider arguments and viewpoints concerning childhood, democracy and the institutions of care and education of young children. This is an international book with global messages, but with exemplars originating in the Antipodean Pacific, distant in geography and culture from Western sites of early childhood discourses. The exemplars stem variously from research projects, policy initiatives, pedagogical innovation, advocacy and protest. The combination of pedagogy, policy, protest, politics and research, as a linked analysis, is a significant contribution to policy discourses. Linda explores the interface of these domains to illustrate, for example, what democratic practice might look like and what it can achieve in terms of policy and practice.

The timeframe spans Linda's own career in education and is indeed a scholarly mirror, probably not intentionally, of her own activism. But a preface writer, and long-time colleague in advocacy, can surely acknowledge Linda as a key player in both shaping early childhood policy in Aotearoa New Zealand: contesting its shortfalls and articulating new debates. This is a distinctive feature of the Aotearoa New Zealand early childhood scene and a clue to its policy successes and innovation, with players like Linda who combines long-term activism, scholarly research and writing and union activism: strategically working with government as well as, at times, sternly critiquing government.

The book was conceptualised in challenging political times amidst the third term of a conservative government that undermined and stalled earlier policy initiatives around free and universal approaches to early childhood, a pathway to 100% qualified teaching staff with equal pay and status with the other education sectors and fledgling understandings of the rights of the young citizen child. But in the late 2017, new political times emerged in Aotearoa New Zealand with the election again of a Labour-led government promising to redress earlier wrongs across the education sector. The timeliness of this book captures the dramatic turnaround in policy and opportunities ahead to again enhance "democratic policies and practices in [the] early childhood centres of Aotearoa New Zealand".

Emeritus Professor, University of Otago   Helen May
Otago, New Zealand

Contents

Introduction 1
1 Overview 2
2 The Child as Citizen 4
3 ECEC in a Mixed Market Economy 5
4 Globalisation 7
5 Why Aotearoa New Zealand as a Case Study? 9
6 A Personal Story 10
7 Layout 11
References 13

Aotearoa New Zealand Within Global Trends in ECEC Policy 17
1 Introduction 18
2 Early History of Aotearoa New Zealand 19
   2.1 Diversity of ECEC Provision 21
3 Advocacy and Participation 23
   3.1 Women's Rights and Integration of Care and Education 23
   3.2 Indigenous Rights and Self-Determination 26
4 Democracy and Social Justice in the Development
   of the Curriculum 28
5 Market Forces and New Right Economic Theories 30
6 ECEC as a Public Good and a Child's Right 33
7 Retrenchment and a Focus on Vulnerable Children 34
   7.1 Continued Growth of Market-Led Provision 35
8 Promising New Directions: The 2017 Coalition Government 36
9 Contrasting Policy Approaches: Constructs of Childhood 38
References 40

Traditions of Democracy in Education 45
1 The Case for Democracy in Education 46
2 Athenian Origins of Democracy 51
3 Transformations in the Meaning of Democracy
   and Citizenship 53

4   Recent Traditions of Democracy in Education   55
5   Democracy in Aotearoa New Zealand's Education
    Traditions and History   58
6   Conclusion   60
References...   61

Weaving a Curriculum   65
1   Te Whāriki...   66
2   Case Study: Nurturing the Mana of the Child   71
    2.1   Values and Beliefs   72
    2.2   A Project Extending Over Time and Place   74
3   Case Study: Iwi Weaving a Curriculum...   77
    3.1   Iwi Curriculum: Mana Whenua...   78
    3.2   Iwi Curriculum: Whakapapa   79
    3.3   Iwi Curriculum: Whanaungatanga   79
    3.4   Iwi Curriculum: Sharing the Kaupapa   80
4   Generating a Curriculum Whāriki and Democracy   81
5   Conclusion   83
References...   83

Assessment and Pedagogical Documentation   87
1   Introduction...   88
2   Approaches to Assessment That Have Democracy in Mind....................   92
3   Assessment to Construct and Highlight Valued Outcomes.......................   95
4   Assessment to Show and Develop Trajectories of Learning.....................   98
5   Assessments to Provide Opportunities for Self–Assessment....................   99
6   Family and Community as Contributors to Assessment...........................   101
7   Conclusion   104
References...   105

Influencing Policy Change through Collective Action   109
1   Introduction...   110
2   The Pathways to Pay Parity..   111
3   The Context and Events of the 1990s   112
    3.1   A Kindergarten Story   113
    3.2   A Childcare (Education and Care) Story   117
4   Future Directions   120
5   Conclusion   122
References...   123

Policy Frameworks and Democratic Participation....................................   125
1   Introduction...   125
2   Policy Frameworks to Support Democratic Participation
    and Pedagogy..   126
3   Strategic Plan for Early Childhood Education...   127
    3.1   Children's Access and Participation..   128
    3.2   A Qualified and Professionally Supported ECE Workforce   131

4   Teachers as Critical Thinkers... 133
5   Conclusion 140
References... 140

Conclusion 145
1   Democratic Ideals 145
2   What Conditions Supported Democratic Practices?............................... 147
3   What Conditions Supported Universal Access?...................................... 151
4   What Changes Are Needed in Aotearoa New Zealand's
    System of ECEC? 153
    4.1   Individual Practitioner Level.. 153
    4.2   Management Level... 154
    4.3   Policy Level... 154
5   A Way Forward 156
    5.1   To Improve the Social Context of Childhood 156
    5.2   To Develop a Democratic Vision for Children
          and the Aims of ECEC.. 157
    5.3   To Retain *Te Whāriki* and Sociocultural Assessment
          Approaches... 159
    5.4   To Shift from a Market Approach to a "Partnership Model"
          of ECEC Provision... 159
    5.5   To Provide Free ECEC as an Entitlement for all Children 161
    5.6   To Improve the Qualifications, Professional Support
          and Remuneration of All Staff 162
6   Conclusion 163
References... 163

Glossary of Māori Terms.. 167

Name Index.. 169

Subject Index... 173

Introduction

Political interest in early childhood education and care (ECEC) has grown in recent times, with governments and international organisations claiming benefits of ECEC to justify particular policy approaches. But increasingly, a narrow view of the purposes of ECEC is held and conveyed in policy texts as a means to address social problems, to prepare children for later academic success and as an economic investment for the good of the country. Missing in these views is an understanding of childhood as socially constructed and an important phase in its own right and of children as citizens who contribute to society. In parallel, neoliberal commitment to the market has swept countries worldwide, including the UK, the Netherlands, the USA, Canada, Australia, Aotearoa New Zealand, the African continent and the Asia Pacific region. Marketisation has had a profound effect on education and accountability systems and particularly ECEC where in many of these countries, private owners of ECEC centres have set up to produce profits for themselves and their investors from their business undertaking. Within this model, resources intended for education have been siphoned off for individual business owner and shareholder profits. Competition between ECEC centres for children has led to a highly inequitable distribution of ECEC provision, where economically richer communities and families who can pay more have been best served. A very old idea and at the same time a new idea for contemporary times are the ideas of education for democracy as an alternative and valuable way to reconceptualise ECEC. The purpose of a democratic education is directed to the good of each person and the common good for society; these purposes are mutually connected and reinforcing. Aotearoa New Zealand is offered as an interesting case study, set within these global trends, because of its extreme adoption of neoliberal principles during the 1980s and 1990s and, in contradiction, its early social justice foundations and its renowned early childhood curriculum, *Te Whāriki*. The curriculum is an inspiration worldwide for the centrality of the concept of whakamana (empowerment or agency) and commitment to biculturalism that originates from the 1840 Tiriti o Waitangi, a treaty between Māori (indigenous people) and the British crown. *Te Whāriki* sets

© Springer Nature Singapore Pte Ltd. 2019
L. Mitchell, *Democratic Policies and Practices in Early Childhood Education*,
International Perspectives on Early Childhood Education and Development 24,
https://doi.org/10.1007/978-981-13-1793-4_1

conditions for democracy to flourish. In this book, I provide examples of political advocacy, policy formulation and pedagogical practice in Aotearoa New Zealand that have resisted neoliberalism and progressed democratic ideals. At the same time, I offer examples from other countries, from which Aotearoa New Zealand has much to learn. These examples are offered, not as blueprints for others to follow, for it is not that we can copy policies and practices from one country to our own. But it gives opportunity to think differently and therefore critically, to enable us to see what we take for granted – these things are of mutual benefit in helping push forward thinking and practice.

1   Overview

This book is an exploration of possibilities for ECEC centres to be conceptualised and supported in policy and practice as sites for democratic citizenship and social justice. The need to explore ideas about the purposes of ECEC has become urgent as more children from younger ages and for longer time periods attend ECEC centres; their wellbeing is dependent on how these centres are run. Those ideas that hold dominance have consequences for policy priorities and hence for how ECEC is organised, provided and funded. In many countries, ideas conveyed by governments and international organisations about the purposes of ECEC have become dangerously narrow. ECEC is increasingly portrayed as serving parental labour force participation (children do not feature in their own right), rescuing children from disadvantage (children are objects of concern; other children do not feature) and promoting the future economic standing of the country (children's wellbeing and contribution at the time of attendance are not given priority). In line with these purposes, technical measurement of limited outcomes of education have become of predominant concern; these measures bypass wider goals for education and are used to label and classify individuals, education institutions and countries. Globally there has been a shift in many societies away from an idea of ECEC as a public good and public responsibility, towards an individualist and competitive model that is driven by the market. Marketisation has consequences for access that privilege the wealthy and dominant group, that are not responsive to diverse families and that reduce possibilities for democratic contribution. Fielding and Moss (2012, p.56) portray the distinction between a marketised system of education where schools are conceptualised as businesses and parents as consumers making individual choices, and "a democratic system of education that treats schools as public institutions and parents and children as citizens, capable of engaging in a democratic way of life and democratic forms of relationship, including participation in the making of collective choices". In this book, I argue for this alternative approach based on the idea of education for democracy. Democracy as a primary value for education raises possibilities for critical thinking about educational policy and practice and possibilities for change.

The book will be of particular interest to readers because of its use of Aotearoa New Zealand ECEC examples of advocacy, policy formulation and pedagogical practice that have worked towards possibilities for ECEC centres as democratic communities. Moss (2007, 2–3 May, p. 33) described Aotearoa New Zealand as "leading the wave" in ECEC having confronted the "wicked issues" through an integrated approach to curriculum, funding, regulations and qualifications. This book uses examples from researching curriculum, pedagogy and assessment practices within Aotearoa New Zealand ECEC settings to illustrate how these settings have enabled democratic and learning-oriented practices to happen. The examples offer a compass not a map; they suggest promising directions, but each party must find their own way. In a similar way, writing from England, Fielding and Moss (2012, p. 3) have argued that the road to transformation to a "radical education" cannot be specified in advance, but signposts can be constructed to point the direction. Moss explains the value of cross-national work:

> . . country A may provide a prism or lens for looking at country B. Adopting a Foucauldian perspective, cross-national work can help us to 'think differently' and therefore critically: the lens of Country A may make it easier to see in Country B what is uncritically taken for granted and make the invisible visible and the familiar strange, so enabling dominant assumptions, discourses and constructions in Country B to be questioned. (Moss, 2000, p. 4)

While offering exemplars of democratic practice and advocacy as sources of optimism, the book also examines challenges and tensions experienced in Aotearoa New Zealand that are common to countries that share capitalist mixed economies of welfare (Lloyd & Penn, 2012) and where competition and marketisation have become dominant principles. Within Aotearoa New Zealand and other countries, unfettered expansion of for-profit provision is occurring. Writing of critical analysis in education, Michael Apple (2013) argues that:

> … its aim is to critically examine current realities with a conceptual/political framework that emphasizes the spaces in which more progressive and counter-hegemonic actions can, or do, go on. This is an absolutely crucial step, since otherwise our research can simply lead to cynicism or despair. (p. 207)

A hope is that the ideas put forward in this book for action around the problematic and unresolved issues of marketisation of ECEC provision in Aotearoa New Zealand will suggest positive ways forward. In Aotearoa New Zealand, a tradition for gaining positive change has been through organised groups (unions and early childhood organisations) working collectively with academics and individuals from the basis of a critical analysis of policy and of preferred policy solutions.

This introductory chapter sets the scene for the book by examining influential contexts for childhood and ECEC: the children's rights movement, the state of ECEC in a mixed market economy and globalisation. These trends have brought with them dominant discourses that are often contradictory, working in opposition and leading to unintended outcomes. The children's rights movement and the articles of the 1989 United Nations Convention on the Rights of the Child (UNCROC), ratified by most countries internationally, have been an advocacy tool for children in education and other social institutions to be regarded as active citizens with agency, as "beings not becomings" and as being entitled to publicly provided provisions that ensure their wellbeing, education and development. By contrast, marketisation and competition have narrowed conceptions of the purposes of education, limited opportunities for access and shaped economic values underpinning educational institutions. In this chapter, I argue for an alternative approach to an individualist and competitive model based on the idea of education for democracy. This chapter ends with my personal story and motivations for writing and a description of the layout of the book.

2   The Child as Citizen

The 1989 United Nations Convention on the Rights of the Child (UNCROC) (United Nations, 1990), ratified by all UN countries except South Sudan and the USA, is a legally binding document. It is wide-ranging in its breadth and applies to children from birth to age 18 years. Children's rights under UNCROC fall into three main categories: provision rights, protection rights and participation rights. Progress made by each country on the UNCROC is monitored each year by the UN Committee on the Rights of the Child. Each country, and often NGOs as well, presents a report on the progress achieved after 2 years and then every 5 years.

The UNCROC and ideas from the sociology of childhood (e.g., James, Jenks, & Prout, 1998; Moss & Petrie, 2002) have offered new ways of representing children that emphasise the diversity of childhoods that are socially constructed and possibilities for children's citizenship. Anne Smith (2016, p. 16) prefers the term "Childhood Studies" to "sociology of childhood" because it emphasises the interdisciplinary nature of the field. She argues:

> There are similar aspirations for children inherent in Children's Rights and Childhood Studies frameworks, such as the importance of constructing children as persons not property, supporting their citizenship and opportunities to participate, treating them as agents rather than passive recipients, and recognising that children constitute multiple voices and not one collective undifferentiated class.

Dahlberg, Moss and Pence (1999, p. 48) described the child produced under the "child as citizen" paradigm as a "co-constructor of knowledge, identity and culture". This view acknowledges that children have agency: they are shaped by society and they also shape it through their own experiences and interactions with others. These ideas about children and childhood connect well with *Te Whāriki*, Aotearoa New Zealand's early childhood curriculum. This vision of children as competent and active contributors to society is a founding aspiration for children in *Te Whāriki*. The core ideas in the concept of "child as citizen" are that the child is a citizen, with rights and responsibilities, a member of a social group, an agent and a voice to be listened to (Moss & Petrie, 2002, p. 101). Children are agents in their own learning and the learning of others. A second core idea is that childhood is important in its own right, and not simply in relation to adulthood.

As a basis for policy and pedagogy, the concept of child as citizen could help build a democratic society and cater better for societal change that is a feature of Western societies. Policy and pedagogy that predominantly emphasise goals of ECEC which support a process of inevitable development, or protect the vulnerable child, or link narrowly to government economic and labour force participation goals, give insufficient weight to provision and possibilities for children's participation.

3   ECEC in a Mixed Market Economy

In a mixed market economy, public services, such as education, health and welfare, are not solely provided by the state but by a mix of state, private for-profit and community-based not-for-profit organisations. Childcare markets are found in the UK, the Netherlands, the USA, Canada, Australia, Aotearoa New Zealand, the African continent and the Asia Pacific region. In a mixed market economy, "the state, private-for-profit and private not-for-profit providers all play a role in the provision, funding and regulation of ECEC" (Lloyd & Penn, 2012, p. 4).

In a marketised system of education, educational institutions are treated as businesses and parents as consumers. Parental choice and efficiencies produced through competition are held out as reasons for governments to take a market approach to ECEC provision. Choice is based on the idea that parents will "vote with their feet" if ECEC is too expensive or of poor quality, and a competitive market will contribute to cost-effectiveness and higher quality. This does not happen as many research studies have shown. Parents are constrained in the choices they might make by what ECEC services are available in their locality, the cost of ECE and responsiveness of available services to cultural aspirations and family circumstances. International evidence (Boag-Munroe & Evangelou, 2011; Mitchell, 2015; Mitchell et al., 2014; Noble, 2007) shows that choice of ECEC service is very constrained by these pragmatic factors, especially for low-income families. Noble (2007) found the opinions and perceptions of other parents using the ECEC service were influential in the choices they made, but choice was mediated by the practical factors. Clearly, in communities where the range of ECEC services is limited, there is little choice. Even if there is choice, moving a child from an ECEC service is likely to be problematic since it involves disrupting relationships and transitions to new relationships. Many concerns have been expressed about the impact of privatisation and competition for all participants in ECEC – children, families, the staff who work in them and community (e.g. Mitchell & Davison, 2010 ; Press & Woodrow, 2009). Within a marketised system, ECEC services are increasingly provided by for-profit providers (Lloyd & Penn, 2012), some of which are now listing on the stock exchange (Penn, 2013). These corporate businesses which have a main interest from a commercial view in making profits for owners or shareholders are positioned at odds with more altruistic aims to invest fully in the service itself.

Internationally, researchers have provided evidence that the influences of competition and marketisation have consequences for ECEC, narrowing opportunities for access that privilege the wealthy and dominant group (Mitchell & Davison, 2010; Noially, Visser, & Grout, 2007; Penn, 2012). Differences in quality between community and for-profit providers have been found in marketised systems, with higher quality in community provision (Cleveland & Krashinsky, 2004; Penn, 2009; Sosinsky, Lord, & Zigler, 2007). In addition, quality differentials tend to favour higher-income communities. The listing of for-profit centres on the stock exchange brings a conflict in interests between the first duty of publicly listed companies to shareholders and accountability to children and families. Australian researchers (Brennan, 2007; Press & Woodrow, 2009; Rush, 2006; Sumsion, 2006, 2012) have carefully researched and documented the rise of corporate publicly listed company ABC within Australia and into New Zealand, the UK, China, Hong Kong, the Philippines and Indonesia and the damaging impact of its subsequent suspension from trading (Sumsion, 2012). It went into voluntary receivership in November 2008 forcing the Australian government to spend AUD$56 million to keep centres open, while a new buyer was found.

Linked to marketisation is a trend towards measureable and predetermined learning outcomes and accountability, which the OECD (2006, p. 61) *Starting Strong 11* report described as "the pre-primary approach to ECEC" that "reinforce school-like learning approaches and content". These are often focused on learning areas emphasised by schools, especially language, print-based literacy skills and numeracy. Such a narrow focus has been influenced by longitudinal research studies, particularly intervention studies in the USA, including the *Abecedarian* study, the *High/Scope Perry Preschool* study, the *Chicago Child-Parent Centre* study and the *Infant Health and Development Program* study. These studies have measured child outcomes in traditional and quantifiably measureable domains and shown statistically significant connections with a range of variables in later life. Such a narrow focus does not recognise and value different outcomes and neglects consideration of context. One concern is that the privileging of these outcomes may be at the expense of others. For example, Kress (2000), writing about literacy modes, has argued that a focus on verbal literacies alone "…has meant a neglect, an overlooking, even a suppression of the potentials of all the representational and communicational modes… and a neglect equally, as a consequence, of the development of theoretical understandings of such modes" (p. 157).

A new approach to learning and teaching does not make distinctions between cognitive, socioemotional and dispositional outcomes as separate domains. Carr, Davis and Cowie's (2015) literature scan, *Continuity of Early Learning: Learning Progress and Outcomes in the Early Years*, explores this alternative approach in relation to assessment; it foregrounds the combination of knowledge/skills and key competencies/learning dispositions that support lifelong learning and takes the idea of the construct of *participation* as encompassing and integrating the two sets of outcomes. These ideas about marketisation and learning outcomes will be shown to link to the theme of democratic practice and policy within this book.

4 Globalisation

Widespread changes are occurring in the way childhood is experienced and the opportunities available to children. Prout (2003, 3–6 September; 2005) described the following childhood changes occurring across Europe and North America; such changes are evident in the Asia Pacific and Australasia regions too.

1. Children are becoming a declining proportion of the population, while life expectancy is increasing and the population is ageing. Social policy analysts (Jensen & Saporiti, 1992) consider that this situation has seen, and will see, the redistribution of social resources away from children towards the elderly. How to give visibility to children's situation in relation to other groups in society, in a way that their interests are not subsumed by majority interest, has become a key ECEC policy question.
2. Children's life circumstances are becoming more differentiated through family change. Children are spending substantial time outside the family and relating to more than one social network, a process described as "dual socialisation" (Dencik, 1989; Prout, 2003, 3-6 September). Dencik (1989) has demonstrated that dual socialisation requires children to make "flexible adjustments" between one environment, such as home and ECEC, and another and as environments shift in time. Children need to make sense of a world in which there are divergent values and perspectives. This constitutes a policy and practice challenge for ECEC: how to support and strengthen continuity with a child's cultural identity, home languages, funds of knowledge and connections from one place to another.
3. Children are spending longer periods of time in early childhood institutions, leading to a rethinking of the relationships between the state, parents and children. In Scandinavian countries children are now regarded as a shared responsibility of the state and parents, rather than the state being regarded as "backup" to parents (Mayall, 1996). The role of the state is another policy issue that will be canvassed in this book and links to views of childhood and marketisation.
4. Growing income inequality and child poverty are features of Western societies. The UNICEF Innocenti Research Centre, which has been tracking child poverty in the European Union and/or OECD since 1988 as part of its focus on child rights, has found child poverty to be growing in most countries (UNICEF Innocenti Research Centre, 2005). Low income affects children's development, health and survival, educational achievement, job prospects and life expectancies. Mayer (2002), who reviewed literature on the influence of parental income on child outcomes, wrote:

Parental income is positively correlated with virtually every dimension of child well-being that social scientists measure, and this is true in every country for which we have data. The children of rich parents are healthier, better behaved, happier and better educated during their childhood and wealthier when they have grown up than are children from poor families. (p. 30)

Poverty limits opportunities for children to access education and health care and participate in family activities and their own culture. Moreover, using evidence from their own and OECD and World Bank data, Wikinson and Pickett (2010) show that a wide range of health and social problems are much more common in societies with bigger income differences between rich and poor. Rather than being confined to the poor, the effects of inequality extend to the vast majority of the population.

5. Childhood is becoming more "transnational" through migration across national borders and through "flows of products, information, values and images that most children routinely engage with" (Prout, 2003, p. 9). Migration is a source of ethnic and racial diversity among children and has direct implications for early childhood settings where culture-bound ideas about children's experiences are inadequate to do justice to the diverse realities of children's lives.

Prout (2003; 2005) argued that these trends as set out above call for new ways of representing children that are responsive to children's experiences. In my view the same argument can be made in the Aotearoa New Zealand context. In fact, McDonald (1978) was an early advocate for putting the child at the centre of research and policy analysis in Aotearoa New Zealand. He argued that from 1979 onwards, the rights and civil status of children were being opened up for debate and that there was a move towards a social justice agenda in children's services.

Giddens (1999) regards globalisation as being influenced by four sets of changes, all of which are interconnected. The first is the "world-wide communication revolution" (p. 1) that began with the first satellite and has spread to an intensification of global communications, the most powerful of which is the Internet. The second, the knowledge economy, is currently led by financial markets. The third is the fall of Soviet communism, influenced by both the communication revolution and transformation to a global electronic economy. The fourth change refers to transformations in everyday life, in particular, growing equality between men and women (with still a way to go).

Globalisation is portrayed as an inescapable force. "For globalisation is not incidental to our lives today. It is a shift in our very life circumstances. It is the way we now live" (Giddens, 1999). Globalisation makes possible communication and interactions across great distances where before the "communication revolution", interactions were held face to face; in so doing this may enable possibilities for greater shared understanding, but it can equally inhibit locally constructed values and views. Globalisation has "universalising tendencies" (Dahlberg, Moss, & Pence, 1999, p. 162), referring to the spread of values, ideas, practices and policies worldwide. This spread is directly relevant to education, which is evident in practice, policy and provision. Hence, it can be seen in the spread of ideas that competition and marketisation of provision produce cost-effectiveness and encourage quality and ideas that what constitutes valued outcomes in ECEC can be universally prescribed and exported from one country to another. Universalising tendencies are seen in the importing of curriculum from a different context and country, such as Head Start and High Scope programmes that have spread to many developing countries through the influence of organisations like the World Bank. Influences of globalisation include the spread of commercial brand products as educational resources, such as the spread of commercially branded equipment by the corporate company ABC in Australia, and the recent development of ePortfolio computer programmes as a template for assessment documentation. These raise troubling questions about whose knowledge goes into the design of such resources.

5 Why Aotearoa New Zealand as a Case Study?

The use of Aotearoa New Zealand ECEC as a case study of policy formulation and practice will highlight exemplars for democratic policy and practice that have worked well in this country and examine the policies and practices supporting these. The Aotearoa New Zealand curriculum, *Te Whāriki*, is based on principles of social justice and respect for rights and an aim to support children growing up in a democracy. The curriculum upholds Māori rights to tino rangatiratanga (absolute authority over their lives and resources). The curriculum sets a context for democratic practice, but other conditions are needed too, in particular national and local policy support for "democratic professionalism" (Oberhuemer, 2005). A second reason for choosing Aotearoa New Zealand as a case study is the advances it has made to integrate childcare services and education services within a common educational administration, a step that began in 1986. Since then further integrations have occurred with respect to teacher education, teacher salaries, funding and regulations. Why and how these integrations occurred will be of interest internationally, and also of interest will be the areas where integration reached stumbling blocks and was not fully realised.

In addition, Aotearoa New Zealand offers an example of ways in which the competitive approach to provision has led to a boom in the number and percentage of for-profit businesses in the childcare sector (both centre-based and home-based). Its extreme market policies and its harsh labour laws during recent periods run contrary to ideals of democracy and are puzzlingly inconsistent with curriculum policies. I will argue that the marketisation of ECEC is an Achilles heel in Aotearoa New Zealand's policy framework that has consequences for access and quality that privilege better off families. These are antidemocratic.

My intention is to provide insights with regard to issues in ECEC policy and practice that are of current concern globally.

6   A Personal Story

The year 1986 when I became general secretary of the union covering kindergarten teachers was the year we celebrated the integration of all ECEC services coming under the administrative umbrella of the Department of Education in Aotearoa New Zealand, hailed as a triumph for women and children. The integration replaced the divided policy approach where kindergartens and playcentres, regarded as "education" services, were administered under this Department and were more generously funded, compared with "childcare", regarded as "welfare" services and administered by the Department of Social Welfare. I remember my job interview, where I was questioned closely about my views of integration and of a model of one union representing the whole ECEC workforce. The idea of integration of all ECEC services made good sense to me, an opportunity for childcare to gain equitable treatment and funding as an education and care service and a chance to work together to gain public valuing and tangible recognition for all of ECEC, always demeaned as being "women's work". Through an integrated ECEC workforce, we could build strength in solidarity and fairness in pay and working conditions. I was offered the job. My 15 years in the union were years of continuous organising, strategising, negotiating and campaigning – particularly around ECEC policy about curriculum, funding, teacher qualifications and teacher pay and working conditions. At first we had only two paid positions in the union me and the president, later joined by the trade union education organiser. These women working with me were bold, inspirational leaders and committed unionists. We did everything – from sitting on the floor, usually on a Friday night, enveloping campaign kits in time to catch the post for delivery to members around the country on Monday morning, to high-level meetings with government ministers. Our union was highly democratic. Teacher members took on many roles as industrial advocates, counsellors, office holders and decision-makers. We had debates within the national executive, branch and annual meetings around deeply considered issues of gay and lesbian rights, structures for Māori decision-making as part of our commitment to Te Tiriti o Waitangi, biculturalism and union amalgamations. Our members participated enthusiastically in eye-catching campaigns to influence government policy. These were organised nationally and delivered locally in idiosyncratic ways. Members of the parliament were visited, and petitions presented. We felt deeply about political issues. We were exhilarated at critical successes; we cried at enormous setbacks. I did a lot of writing at that time: submissions to the government, newsletters to members and policy proposals – I came to regard highly the power of the pen. During these years, we forged two amalgamations to become a stronger united education union, we developed strategies for pay parity for teachers in kindergartens and "childcare", we led collaborations with other ECEC organisations to set an agenda for a long-term strategic plan for ECEC. I represented the union on many working groups, in meetings with politicians and government officials. At times we collaborated with the government and worked closely with politicians; at other times we resisted and condemned the policies. We worked collectively as a union, sometimes in tandem with other organisations – our efforts were united. My love of writing and research and ECEC led me to work as a researcher at the New Zealand Council for Educational Research and as a university academic in the Faculty of Education at the University of Waikato. In the last 17 years, I've written and researched about ECEC policy and pedagogy in Aotearoa New Zealand, as both a critic and supporter of what we do here. In 2001, I visited Denmark, Sweden and England and heard about the "child rights movement" that was sweeping Europe. Back in Aotearoa New Zealand, I called for a new debate about children and childhood and for ECEC institutions to be conceptualised as community organisations playing an important role in fostering a democratic society. This is essentially what my book is about.

7   Layout

Chapter "Aotearoa New Zealand Within Global Trends in ECEC Policy", Global Trends in ECEC Policy, will focus on a narrative of the history and current situation of Aotearoa New Zealand early childhood education, including a critical account and assessment of the reform process. This will discuss the goals and values in the original reforms and cover some of the tensions and issues that have arisen during implementation, including those arising from marketisation and privatisation. This chapter gives an indication of the significance of the Aotearoa New Zealand reforms from an international perspective.

Chapter "Traditions of Democracy in Education" turns to a conception of ECEC that takes as its foundational values that children are citizens and that education is valued as a public good and is a child's right. These ideas are analysed within an overarching framework of democracy, going back to the Athenian origins of democracy and including recent writers on meanings and traditions of democracy in education. It takes core ideas from Dewey (1915) that democracy is something that has to be made and remade by each generation and of the capacity of education to build democratic society rather than reproduce society. Giroux (1992) takes these ideas further in emphasising social criticism and struggle in his definition of democracy, while Apple (2005) emphasises a commitment to "thick" collective forms of democracy. This chapter will also include a specific section on democracy in Aotearoa New Zealand's educational traditions and history, including how democracy weaves with *Te Whāriki* and other aspects of reform. It examines whether democracy is implicit or explicit and how democracy relates to the key values in *Te Whāriki*. This chapter also sets a framing for analysis in subsequent chapters.

In Chapter "Weaving a Curriculum" curriculum principles for ECEC are examined, and Aotearoa New Zealand's curriculum, *Te Whāriki*, is used as an example to highlight affordances of curriculum to enable local and community democratic practice. Research-based case studies are used to examine curriculum in action in Aotearoa New Zealand, where curriculum strands and valued learning are woven into the curriculum whāriki (weaving) through democratic discussion and contribution. The case studies are drawn from and extend examples from the author's

Aotearoa New Zealand studies and include an iwi-based ECEC centre where local whānau/hapū/iwi[1] decide what knowledge should be available and how it should be made accessible (Mitchell, Meagher-Lundberg, Arndt, and Kara 2016b), and a rural kindergarten, where children plan a project to make a concrete path in their kindergarten and elicit support from families and local community to enable them to do this (Mitchell, 2007). The chapter argues that the Aotearoa New Zealand curriculum framework offers opportunity for democratic participation by conceptualising children as competent and active participants and agents in their own lives and taking responsibility for others and by recognising the powerful contribution of families to children's learning and wellbeing.

Chapter "Assessment and Pedagogical Documentation" examines the role of teachers, pedagogy and assessment. Tensions in assessment between a focus on measureable learning outcomes particularly in literacy and numeracy and formative assessment for learning are highlighted. It argues that ideas about outcomes and how these should be assessed reflect ideas about what learning is valued and the nature of knowledge. The chapter analyses a fear of "schoolification" of ECEC and the push down of standards applying to the schools sector to ECEC globally and in Aotearoa New Zealand. It uses examples of Aotearoa New Zealand pedagogy and assessment to demonstrate an approach designed to emphasise and construct a democratic educational culture. The chapter argues that assessment practices that have democracy in mind will include the views of those being assessed, build a culture of success and be open to contribution from children, families and community. A democratic community might be a place where all these participants are able to belong and make a contribution that makes a difference for learning; where they collectively "create a world" a term used by Bruner (1998). This requires teachers to establish productive partnerships with children, families and communities that facilitates, values and utilises children's and families' funds of knowledge. Valued outcomes will include knowledge, skills, learning dispositions and working theories that support lifelong learning.

Chapter "Influencing Policy Change Through Collective Action" is about advocacy. Many writers have argued that we need to debate values about children and childhood as a basis for ECEC provision (Brostrom, 2013; Mitchell, 2007; Moss & Petrie, 1997; Prout, 2005). Citizenry rights and living in a democracy is a good place to start. Aotearoa New Zealand academics, unionists and activists have a history of acting collectively to debate, formulate and progress their collectively desired ECEC policy directions. Advocates from the early childhood teachers' union harnessing support from families and community, and working with national early childhood organisations and academics, have been highly influential in influencing policy change through collective action. Stories of advocacy to influence policy are told in this chapter. The first is a story of collective strategising and action to achieve pay parity of kindergarten teachers' salaries with the salaries of primary and secondary teachers and a parallel story about teachers in education and care (childcare settings) where only partial pay parity was achieved. The reasons for

---

[1] Whānau is the Māori word for extended family; hapū is a clan or sub-group; and iwi is a tribe.

different results are analysed. The second is a story of a collective group formed by the union for policy development that resulted in the publication and widespread endorsement of the report *Future Directions: Early Childhood Education in New Zealand* (Early Childhood Education Project, 1996; Wells, 1999). This pointed the processes of consultation and direction for the subsequent government initiated Strategic Plan for ECE: Ngā Haurahi Arataki.

The people who staff ECEC services and are in direct interaction with children and families are key players in ECEC. Oberhuemer, Schreyer and Neuman's (Oberhuemer, Schreyer, & Neuman 2010) analysis of professionals in 27 ECEC systems across Europe highlights many issues, including variable and often low pay rates, unsupportive conditions of employment, a gendered workforce, variable qualification levels and opportunities for professional development and recruitment and retention issues. Considerable interest has emerged in policy frameworks to sustain and encourage democratic participation and responsive pedagogy in ECEC. Using findings from an evaluation of New Zealand's strategic plan for early childhood education (Mitchell, Meagher-Lundberg, Mara, Cubey, & Whitford 2011), Chapter "Policy Frameworks and Democratic Participation" highlights ways in which policy initiatives interacted to support such processes. A range of initiatives aimed at improving teacher qualifications and professional capabilities supported teachers to think critically, encouraged teachers to experiment with innovative teaching and learning practices and contributed to enhanced quality. A key argument is that benefits came from policies that were universally available and coherently organised around an understanding of children, families and communities as participants.

The final chapter is the "Conclusion", and it argues that Aotearoa New Zealand, like many countries, is at a critical time in ECEC. The chapter examines the tensions and oppositions that have arisen in Aotearoa New Zealand between aspirations for democratic and universal ECEC and oppositional influences of marketisation and privatisation. In particular, it brings together findings from the chapters to examine what conditions might be needed for an integrated and democratic early childhood education system in Aotearoa New Zealand, the progress made to date, and what changes are needed for the future. It ends with an expression of hope that with support from ECEC advocates, the newly elected Labour-led government in Aotearoa New Zealand will take the ECEC sector on a pathway to a democratic and public education system.

References

Apple, M. (2005). Education, markets, and an audit culture. *Critical Quarterly, 47*(1–2), 11–29.
Apple, M. (2013). Between traditions: Stephen Ball and the critical sociology of education. *London Review of Education, 11*(3), 206–217.
Boag-Munroe, G., & Evangelou, M. (2011). From hard to reach to how-to-reach: A systematic review of the literature on hard-to-reach families. *Research Papers in Education, 27*(2), 209–239.

Brennan, D. (2007). The ABC of child care politics. *Australian Journal of Social Issues, 42*(2), 212–225.

Brostrom, S. (2013). Understanding *Te Whāriki* from a Danish perspective. In J. Nuttall (Ed.), *Weaving Te Whāriki. Aotearoa New Zealand's early childhood curriculum document in theory and practice.* (2nd ed., pp. 239-257). Wellington, New Zealand: New Zealand Council for Educational Research.

Bruner, J. (1998). Each place has its own spirit and its own aspirations. *RE Child, 3*(January), 6.

Carr, M., Davis, K., & Cowie, B. (2015). *Continuity of early learning: Learning progress and outcomes in the early years. Report on the literature scan.* Retrieved from https://www.educationcounts.govt.nz/publications/ECE/continuity-of-early-learning-literature-scan

Cleveland, G., & Krashinsky, M. (2004). *The quality gap: A study of nonprofit and commercial child care centres in Canada.* Toronto, Canada: University of Toronto at Scarborough.

Dahlberg, G., Moss, P., & Pence, A. (1999). *Beyond quality in early childhood education and care. Post modern perspectives* (1st ed.). London: Falmer Press.

Dencik, L. (1989). Growing up in the post-modern age: On the child's situation in the modern family, and on the position of the family in the modern welfare state. *Acta Sociologica, 32*(2), 155–180.

Dewey, J. (1915). *School and society.* Chicago: The University of Chicago Press.

Early Childhood Education Project. (1996). *Future directions: Early childhood education in New Zealand.* Wellington, New Zealand: New Zealand Educational Institute Te Riu Roa.

Fielding, M., & Moss, P. (2012). *Radical education and the common school. A democratic alternative.* London: Routledge.

Giddens, A. (1999). *Runaway: World BBC Reith lectures 1999.* Retrieved from http://www.looooker.com/wp-content/uploads/2013/05/Giddens-lectures-in-london.pdf

Giroux, H. (1992). *Border crossings. Cultural workers and the politics of education.* London: Routledge.

James, A., Jenks, C., & Prout, A. (1998). *Theorizing childhood.* Cambridge, UK: Polity Press.

Jensen, A., & Saporiti, A. (1992). *Do children count? Childhood as a social phenomenon. A statistical compendium.* Vienna: European Centre for Social Welfare Policy and Research.

Kress, G. (2000). Design and transformation: New theories of meaning. In B. Cope & M. Kalantzis (Eds.), *Multiliteracies: Literacy learning and the design of social futures* (pp. 153–161). London: Routledge.

Lloyd, E., & Penn, H. (Eds.). (2012). *Childcare markets: Can they deliver an equitable service.* Bristol, UK: The Policy Press.

Mayall, B. (1996). *Children, health and the social order.* Buckingham, UK: Open University Press.

Mayer, S. (2002). *Parental incomes and children's outcomes.* Retrieved from http://www.msd.govt.nz/documents/publications/csre/influence-of-parental-income.pdf

McDonald, D. (1978). Children and young persons in New Zealand society. In P. Koopman-Boyden (Ed.), *Families in New Zealand society* (pp. 44–56). Wellington, New Zealand: Methuen Publications (NZ) Ltd.

Mitchell, L. (2007). *A new debate about children and childhood. Could it make a difference to early childhood pedagogy and policy?* Doctoral thesis. Wellington, New Zealand: Victoria University of Wellington. Retrieved from http://researcharchive.vuw.ac.nz/handle/10063/347

Mitchell, L. (2015). *Engaging priority children in ECE, creating opportunities for families.* Paper presented at the Coming Together for Australia's Children Conference, Australian Research Alliance for Children and Youth Hobart, Tasmania.

Mitchell, L., & Davison, C. (2010). Early childhood education as sites for children's citizenship: Tensions, challenges and possibilities in New Zealand's policy framing. *International Journal of Equity and Innovation in Early Childhood, 8*(1), 12–23.

Mitchell, L., Meagher-Lundberg, P., Arndt, S., & Kara, H. (2016b). *ECE Participation Programme evaluation. Stage 4.* Retrieved from https://www.educationcounts.govt.nz/publications/ECE/ece-participation-programme-evaluation-stage-4

Mitchell, L., Meagher-Lundberg, P., Caulcutt, T., Taylor, M., Archard, S., Kara, H., et al. (2014). *ECE Participation Programme evaluation. Delivery of the ECE participation initiatives: Stage 2*. Retrieved from http://www.educationcounts.govt.nz/publications/ECE/148513

Mitchell, L., Meagher-Lundberg, P., Mara, D., Cubey, P., & Whitford, M. (2011). *Locality-based evaluation of Pathways to the Future – Nga Huarahi Arataki. Integrated report 2004, 2006 and 2009*. Retrieved from http://www.educationcounts.govt.nz/publications/ece/locality-based-evaluation-of-pathways-to-the-future-ng-huarahi-arataki

Moss, P. (2000). *Workforce issues in early childhood education and care staff. For consultative meeting on International Developments in Early Childhood Education and Care*. The Institute for Child and Family Policy, Columbia University, New York, May 11–12.

Moss, P. (2007). International connections. In Ministry of Education (Ed.), *Travelling pathways to the future: Ngä Huarahi Arataki*. Wellington, New Zealand: Ministry of Education. Retrieved from www.minedu.govt.nz.oss

Moss, P., & Petrie, P. (1997). *Children's services: Time for a new approach*. London: Institute of Education, University of London.

Moss, P., & Petrie, P. (2002). *From children's services to children's spaces*. London: Routledge Falmer.

Noble, K. (2007). Parent choice of early childhood education and care services. *Australian Journal of Early Childhood, 32*(2), 51–57.

Noially, J., Visser, S., & Grout, P. (2007). *The impact of market forces on the provision of child-care: Insights from the 2005 Childcare Act in the Netherlands* (CPB Memorandum 176). The Hague, The Netherlands, CPB Netherlands Bureau for Economic Policy Analysis. www.cpb.nl/nl/

Oberhuemer, P. (2005). Conceptualising the early childhood pedagogue: Policy approaches and issues of professionalism. *European Early Childhood Education Research Journal, 13*(1), 5–16.

Oberhuemer, P., Schreyer, I., & Neuman, M. J. (2010). *Professionals in early childhood education and care systems*. Opladen and Farmington Hills: Barbara Budrich Publishers.

OECD. (2006). *Starting strong 11: Early childhood education and care*. Paris, France: Organisation for Economic Cooperation and Development.

Penn, H. (2009). International perspectives on quality in mixed economies of childcare. *National Institute Economic Review 207, 83*(7). Retrieved from: http://find.galegroup.com.ezproxy.waikato.ac.nz/itx/start.do?prodId=ITOF

Penn, H. (2012). Raw and emerging childcare markets. In E. Lloyd & H. Penn (Eds.), *Childcare markets. Can they deliver an equitable service?* (pp. 173–187). Bristol, UK: The Policy Press.

Penn, H. (2013). The business of childcare in Europe. *European Early Childhood Education Research Journal, 22*(4), 432–456. https://doi.org/10.1080/1350293X.2013.7883300.

Press, F., & Woodrow, C. (2009). The giant in the playground: Investigating the reach and implications of the corporatisation of child care provision. In D. King & G. Meagher (Eds.), *Paid care in Australia: Politics, profits, practice*. Sydney, Australia: Sydney University Press.

Prout, A. (2003, September). *Children, representation and social change*. Paper presented at the European Early Childhood Education Research Association 13th Annual Conference, Glasgow, Scotland.

Prout, A. (2005). *The future of childhood*. London: RoutledgeFalmer.

Rush, E. (2006). *Child care quality in Australia* (Discussion paper Number 84). Victoria, Australia: The Australia Institute.

Smith, A. B. (2016). *Children's rights. Towards social justice*. New York: Momentum Press.

Sosinsky, L., Lord, H., & Zigler, E. (2007). For-profit/non-profit differences in center-based child care quality: Results from the National Institute of Child Health and Human Development study of early child care and youth development. *Journal of Applied Developmental Psychology, 28*(5), 390–410.

Sumsion, J. (2006). The corporatization of Australian childcare: Towards an ethical audit and research agenda. *Journal of Early Childhood Research, 4*(2), 99–120.

Sumsion, J. (2012). ABC Learning and Australian early education and care. In E. Lloyd & H. Penn (Eds.), *Childcare markets. Can they deliver an equitable service?* (pp. 209–225). Bristol, UK: The Policy Press.

UNICEF Innocenti Research Centre. (2005). *Report Card No 6. Child poverty in rich countries 2005.* Retrieved Oct 25, 2005 from http://www.unicef-icdc.org/publications/

United Nations. (1990). *Convention on the Rights of the Child* Retrieved from http://www2.ohchr.org/english/law/crc.htm

Wells, C. (1999). Future directions: Shaping early childhood policy for the 21st century – a personal perspective. *New Zealand Annual Review of Education, 8,* 45–60.

Wikinson, R., & Pickett, K. (2010). *Spirit level: Why equality is better for everyone.* London: Penguin Books.

Aotearoa New Zealand Within Global Trends in ECEC Policy

Aotearoa New Zealand is distinguished for its social justice foundations, its world-wide leadership in the early suffrage of women and its radical policies in response to economic and social problems following the Great Depression. Yet in a curious reversal of liberal trends, in recent years it is also marked for its extreme neoliberal policies applied in the 1980s and 1990s across most areas of interest to the state. Inequities in wealth distribution and access to basic education, health and social services have been a result. In this chapter, I discuss the social justice foundations and struggles within the early history of Aotearoa New Zealand to set a scene for the development of ECEC (early childhood education and care) and the curriculum, where advocacy by organisations and individuals played an influential role. Neoliberal ideologies swept Aotearoa New Zealand in the 1980s and had major impacts on the social context of society. New right economic theory was applied to reforms in education and particularly to the ECEC sector, which became increasingly privatised. ECEC policy has taken different turns since then, paralleling changes in political leadership, with a marked shift from 1999 to 2008 from minimal state support to a supportive state where providing ECEC is seen as a co-operative effort amongst the state, families, teachers and community. This saw positive moves to conceptualising ECEC as a universal public good, only to be unravelled by a right-leaning government from 2009 to 2017 that focused attention on priority children. A new government, elected in November 2017, holds out promise for tackling the big issues of child poverty, environmental climate change, inadequate housing and poor health services. Education is on the agenda, and promising moves have already happened in schools and tertiary education that signal a shift to a strongly privileged public education system. ECEC policy is still to be unravelled and enacted. This book points the directions for what policy to support a democratic system of ECEC might possibly look like.

© Springer Nature Singapore Pte Ltd. 2019
L. Mitchell, *Democratic Policies and Practices in Early Childhood Education*,
International Perspectives on Early Childhood Education and Development 24,
https://doi.org/10.1007/978-981-13-1793-4_2

1   Introduction

Helen May has written about the history of ECEC in Aotearoa New Zealand (May, 2009, 2013) from the formation of the first childcare services and kindergartens in the late nineteenth century, focusing on social and political change and the changing role of the state. This chapter analyses the recent history of ECEC from the 1980s, discussing the goals and values in the reforms over the last three decades and covering the tensions and issues that have arisen during implementation. The significance of the Aotearoa New Zealand reforms within global trends in ECEC policy is highlighted. These decades were periods of political change in Aotearoa New Zealand, with new ideologies played out in different policy approaches to children and families, as the significance of ECEC for children's learning and development, economic development and workforce participation was made visible by a raft of policies and publications. The trends observed in Aotearoa New Zealand in these decades can be linked to the global spread of ideas and movements and to Aotearoa New Zealand's unique context and heritage.

In relation to ECEC, the global rights movements have been particularly influential in Aotearoa New Zealand and elsewhere. These include the rights for women in the home, workplace and society; the rights of indigenous people especially in colonised countries like Aotearoa New Zealand where colonisers have instituted monocultural educational systems, devaluing indigenous knowledge, languages and practices; children's rights and the adoption of the *United Nations Convention on the Rights of the Child in 1989* (United Nations, 1990) and its subsequent ratification by most countries (New Zealand ratified this in 1993); and the influence of increasing migration and calls for rights of ethnic minority groups to be upheld through culturally responsive pedagogy. These have been especially dominant at different times, linked to the prevailing government ideology and advocacy from community groups and individuals.

New right economic theories have been another and competing powerful global influence on the ways in which ECEC is provided, funded and regulated in New Zealand and other English-speaking countries. Associated with this influence is the global spread of ideas about the purpose of ECEC, the nature of curriculum and assessment and what constitutes valued outcomes of ECEC. Standardised testing regimes such as Programme for International Student Assessment (PISA) are providing benchmarks against which countries can compare results and are increasingly linked to high-stakes outcomes. Ideas that outcomes need to be measureable and the privileging of some learning domains are now moving more widely into the ECEC world are fuelled by initiatives such as the OECD's International Early Learning Study (IELS) (OECD, 2016, 2017).

Within the policy framings emerging from these perspectives are contradictory views of ECEC: the one, from a rights perspective, of ECEC as a public good, a child's right and entitlement and an institution in civil society founded on democratic participation, and the other, influenced by economic theories, of ECEC as an individual choice, a product for purchase and a business opportunity whose operation is determined by management owners. Associated with the marketised approach is a demand for measurement of standardised predetermined child outcomes as a form of accountability.

Aligned with these positions are different ideas about the role of the state, children and childhood that have far-reaching consequences for ECEC access, quality and democratic participation. They are linked to wider societal systems that affect childhood and ECEC, the levels of poverty and more especially the extent of poverty differentials between rich and poor in society and conditions to support parents in their childrearing, including provisions for paid parental leave and whether and how leave provisions are equitably shared between men and women – these are notable influences on the situation of preschool children and their families. These major influences from the rights movements, economic theorising and ideas about valued outcomes and assessment regimes coexist uncomfortably in New Zealand's ECEC landscape, producing exciting possibilities, as well as contradictions and unintended consequences for ECEC.

Before considering these trends and influences, the early history of Aotearoa New Zealand is discussed as a background to highlight foundational values that are intended to support children growing up in a democracy and provide a basis for a bicultural society. I shall argue that these values have shaped the diversity of early childhood care and education provision that currently exists and the development of the ECEC curriculum, *Te Whāriki* (Ministry of Education, 1996, 2017), and that the collective voice of rights advocates and early childhood advocates, supported by key politicians and workers inside of government, have contributed to the shaping of ECEC policy.

2 Early History of Aotearoa New Zealand

Aotearoa New Zealand is a small geographically remote island country located in the southern Pacific Ocean. Its population is 4.5 million. Eastern Polynesian migrants came in canoe groups probably in the thirteenth century AD, although some historians put the date earlier than this (King, 2003). Its name "Aotearoa" refers to the long white cloud seen enshrouding the North Island as the voyagers approached. The first settlers and indigenous people of Aotearoa New Zealand are Māori.

The first Europeans with Abel Tasman of the Dutch East India Company sighted Aotearoa New Zealand in 1642. Over 100 years later, in 1769, the British Royal Navy Lieutenant James Cook rediscovered Aotearoa New Zealand and Europeans landed and began settling there. By the late 1830s, there were approximately 125,000 Māori in Aotearoa New Zealand and about 2000 settlers. More immigrants were arriving all the time, but British law did not extend to controlling British subjects in Aotearoa New Zealand. Therefore, a British emissary was sent to act for the British Crown in the negotiation of a treaty between the Crown and Māori. On 6 February 1840, the Treaty of Waitangi (Te Tiriti o Waitangi) was signed at Waitangi in the Bay of Islands by a representative of the British government, William Hobson, several English residents and more than 40 Māori rangatira (chiefs). Several hand-written copies of Te Tiriti were taken around Aotearoa New Zealand, and by the end of that year, over 500 Māori rangatira, some of them women, had signed it. Te Tiriti represented "an agreement in which Māori gave the Crown rights to govern and to develop British settlement, while the Crown guaranteed Māori full protection of their interests and status, and full citizenship rights" (Waitangi Tribunal, 2012a). The principles of the treaty are referred to by the Waitangi Tribunal as "the principle of active protection, the tribal right to self-regulation, the right of redress for past breaches, and the duty to consult. The recognition and adherence to these principles ensure the 'active protection' of Māori language and culture" (Waitangi Tribunal, 2012b). In fact, the process of colonisation led to the marginalisation of Māori, and many serious breaches of promises made in Te Tiriti. Nevertheless, Te Tiriti o Waitangi was to provide a foundation for a country with two official languages, Māori and English, and a vision of a bicultural society. These principles have been carried forward into the development of the ECEC curriculum, *Te Whāriki*.

Aotearoa New Zealand was called the "social laboratory of the world" for its welfare state policies following the Great Depression of the 1930s. It became a self-governing democracy in 1856 and in 1893 was the first country in the world to give women the vote. Nevertheless, it was not until 1919 that the restrictions on women standing for parliament were repealed (Wilson, 1997). Wilson has argued that equality as a value and goal in Aotearoa New Zealand society arose from struggles of people for free and equal participation in their country's civil and political institutions.

These social justice foundations and struggles are evident now in more recent development of ECEC provision and the curriculum. Playcentre is an internation-ally recognised and uniquely Aotearoa New Zealand ECEC provision that began during the Second World War in 1941. It was intended to be a support service for women with young children who were often isolated, of low income and on their own raising their children. This was a democratic movement, with groups of moth-ers rostering themselves to care for children in a community hall and managing themselves as a group. The aims were to "provide leisure for mothers and opportu-nities for the social development of the preschool child" (Stover, 1998, p. 3). A parallel emphasis was on parent education. Maureen Woodhams (2010) has described the origins of playcentre as "a site for women's empowerment and femi-nist thought" (p. 265).

Global values from the women's liberation movement concerning the rights of women in the late 1960s and early 1970s spread to Aotearoa New Zealand and influ-enced the expansion of government support and integration of ECEC. In a country where many Māori could not speak the Māori language and were not knowledge-able about tikanga Māori (values, beliefs, spirituality and culture), growing advo-cacy was mounted for the government to support the revitalisation of Māori language and culture. The first kōhanga reo (Māori language nest) was established in 1982 and became "a national movement embracing the Māori nation in a united vision of language revitalisation and regeneration" (Lee, Carr, Soutar, & Mitchell, 2013,

p. 34). Valuing and promoting diversity and upholding Māori rights to tino rangatiratanga (absolute authority over their lives and resources) can be seen within the
story of much of the development of ECEC provision in Aotearoa New Zealand.
Alongside this story, generous government subsidies and marketisation have
resulted in an exponential rise in ECEC provided by business owners, where aims
to make a profit are at odds with more altruistic aims to invest fully in the service
and respond to community values.

2.1 Diversity of ECEC Provision

Early childhood education and care in Aotearoa New Zealand covers the period
from birth to school starting age (usually age 5 but compulsory at age 6). A diversity
of provision and freedom of philosophy emerged mainly from grassroots community initiatives and is highly valued. Recently, for policy purposes, ECEC services
have been categorised broadly as teacher-led and parent–/whānau-led (whānau
means extended family) to differentiate between how the services operate and are
funded.

2.1.1 Teacher-Led Services

A teacher-led service is one where one or more qualified teachers are responsible
for the overall programme in the service. They are required to have a person responsible who is a registered, early childhood education qualified teacher (equivalent to
a 3-year specialist degree or diploma), and meet the government's regulation that 50
percent of required staff must hold this recognised qualification. As an incentive to
employ more than the minimum 50 percent of qualified teachers and as recognition
of employment costs, services attract higher funding rates for employing 50–79
percent registered teachers. Until 2009, further financial incentives were available
for services employing 80 to 89 percent registered teachers and 100 percent registered teachers. Kindergartens receive higher funding rates to compensate for an
employment contract to which the Ministry of Education is a party that gives kindergarten teachers parity with school teachers' pay.

  Within the teacher-led service grouping, education and care centres (childcare
centres) cater for the largest number of children and offer full-day, sessional or half-
day provision. These centres may be based on particular philosophies, such as
Rudolf Steiner, Montessori and Reggio Emilia. They provide for children from birth
to school starting age. Home-based services (family daycare) tend to be flexible,
providing an educator to work with children in the educator's home or the child's
home at hours to suit parents. Although termed "teacher-led", it is only the co-
ordinator who is required to be a qualified, registered teacher; educators working
directly with children do not have this requirement. Kindergartens traditionally have

been sessional services for 3- and 4-year-olds. In the 2000s, many expanded their hours to school day or full-day provision in response to funding incentives and community needs, including needs of women for their child to be in ECEC, while they are in paid employment (Davison, Mitchell, & Peter, 2011). The correspondence school is a distance education service and as a school is the only ECEC service that is directly provided by the state. There are also some ECEC services located in hospitals for hospitalised children.

2.1.2 Parent–/Whānau–Led Services

Parent–/whānau-led services have high levels of parent and/or whānau involvement in providing education and care for children. They do not have to meet teacher registration targets, but the licensed parent-/whānau-led services have their own service-specific qualification requirements.

Kōhanga reo (Māori immersion language nests) were established in 1982 and have been described as "the most vigorous and innovative educational movement in this country (dare I say in the world)" (Reedy, 2003, p. 65). These offer total immersion Māori and are managed by whānau. The kōhanga reo philosophy centres around fostering Māori language and cultural identity and self-determination. A core aim is "passing on the Māori way of life to future generations" (Government Review Team, 1988, p. 19). Most kōhanga reo operate for 30 or more hours per week. Kōhanga Reo National Trust provides kōhanga-specific training.

Pacific early childhood groups are total immersion or bilingual in their home Pacific language. They may be sessional or full day. The impetus for setting up these services arose mainly from a desire by Pacific women to ensure that their Pacific languages and traditions were passed on to succeeding New Zealand-born generations (Mitchell, Royal Tangaere, Mara, & Wylie, 2006, p. 43). Some are staffed by qualified teachers and in this case are termed "teacher-led".

Playcentres are a uniquely Aotearoa New Zealand service and based on a belief in the family as the most important setting for the care and education of the child. Parents undertake all roles, including curriculum implementation, management and administration. Parents undertake playcentre training to be educators of their children (Hill, Reid, & Stover, 2000).

Sessional playgroups are also run by parents, but unlike in playcentres, parents require no training. They are usually small, often operating in community halls. Playgroups include Māori immersion and community language playgroups for different ethnic communities, as well as general playgroups.

Smith and May (2006) have linked the "paradigm of diversity" to Aotearoa New Zealand's historical context, particularly the Polynesian migration approximately 800 years ago; European colonisation in the nineteenth century and immigration during post-war years, especially from Pacific Island nations; but more recently from other countries.

3 Advocacy and Participation

Before moving into a more critical account of ECEC reform processes in Aotearoa New Zealand, this section discusses the advocacy, values and participation of people who, as individuals and within their collective organisations, held a vision and struggled for new alternatives for ECEC that were grounded in rights and offered promise of fair and empowering practice.

3.1 Women's Rights and Integration of Care and Education

The period in Aotearoa New Zealand from the late 1960s to the 1980s was described by May (2001) as a time when "The language of 'order' and 'adjustment' was overlaid by the language of 'rights' and 'liberation'.. .. demands arose for early childhood institutions to broaden their functions. Campaigns concerning Māori grievances, women's rights and the status of early childhood teachers and workers introduced a new militancy to the politics of early childhood" (p. 103–104). This new emphasis in rights and advocacy resulted in advances in ECEC policy that placed Aotearoa New Zealand as a world leader in its policy to structurally integrate all its ECEC services under an education administration. In 1986, all ECEC services were brought under the administration of the Department of Education. Prior to this, childcare centres were administered by the Department of Social Welfare, where they were regarded and funded primarily as services for the disadvantaged and needy. Home-based care was a matter of informal arrangements with relatives or carers (backyard baby-sitting), was not regulated and was privately funded. Kindergartens and playcentres were deemed to be education services, had more generous government subsidies and were administered by the Department of Education. Kōhanga reo, which were under the administration of the Department of Māori Affairs, remained with this department until 1990 – they were conceived to be "more than a language nest" (Royal-Tangaere, 1997) as discussed in the next section.

What brought about the shift in approach to government thinking? The integration of childcare into the Department of Education was over 10 years in the making and originated in feminist movements of the 1970s and concerted advocacy by women. Many were educated women, in paid employment, wanting childcare services that, like kindergartens, were educational but also offered full-day hours to fit with their employment. Achieving the integration was a long-winded process. Geraldine McDonald (1981) tells the story of the passage of the recommendation for integration passed by the Child Care Syndicate of the Conference on Women and Social and Economic Development held in March 1976 to mark the end of International Women's Year. This followed a recommendation for childcare to be transferred from the Department of Social Welfare to the Department of Education from the 1975 Select Committee on Women's Rights and a similar recommendation passed at the Seminar on Equality and the Education of the Sexes in 1975. The later 1976 recommendation was broader and more concrete. It sought a working group to be set up to look at ECEC in Aotearoa New Zealand and for organisations, including women's organisations to be consulted. "In essence it said, on behalf of women, 'consult us' and 'bring child care into the range of funded services'" (p. 162). Although a working group was established by the State Services Commission, its terms of reference became distorted through inadequate briefing, and women were not organised as a group to see the recommendations through. McDonald (1981) argued that "the original intention of those who passed the recommendation became pressed out of shape by 'the system'" (p. 169). Its draft report was widely criticised by early childhood organisations who were concerned about lack of consultation and took a delegation to the Minister of State Services to express their views. A reconstituted working group with a new chair and including Geraldine McDonald was then established. Its main recommendations were set out in the State Services Commission Report on Early Childhood Care and Education released in 1980:

• That there be three early childhood services (playcentre, kindergarten and child-care) with administrative responsibility in the Department of Education.
• That there be "equitable" funding for childcare and that this be based not on the "welfare" principle but on the principle of a contribution to a recognised service.
• That the government eventually subsidise up to 50% of the cost to parents. (May, 2001, p.148).

The values in these reforms shifted over time, from a focus on liberation of mothers, which antagonised some people, to arguments that breaking the artificial division between care and education services was in the best interests of children (Meade & Podmore, 2002). The State Services Commission Working Party report provided a rationale for the latter in stating:

> Whatever is provided for young children is in one sense care, and in another sense education. The two things in relation to the young child cannot be easily be distinguished. One cannot provide care for young children without their learning ideas, habits and attitudes; nor can one educate them without at the same time providing them with care. (State Services Commission, 1980, pp. 3–4).

Like many reforms in Aotearoa New Zealand, advocacy played a major role in identifying the nature of reform that was sought; collective organisation, rather than organisations or individuals acting separately, was a catalyst for seeing specific reform recommendations made and implemented. Advocates were persistent over a 10-year period, not losing sight of their goals for reform and refusing to accept unsatisfactory political responses. Before the publication of the United Nations Convention on the Rights of the Child, but during a decade when a children's rights focus was being broadened and clarified following the International Year of the Child in 1979 (Smith, 2016), the vision and argument about the "best interests of the child" captured imaginations and minds. Advocates' insistence on consultation in policy development with those working at the grassroots level was another reason why sound policies were eventually developed.

While the consultation brought out opponents to the transfer, the advocacy had influenced the opposition Labour Party to adopt the recommendations in its policy. In 1984, when the Labour government was elected, it announced that childcare would transfer to the Department of Education. The actual transfer happened in 1986.

Integration is now recognised as one of the core elements of a successful early childhood policy (OECD, 2001). The OECD (2001, 2006) has proposed that those countries with strong early childhood education and care systems have developed "a systematic and integrated approach to policy centring predominantly on children as a social group with rights". Benefits of a unified approach were said to include an enhanced ability to address inequalities and facilitate policy cohesion, e.g. in social and pedagogical objectives, budgets, regulation, funding, staffing and parental costs. The principle of integrated action refers to structural integration of policy and conceptual integration within policy and pedagogy (Cohen, Moss, Petrie, & Wallace, 2004).

Integration was significant in Aotearoa New Zealand in acknowledging the inseparability of care and education and promising an educational focus in all early childhood services. In terms of children's rights, integration was intended to offer a basis for a good-quality education for all children in whatever service they attend but needed other policy (including provision, curriculum, staffing, advisory support, and funding) to support this goal. These policies began to happen under the Labour government's terms of office (1984 to 1989).

Other integrations occurring in the late 1980s were to help to unify the sector.

In 1988, 3-year integrated training in colleges of education for teachers in childcare centres and kindergartens was introduced, replacing 2-year training for kindergarten teachers and 1-year training for childcare teachers. In the previous divided approach, there was an implicit view that childcare was a welfare service offering "care for the needy", while kindergartens and playcentres were "education" services (Dalli, 1992; May Cook, 1985; May, 1992). New teacher training programmes were required to "be inclusive of care and education, cover programmes for the care of babies and have more emphasis on education studies and the cultural and family contexts of children's lives" (May, 2009, p. 207).

Outside of government initiatives, in 1990, the two early childhood unions, the Kindergarten Teachers Association and Early Childhood Workers Union, amalgamated. Underlying the amalgamation was a goal, debated within the membership and by the national executives of each union over a period of 5 years, to form a strong united voice for staff in kindergartens and education and care centres to work collectively to influence policy and equitable employment conditions. The story of collective advocacy, the rights of workers and unionism is told more fully in chapter "Policy Frameworks and Democratic Participation".

This new era of equity became compromised by the powerful force of new right economic theories. Further integrations were to occur with respect to curriculum, teacher qualifications, funding and teacher pay, but market mechanisms somewhat jeopardised their coverage, adequacy and sustainability.

3.2   Indigenous Rights and Self-Determination

Helen May writes of the development of kōhanga reo:

> Liberation politics of the late 1960s–70s created the climate for a more radical analysis of Māori as an almost landless minority people, whose language and culture were besieged. The challenges to older cultural policies of assimilation and integration were driven initially by young Māori radicals comfortable with the strategies of protest and conscious of their connected plight to other indigenous people. The challenge was pervasive across the economic, political, social and educational institutions of Aotearoa New Zealand. (May, 2001, p. 176)

A story in *Te Ara, the Encyclopedia of New Zealand*, about Ngā rōpū tautohetohe – Māori protest movements – explains that the protests emerging during the 1960s and becoming more radical in the 1970s were "informed by awareness not only of historical injustices, but also the methods used historically by tīpuna (ancestors) to protest" (Keane, 2012, p. 1). Many nineteenth-century protests were about land confiscations, and methods included pulling out survey pegs and occupations, ploughing land, and petitioning parliament. The late 1960s and 1970s saw a dramatic increase in awareness of injustices and in Māori political activism. Māori land marches and protests at Waitangi Day celebrations over breaches of the Treaty of Waitangi were common. By this time, assimilationist policies and racist attitudes had resulted in an over-representation of Māori compared with Pākehā (white New Zealanders) on negative social statistics of justice, housing, health, education and employment (Poutu, 2004, cited in Lee et al., 2013, p. 33). In relation to education, in the 1980s and 1990s, "Notwithstanding countless recommendations and reports, the education policies and systems, when taken in their wider context, continued to marginalise and devalue Māori cultural traditions (tikanga Māori), Māori language (te reo Māori) and Māori ways of knowing (mātauranga Māori) within teaching and learning practices, protocols and policy-making" (Macfarlane, 2015). Macfarlane termed the emergence of kōhanga reo in 1982, and subsequently kura kaupapa Māori (total immersion primary schools) in 1986, as "exemplary resistance initiatives".

Royal Tangaere, writing in a Ministry of Education commissioned report on quality of education in parent-/whanau-led services, describes the underpinning kaupapa or philosophy of kōhanga as centring around:

> "te mana o te whānau" (the dignity of the family, including the extended family). Tino rangatiratanga (self determination), a fundamental principle of Te Tiriti o Waitangi, is also the foundation of the kōhanga movement. Embodied in Te Korowai are four pou (or posts) which are the cornerstones of the kaupapa: total immersion in te reo Māori, whānau decision-making, management and responsibility, accountability to all cultural, financial

and whānau members and groups, and ensuring the health and well-being of the mokopuna and the whānau.

The educational programme is based on *Te Whāriki*. In addition the kōhanga model emphasises the importance of strong spiritual and cultural wellbeing of the child and the whānau. It focuses on quality cultural interactions between adults, between adults and children, and between children. Whakapapa and genealogy of the child and whānau are important and mihimihi (or greetings) are an important part of the programme. (Mitchell et al., 2006, p. 28)

The idea for kōhanga reo originated from a Department of Māori Affairs forum in 1980, where Māori elders decided it was time for Maoridom "to take control of the future destiny of the language and to plan for its survival" (Royal-Tangaere, 1997, p. 42). Kaumatua and kuia (elders) who are native speakers of Māori are essential in kōhanga reo because it is usually the older generations who have the reo and tikanga knowledge to be passed on. Kōhanga reo challenge mainstream views, validate Māori knowledge and methods of teaching and learning and provide an alternative education system determined by Māori and for Māori. This reform was developed to assert Māori cultural values, practices and beliefs and revitalise language through total immersion.

After establishment in 1982, the number of kōhanga reo grew rapidly to 809 in 1993, serving 14,514 children, but the number has since declined to 450, serving 8860 children in 2015. In 2011, Te Kōhanga Reo National Trust made a claim to the Waitangi Tribunal that the Crown's actions and failure to uphold the principles of Te Tiriti o Waitangi in relation to kōhanga reo to operate effectively in ensuring the transmission of te reo me ngā tikanga had led to the decline in number of kōhanga reo and number of children enrolled. The tribunal found that transfer of responsibility for kōhanga reo during 1990 from the Department of Māori Affairs to the Ministry of Education brought the trust and kōhanga reo under "a more rigid, rules-based ECE compliance regime" and a staff who "knew little about the kōhanga reo kaupapa and culture and focused more narrowly on educational objectives" (Waitangi Tribunal, 2013, p. 19). It found further that early childhood policy changes from 2002 put kōhanga reo at a disadvantage by assessing quality against standards for general early childhood centres rather than their own quality criteria. It cited a qualitative study that included six kōhanga reo undertaken in 2005 (Mitchell et al., 2006), where Royal-Tangaere (the author of the section on kōhanga reo) found that when assessed against their own values and philosophy, kōhanga reo were performing well. The predominant strengths of kōhanga reo were clearly recognised as te reo and tikanga Māori (Māori language and culture) learning (children and adults) and children learning to care for and socialise with each other. Some changes towards more limited parent involvement had also occurred and were a reflection of the reality that many parents in kōhanga reo were not able to participate with the children on a regular basis during the day because of work commitments or limited competency in te reo Māori (Māori language), making them feel whakamā or embarrassed. Parent and whānau (extended family) were highly involved through management and decision-making; participation in kura reo (Māori language learning opportunities) and other wananga (educational forums), language and cultural support; and supporting the kōhanga reo through fundraising and working bees.

In summary, the kōhanga movement was born from resistance politics but on its path has faced policy decisions that have not been sufficiently supportive of its distinct kaupapa and needs. The movement highlights the importance of culturally determined values for that community, time and place holding centrality within the programme. In respect to policy, standardised solutions do not fit all services.

4   Democracy and Social Justice in the Development of the Curriculum

The unifying processes of the 1980s provided a platform for an integrated approach to curriculum (Lee et al., 2013). The 1988 Lopdell Curriculum Statement identified 15 basic curriculum statements which were reflected in the strands of *Te Whāriki* and the following definition of curriculum as "the sum total of the child's direct and indirect learning experiences". This was expanded in *Te Whāriki* as "The term curriculum is used in this document to describe the sum total of the experiences, activities, and events, whether direct or indirect, which occur within an environment designed to foster children's learning and development" (Ministry of Education, 1996, p. 10).

Social justice values are reflected in *Te Whāriki*'s focus on equity and respect for children's rights and an aim to support children growing up in a democracy:

> In particular early childhood curriculum supports the renaissance of Māori language. It looks ahead to citizens who can make responsible and informed choices, respect the ideas and beliefs of others, include diversity in their world view, and have an understanding of both the major cultures and languages. (Lee et al., 2013, p. 9)

It was within the context of a centre-right government that took office in late 1989 that the ECEC curriculum was developed. The government's revision of the school curriculum in, 1991 included development of achievement initiatives for different ages for each subject level. When the government turned its attention to an early childhood curriculum, early childhood organisations were concerned that an early childhood curriculum might promote a standardised approach and cut across the diversity that is a hallmark of Aotearoa New Zealand's early childhood sector. There was a fear that testing of 5-year-olds and the national curriculum for schools might push downward. The awarding of the curriculum contract writing to Helen May and Margaret Carr from the University of Waikato had the full backing of early childhood organisations "who saw it was timely to define the curriculum in more detail to both protect and promote the early childhood philosophy" (Carr & May, 1993a, p. 47). From the outset, the writers argued for a bicultural approach to curriculum development and content and for diverse services to be able to negotiate their own curriculum.

The curriculum development was undertaken with very close consultation and in partnership with Te Kōhanga Reo National Trust (the overall umbrella organisation for Māori immersion kōhanga reo). This intensive consultation and collaboration were crucial to the widespread support engendered for the curriculum document. Carr and May (2000) have argued they needed to negotiate between three voices: government interests in an efficient and competitive economy, early childhood practitioners and families from a diversity of services and cultural perspectives and national and international early childhood voices "advocating for equitable educational opportunities and quality early childhood policies and practices" (p. 53). The curriculum development process was organised to ensure dialogue with all parties having an interest in early childhood education. Representatives from all national early childhood organisations, government agencies, universities, and research and teacher training institutions were on an Advisory Group and gave feedback on all papers. A review group was established by the Ministry of Education to represent the government and evaluate the document (Carr & May, 1993c).

A curriculum development team of 15 practitioners, trainers and nationally recognised individuals formed the core working group. The curriculum was structured to enable the development of common principles, aims and goals and also to provide opportunity to negotiate the identity of diverse provision within the curriculum framework.

> The team had two working groups: the infant and toddler and the young child, along with the co-ordinators of four specialist working groups: Māori Immersion, Curricula for Pacific Island Children – Tageta Pasifika, Including Children with Special needs, and Home Based Programmes. (Carr & May, 1993c, p. 133)

In this process, the partnership formed with Te Kōhanga Reo National Trust was of vital importance. Tilly Reedy and Tamati Reedy were appointed as two Māori lead writers and were responsible for writing the Māori immersion curriculum for ngā kōhanga reo. Tilly and Tamati Reedy met often with Helen May and Margaret Carr to discuss how to weave the Māori and Pākehā concepts together (Te One, 2003, p. 29).

From 1991 to 1993, the writers tested out their ideas through a series of working papers which they circulated for feedback. They also made many conference presentations in Aotearoa New Zealand and internationally where they gained more feedback. It was through this process of intensive consultation that consensus concerning the proposed curriculum principles and the aims and goals for children was able to be reached amongst the diverse early childhood services (Carr & May, 1993b). *Te Whāriki* was published in 1996 (Ministry of Education, 1996). Dalli and Te One (2003) have argued that, throughout the 1990s, the community-based early childhood sector remained active, articulate and united about pedagogic principles, influencing the development of *Te Whāriki* and the subsequent assessment and evaluation approach using teaching and learning stories (Carr, May, & Podmore, 1998; Carr et al., 2000).

The ways in which democracy weaves with the principles, strands and goals of *Te Whāriki* are discussed in chapter "Traditions of Democracy in Education". As a curriculum, *Te Whāriki* was able to both protect and promote the early childhood philosophy. It acknowledges that the learning environment in the early years is different from that in the school sector. The roles of key players kept alive ideals of biculturalism, equity and quality during this time. However, having a visionary curriculum is not in itself sufficient for ECEC. The conditions, training and professional support of the adults working in early childhood services are of vital importance. Poverty and inequality of opportunity are wider societal influences that profoundly impact on the child and family.

5 Market Forces and New Right Economic Theories

During the 1980s, new right economic theory was becoming influential internationally. The key beliefs are that private sector approaches and market forces will produce cost-effectiveness and be more efficient than the state; therefore private provision should be encouraged and state provision reduced. Consumer choice would encourage competition, and consumers would "vote with their feet" if provision did not meet their needs. In this way, responsive and effective services would thrive, and unresponsive and ineffective services would fail. During the Labour government's term of office (1984–1989), these ideas were adopted single-mindedly across many spheres of operation and then continued in the 1990s under a National government in what has come to be known as "the New Zealand experiment" (Kelsey, 1997). State services were privatised, including Ports of Auckland, Air New Zealand, Bank of New Zealand, Telecommunications, New Zealand Railways, Auckland International Airport and various power companies. There were severe reductions in benefit levels announced in the 1991 government budget, to the extent that benefit rates were judged by the New Zealand Treasury to have fallen below the poverty threshold. User pays was implemented for social services. The tax base was "broadened" meaning that taxation levels for the rich were reduced and those for the poor were increased. The labour market was deregulated: the *1991 Employment Contracts Act* (New Zealand Government, 1991) actively favoured individual over collective bargaining and removed good faith bargaining provisions and union rights of workplace access. Kelsey writes of the impact: "What were once basic priorities – collective responsibility, redistribution of resources and power, social stability, democratic participation, and the belief that human beings were entitled to live and work in security and dignity – seemed to have been left far behind. Poverty, division and alienation had become permanent features of New Zealand's social landscape" (Kelsey, 1999, p. 3). The gap between rich and poor steadily increased in those years and continued to do so until 2004, when a policy intervention "Working for Families" reduced inequalities marginally, but it has since risen. Using evidence from their own research, OECD data, and World Bank data, Wikinson and Pickett (2010) show that a wide range of health and social problems are much more common in societies with bigger income differences between rich and poor.

The same pattern can be seen at all levels of economic development regardless of culture. Whether you look at violence, drug addiction, lack of community life, mental illness, or low levels of child wellbeing, more unequal societies come close to being socially dysfunctional. Problems such as these may be anything from twice as common to ten times as common in more unequal societies because, rather than being confined to the poor, the effects of inequality extend to the vast majority of the population. (Wikinson & Pickett, 2014)

Over this same period, new right economic theory was applied to reforms taking place in the education sector, where individual schools became self-managing. The education reforms could be termed "liberal welfare" and are comparable in their underlying basis to those produced in England and Scotland during the 1980s and 1990s (Moss & Petrie, 2002). New right theories were applied most rigorously in the early childhood sector. *Before Five* (Lange, 1988), the government policy document for ECEC emerging from these reforms in 1989, promised equal status for early childhood education with other education sectors. United advocacy through a funding campaign, coupled with work from "insiders" in parliament, resulted in funding to early childhood education being increased by 125 percent – a remarkable achievement at a time when there was pressure to reduce government expenditure (Meade, 1990). But the aim for equity was subverted by fundamentally problematic market mechanisms that were applied to staffing, provision and funding. Changes resulting from these policy developments were easily withdrawn because they simply involved a supply of additional resources rather than a shift in values and structures.

Minimum standards only were set in regulation for staff qualifications and staff/child ratios, leaving it up to providers to decide (or not) on higher standards. For-profit providers campaigned actively against higher regulated standards. The government had no direct role in planning and provision of services and offered only a very small pool of discretionary grant funding for capital works for some eligible community-owned services. New services could be established and receive child-based government funding without having to show that they would meet community needs or be sustainable. Per child bulk funding was allocated to early childhood services to enable them to act autonomously, rather than through state employment of staff or state infrastructure (Wylie, 1998). When implemented in the 1990s, consistent with economic theories, funding was largely the same for all services regardless of intake (children) or of costs of operation. The main funding source (bulk funding) was not tagged for particular spending purposes, and management had wide discretion about how it was spent. In the absence of linkages to costs and because there was no transparent formula specifying what the funding was intended to cover, levels of funding were easily reduced, and overall funding did not keep up with price increases. Another consequence was that for-profit providers, with little accountability for spending, could maximise their profits by reducing staff numbers to the minimum required, employing cheaper unqualified staff and cutting back on employment conditions. Government distanced itself. It saw itself as a purchaser of education rather than a provider. "Under current policies the government buys educational hours of a particular quality from early childhood centres and overall is neutral in terms of service type" (Ministry of Education, 1995).

Under the *Employment Contracts Act (1991)* (New Zealand Government, 1991), the bargaining arrangements for teachers/educators in childcare centres became fragmented when a national award specifying minimum employment conditions collapsed because employers refused to bargain (Mitchell & Wells, 1997). In 1997 kindergarten teachers, previously paid by the state, were removed from the State Sector Act, their pay and conditions becoming the responsibility of individual employers. A national employment contract for all teachers splintered into 18 separate contracts as kindergarten associations negotiated separately.

The free market approach assumes that the community or business sector will respond to community needs, and the operation of the market will ensure appropriate provision. This did not occur: there was growing evidence of major problems with the approach. By the mid-1990s, there were gaps and duplications in service provision, and access by different groups in the community was variable, with low-income families, Māori and Pasifika families having lower levels of participation than Pākehā New Zealanders (non-Māori of European extraction) (Department of Labour and National Advisory Council on the Employment of Women, 1999; Early Childhood Education Project, 1996; Hanna, 1994; Mitchell, 1996). Spurred by the access to government funding, the number of privately owned,[1] profit-making education and care (childcare) centres and home-based services grew quickly, a trend that has continued under subsequent governments. The percentage of privately owned education and care centres rose from 41% in 1992 to 51% in 2001, 57% in 2007, 64% in 2010 and 67% in 2016. In 2016, home-based services are mainly in private ownership with 88% of the 472 privately owned (Ministry of Education, 2016).

During the 1990s, services were found to be of variable quality, and the early childhood workforce continued to be underpaid and undervalued. Services were fragmented, especially those which were not part of a larger umbrella organisation operating to support them. There was no coherent policy framework, and sector representatives had little involvement in policy-making, the exception being the consultation over *Te Whāriki*.

---

[1]A private provider is "any person or persons either managing or owning an early childhood service who invest their own personal income and/or capital into the service with any profits made being paid back to the investor either jointly or severally for their private purposes" (Ministry of Education, 1992). Community-owned services are prohibited through their constitution from making financial gains that are distributed to members.

6   ECEC as a Public Good and a Child's Right

When it came into office in late 1999, the Labour-led government worked in a highly consultative way with the early childhood sector on developing a strategic plan for early childhood education. The idea for the strategic plan and for a consultative approach to be taken to its development came from a union initiative to bring together ECEC national organisations to make recommendations for ECEC policy. Chapter 6, "Influencing Policy Change through Collective Action" tells the story of this initiative, termed *Future Directions: Early childhood Education in New Zealand*, and the collective advocacy that saw its agenda advanced. The strategic plan, *Pathways to the Future: Ngā Huarahi Arataki* (Ministry of Education, 2002), led to far-reaching changes to ECEC that focused directly on three main goals: to improve the quality of ECEC, increase participation in quality ECEC and promote collaborative relationships between ECEC and schools and with families and health and social services. The government's vision was "for all children to participate in early childhood education no matter their circumstances" (Ministry of Education, 2002, p. 1). This was a marked change in thinking from the minimal state support under the previous governments (Mitchell, 2005). Its high-level overarching goals were aspirational for the government and the sector. The strategic plan was intended to provide an integrated structure of support through linking the three main goals with strategies to achieve them. Over the period 2002 to 2009, new policy initiatives were put into place to support each goal. These focused mainly on increasing funding levels and improving funding mechanisms to increase child participation and enhancing teacher qualifications, teacher pay and professional resources and professional development to improve quality. Supported by government incentives, striking increases in the percentage of qualified teachers staffing teacher-led services were made in this time: from 37.3 percent in 2004 to 56.4 percent in 2006 and to 64% in 2009. The percentage rose to 76% in 2013. In chapter "Policy Frameworks and Democratic Participation", specific policy initiatives and findings from policy evaluations are discussed.

Yet from a child rights and democratic perspective, New Zealand's strategic plan did not deal well with the "wicked issue" of ECEC provision. The government reliance on the market approach to ECEC provision without necessity for planning continued the inequitable distribution of services throughout Aotearoa New Zealand. Despite progress in regard to ECEC affordability, children from low-income communities were still more likely to miss out on attending ECEC (Mitchell & Davison, 2010). The assumption that the market will provide and that what it provides will be appropriate was at odds with the strategic plan vision of access for all children no matter their circumstances.

7   Retrenchment and a Focus on Vulnerable Children

While the period 1999 to 2008 represented movement towards a view of ECEC as a child's right and support for a professionally qualified and reflective ECEC workforce, new and conflicting policy agendas are being enacted under the centre-right National-led government. This government was elected in November 2008 and finished its third term in September 2017. These agendas have moved ECEC policy from a universal to a more targeted approach that has focused on increasing participation for "priority" children.

Within weeks of being elected, the *Strategic Plan for Early Childhood Education* was removed from the Ministry of Education website, a sign that this was a new political regime. The *Briefing to the Treasury to the Incoming Minister of Finance in 2008* (The Treasury, 2008) foreshadowed some of the policy directions that were to come. Within the education system, The Treasury argued there was no need to improve levels of ECEC funding, but instead the focus should be on improving "how funding is linked to performance through improved targeting, stronger accountability for outcomes and incentives for responsiveness in the early childhood, schooling and the tertiary sectors". In the same section, it also highlighted the welfare benefit system and its view that expectations/sanctions are critical to reducing beneficiary numbers and making long-term gains, a linking between benefits and early childhood education that later was to be played out.

Funding principles were quickly altered by the new government, funding levels were reduced and policy initiatives to improve quality were removed or lessened. A further change announced in 2011 was to allow ECEC centres to operate with 150 children over 2 years and 75 children under 1 year, replacing maximum centre sizes of 50 and 25 children, respectively. The maximum centre size has been the only regulated way in which numbers of children in a group have been constrained.

Aotearoa New Zealand has a relatively high rate of ECEC participation, but lower levels of participation are associated with ethnicity and income levels. While cuts were being made to policies intended to support quality, a new emphasis emerged on targeted policies to support participation of children deemed to be "priority" (Māori, Pasifika and children from low socio-economic homes and who are not yet attending early childhood education). The main government initiative during this time was the "ECE Participation Programme", introduced in 2010, targeting local areas where high numbers of children starting school have not taken part in early childhood education. This programme is made up of six initiatives that aim to support priority families to enrol their children in ECEC.

An evaluation of the ECE Participation Programme (Mitchell et al., 2014; Mitchell, Meagher-Lundberg, Davison, Kara, & Kalavite, 2016; Mitchell et al., 2013) found out much about barriers to participation of priority families and whether and how the initiatives are addressing these. ECEC services in the evaluation that were doing well in catering for priority families were developed as an integrated service that housed or brokered support by bringing together interdisciplinary teams for families/whānau to access. The integrated services drew on the funds of knowledge residing in families/whānau and communities, employed staff from the cultural backgrounds of families/whānau and offered relevant professional support.

In parallel to the implementation of the Participation Programme administered by the Ministry of Education, ECEC developments were occurring under the Ministry of Social Development. Early childhood education became a social obligation for beneficiaries with preschool children under the *Social Security (Benefit Categories and Work Focus) Amendment Act* (New Zealand Government, 2013), passed in April 2013. Specifically, beneficiaries with a child age 3 years or 4 years are required to "take all reasonable steps" to enrol their child in a recognised early childhood education programme and ensure attendance. If the beneficiary does not comply, their benefit could be reduced by 50 percent. If a beneficiary has another child while on the benefit, he/she is required to be "work ready" when that second child turns 1 year old.

The act was contentious and subject to widespread criticism by early childhood organisations who argued amongst other matters that making ECEC compulsory would undermine trusting and respectful relationships between beneficiaries and ECEC services. The interrelated reasons why families do not participate in ECEC suggest barriers to participation need to be addressed in a range of ways. A University of Waikato masters student, Randall (2015), recently undertook a study of the views and experiences of the beneficiaries who were affected by the policy and of ECEC service managers working with beneficiaries. Her study found that Work and Income New Zealand staff members, who administer the policy, were not trained or equipped to provide sound information to parents about ECEC. Staff members did not know what ECEC programmes were available or have details about the different types of ECEC services. Additionally, some beneficiary participants recounted administration errors, staff disregarding individual needs and circumstances and treating beneficiaries with a lack of respect. Randall argued that matters concerning ECEC should remain under the administration of the Ministry of Education and that the principle of integration has been undermined through this policy. The beneficiary participants and ECEC service managers were critical of the labelling of children as vulnerable, and the lack of autonomy afforded families to make their own decisions about ECEC as does every other family in Aotearoa New Zealand. The consequences of having a benefit halved for non-compliance would undoubtedly be harmful for children as the family's financial means would dip well below the poverty level.

7.1 Continued Growth of Market-Led Provision

The National-led government removed the only funding differentials between community-based and privately owned ECEC services. Equity funding became available to the private sector. Targeted Assistance for Participation grants replaced discretionary grants in offering capital works funding. They were made available to for-profit corporate owners as well as community-based services, making Aotearoa New Zealand infamous for providing taxpayer funding for privately owned assets.

These developments are highly problematic. Earlier research has shown quality differentials between privately owned and community-based ECEC services favouring the community sector (Mitchell, 2002; Mitchell & Brooking, 2007) and that private centres are more likely to be in high-income areas where fees could be charged. The 2006 OECD study of 20 countries (OECD, 2006) suggested that a reliance on privatised provision of early childhood education will almost certainly lead to inequities in provision in poorer communities because commercial providers are reluctant to invest in such communities.

In late 2014 a publicly listed company, Evolve Education Group, bought two large ECEC companies, Lollipops Educare with 30 education and care centres and Porse, an accredited home-based provider and trainer. It also bought an additional 55 education and care centres and an ECEC management organisation and has stated its intention to expand. In a comment to a national newspaper (Mitchell, 2 December, 2014), I argued that government ECEC funding and parent fees intended for children's education will pay for the dividend yields of shareholders. The *Evolve Education Group Prospectus* foregrounded money-making potentials of ECEC and in so doing conceptualised ECEC as a business opportunity, selling a commodity to parent consumers as they participate in the workforce. The first duty of Evolve as a listed company is to shareholders, and this main interest from a commercial view in making profits for owners or shareholders positions Evolve Education Group at odds with community-spirited aims to invest fully in the service itself. Profitability is a key selection and acquisition criteria.

The New Zealand Government over time has been unwilling to impose conditions on receipt of government funding that would restrict providers from charging what they like or being listed on the share market – an indication of its adherence to free market principles. This makes high standards of regulation crucially important to offer some safeguards over structural elements of quality, but these have been undermined in the National-led government approach.

8   Promising New Directions: The 2017 Coalition Government

A left-leaning Labour-led and New Zealand First coalition government was elected in October 2017 to hold office for 3 years. The Green Party supports this coalition government with a confidence and supply agreement. That significant change was in the air, was first signalled by the New Zealand First leader, Winston Peters, whose choice was to form a coalition with the governing national party, which he described as a "modified status quo" or side with Labour for significant "change". In particular, he highlighted the need for capitalism to "regain its human face". Notably, the new government has pledged to urgently address child poverty, inadequate housing, poor health services and environmental climate change. Prime Minister Jacinda Ardern told her caucus, "A country where our environment is protected, where we look after the most vulnerable, where we support our families, where we make sure people have the most basic of needs, like a roof over their head." Improving women's lives is a top priority. Ardern is committed to having 50 percent of her caucus made up of women and to supporting women in the home and workplace. "I have great ambition as a woman and as prime minister elect that we will make great gains as a government in issues like equal pay, in issues like supporting women in the roles they choose to take, whether they be work or in caring roles ... I hold that issue close to my heart." Her happy announcements in January 2018 are that she and her partner are expecting their first child, that she will continue with her full prime ministerial duties after 6-week maternity leave ("I'm just pregnant, not incapacitated", she said. "Like everyone else who has found themselves pregnant before, I'm just keeping on going" she told TV1 News on 26 January 2018) and that her partner Clarke Gayford will be the at-home carer and offer to be a positive role model for gender equality.

The new government has been quick to act in its first 100 days of office. Radical policy measures already set in place are to raise the incomes of low-income families, extend paid parental leave, raise the minimum wage and set targets for reduction in child poverty. In the education sector, the government has moved quickly to make the first year of tertiary education free and remove national standards from primary schools (these require schools to make and report teacher judgements about children's levels of reading, writing and mathematics achievement at different times in the first 8 years of primary schooling and are discussed in chapter "Assessment and Pedagogical Documentation"). It has introduced a government bill to end charter schools and to require staff and student representatives on Tertiary Education Institution councils. These changes in the schooling and tertiary education sectors demonstrate a willingness to listen to teachers and other staff in more democratic decision-making processes, to trust teachers as professionals to make decisions about assessment and to reinforce the values of public education and full government support for it.

Some of Labour's policy for the ECE sector is a continuation of what happened under the earlier Labour-led government – reinstating funding levels cut in 2009 and returning to a target of 100% qualified teachers in teacher-led services. Potential extensions of previous policy directions and new policy developments lie in several areas:

- A promise to develop through a consultative process, a second version of Nga Huarahi Arataki – Pathways to the Future, a 10-year strategic plan for early childhood education (herein lie opportunities for new policy directions). The Minister of Education has stated his intention to establish a strategic plan working group, with proposed terms of reference and potential membership reported to the Cabinet in March 2018 (Hipkins, 2018). He has noted that "an important part of the strategic plan will be creating a shared vision for what early learning should achieve for children and exploring what settings best support these outcomes. **This includes the nature of the early childhood education market, along with the network which underpins it and the role of government in managing provision**" (Clause 54, p. 10) [my highlighting]. This is the first time in policy development for early childhood education that the education market and role of government have been an explicit focus. It opens the door for rigorous and research-based analysis of the problems with a market approach and for-profit provision and a move towards public responsibility.

- Support for the establishment of new public early childhood centres in areas of low provision through targeted establishment grants and only provide taxpayer subsidies for new early childhood centres if there is an established need in the proposed location (a welcome emphasis on public and planned provision and shift from a market approach to provision).
- Developing a network of high-quality centre-based early intervention programmes addressing the needs of vulnerable children in the most deprived areas (potentially problematic with its deficit connotations).
- Improving group size and teacher/child ratios for infants and toddlers (a welcome emphasis on structural requirements and quality of ECEC provision for infants and toddlers which has been an ongoing concern).
- To work with the school sector to trial giving schools the option of implementing *Te Whāriki* in the first 2 years of schooling to enhance the transition from early childhood education to schooling (an exciting possibility for the ECEC curriculum and philosophy to become foundational in primary schools).

Taken as a whole, these policies indicate a shift towards the universal and rights-based approach of the previous Labour-led government and go further. They suggest a privileging of public provision in ECEC and a more planned approach to provision and an upward spread of ECEC principles and values into schools.

9   Contrasting Policy Approaches: Constructs of Childhood

Moss and Petrie (1997, 2002) have argued that making explicit the constructs of childhood that underpin policy and pedagogical approaches can open these up to scrutiny and change. Over three decades, different approaches to ECEC policy have been enacted in Aotearoa New Zealand.

The approach to policy in the period 1984 to 1999 could be characterised as a market approach, following new right economic theories, with ECEC regarded as a parental choice. Conceptually, the child is located within the private domain – the child is a dependant of the family, a positioning that curtails the role of the state. The state is as a purchaser of education from an increasingly privatised sector. Associated with this approach is an unwillingness to regulate high standards and impose restrictions on how services are managed. But, against these odds, and in stark contrast, major achievements of integration of ECEC within an education administration and development and publication of the curriculum, *Te Whāriki*, occurred during this time – the former, a result of many years of advocacy by women, and the latter of shrewd strategising, collective ECEC sector support and a commitment to social justice, biculturalism and consultation. Te kōhanga reo were established as "a national desire amongst Māori to save and nurture the language was embraced" (Lee et al., 2013, p. 34). In each of these developments, a focus is on mana, being strong, and a holistic understanding of childhood as fundamental principles.

The approach under the Labour-led government 1999 to 2008 could be characterised as a universal approach where ECEC is viewed as (almost) "a right for the young child citizen" (May, 2014, p. 166). The role of the state is as "a supportive state" (Royal Commission on Social Policy, 1988, p. 128) where providing ECEC is seen as a co-operative effort amongst the state, families, teachers and community. In this approach, credit is given to the views, expertise and experiences of participants, as in the construction of the strategic plan for ECEC, the tangible support and encouragement for teachers to research their own practice and learn from each other and the construction of children and families as participants within curriculum, assessment and pedagogy. Quality is emphasised in tandem with participation. The collaborative relationships goal of the strategic plan showed an understanding of the importance of connections between the major settings that impact on family lives – a holistic understanding of childhood. But nevertheless, a market approach to provision remained.

The third approach could be characterised as social interventionist (May, 2014; Penn, 2011) where ECEC is viewed as most beneficial for vulnerable children from "priority families" and the role of the state is to pick up and support where families cannot provide adequately. At its extreme, this is seen in the social obligations of beneficiaries with preschool children to enrol their child in ECEC. Associated with this approach is a predominant focus on participation by priority families and a neglect of policy measures to support good quality. Alongside is a governmental focus on measurable child outcomes as a form of accountability. The influence of such policies have consequences for ECEC, narrowing opportunities for access that privilege the wealthy and dominant group and shrinking possibilities for an education for lifelong learning.

The approach under the Labour-led government of 2017–current looks promising. Strong indications are that it will continue as a universal and rights-based approach inherited from the previous Labour-led government, focus on quality and go further in dealing with the unresolved and problematic issues caused by a reliance on the market and creeping privatisation in relation to provision and potentially teacher pay. Penn (2011) has argued that a child rights approach "offers challenges to current futuristic thinking" and that from this perspective "ECEC services need to be rethought" (p. 13). There is a way forward; this book pinpoints where the new directions under the 2017 Labour-led government might be taken and uses examples from Aotearoa New Zealand policy and practice as signposts of what might be possible.

References

Carr, M., & May, H. (1993a). The role of government in early childhood curriculum in Aotearoa – New Zealand. In V. N. Podmore (Ed.), *What is government's role in early childhood education? Papers presented at the 1993 NZCER invitational seminar* (pp. 42–50). Wellington, New Zealand: New Zealand Council for Educational Research.

Carr, M., & May, H. (1993b). *Te Whāriki curriculum papers. Early Childhood Curriculum Project.* Hamilton, New Zealand: University of Waikato.

Carr, M., & May, H. (1993c). Te Whāriki: National early childhood curriculum guidelines. Paper presented by Helen May at the International Conference Workshop on Preschool Education: A Change towards the Twenty-first Century, Hong Kong and Hainan, March 20–26. In M. Carr & H. May (Eds.), *Te Whāriki curriculum papers.* Hamilton, New Zealand: University of Waikato.

Carr, M., & May, H. (2000). Te Whāriki: Curriculm voices. In H. Penn (Ed.), *Early childhood services. Theory, policy and practice* (pp. 53–73). Buckingham, England: Open University Press.

Carr, M., May, H., & Podmore, V. (1998). *Learning and teaching stories. New approaches to assessment and evaluation in relation to Te Whaariki.* Paper presented at the Symposium for 8th European Conference on Quality in Early Childhood Settings, Santiago de Compostela, Spain.

Carr, M., May, H., Podmore, V., Cubey, P., Hatherly, A., & Macartney, B. (2000). *Learning and Teaching Stories: Action research on evaluation in early childhood education.* Wellington, New Zealand: New Zealand Council for Educational Research.

Cohen, B., Moss, P., Petrie, P., & Wallace, J. (2004). *A new deal for children? Re-forming education and care in England, Scotland and Sweden.* Bristol, England: The Policy Press.

Dalli, C. (1992). Policy agendas for children's lives. *New Zealand Journal of Educational Studies, 27*(1), 53–67.

Dalli, C., & Te One, S. (2003). Early childhood education in 2002. In I. Livingstone (Ed.), *New Zealand Annual Review of Education* (pp. 177–202). Wellington, New Zealand: School of Education, Victoria University of Wellington.

Davison, C., Mitchell, L., & Peter, M. (2011). *Survey of kindergarten provision. Results of a 2010 survey of New Zealand Kindergartens Inc kindergarten associations.* Retrieved from http://www.waikato.ac.nz/wmier/publications/reports/survey-of-kindergarten-provision-results-of-a-2010-survey-of-new-zealand-kindergartens-inc.-kindergarten-associations

Department of Labour and National Advisory Council on the Employment of Women. (1999). *Childcare, families and work. The New Zealand Childcare Survey 1998: A survey of early childhood education and care arrangements for children.* Wellington, New Zealand: Labour Market Policy Group.

Early Childhood Education Project. (1996). *Future directions: Early childhood education in New Zealand.* Wellington, New Zealand: New Zealand Educational Institute Te Riu Roa.

Government Review Team. (1988). *Government review of Te Kōhanga Reo: Language is the life force of the people.* Wellington, New Zealand: Te Kōhanga Reo National Trust.

Hanna, P. (1994). *A report of the 1994 "Speaking Directly" early childhood education conference.* Wellington, New Zealand: Ministry of Education.

Hill, D., Reid, R., & Stover, S. (2000). More than educating children: The evolutionary nature of 'laycentre's philosophy of education. In S. Stover (Ed.), *Good clean fun: New Zealand's playcentre movement* (pp. 30–38). Wellington, New Zealand: New Zealand Playcentre Federation.

Hipkins, C. (2018). *Education portfolio workplan: Purpose, objectives and overview.* Wellington, New Zealand. Retrieved from http://www.education.govt.nz/assets/Documents/Ministry/Information-releases/R-Education-Portfolio-Work-Programme-Purpose-Objectives-and-Overview.pdf.

Keane, B. (2012). Ngā rōpū tautohetohe – Māori protest movements. Te Ara. The Encyclopedia of New Zealand. Wellington, New Zealand. Retrieved from http://www.teara.govt.nz/en/nga-ropu-tautohetohe-maori-protest-movements/page-1.

Kelsey, J. (1997). *The New Zealand experiment: A world model for structural adjustment?* Auckland, New Zealand: Auckland University Press: Bridget Williams Books.

Kelsey, J. (1999). New Zealand's "experiment" a colossal failure. Retrieved January 1, 2017, from http://www.converge.org.nz/pma/apfail.htm

King, M. (2003). *The Penguin history of New Zealand.* Auckland, New Zealand: Penguin.

Lange, D. (1988). *Before Five.* Wellington, New Zealand: Government Print.

Lee, W., Carr, M., Soutar, B., & Mitchell, L. (2013). *Understanding the Te Whāriki approach.* London: Routledge.

Macfarlane, A. H. (2015). Restlessness, resoluteness and reason: Looking back at 50 years of Māori education. *NZ J Educ Stud, 50*, 177. https://doi.org/10.1007/s40841-015-0023-y.

May Cook, H. (1985). *Mind that Child.* Wellington, New Zealand: Blackberry Press.

May, H. (1992). After 'Before Five': The politics of early childhood care and education in the nineties. *New Zealand Women's Studies Journal, 8*(2), 83–100.

May, H. (2001). *Politics in the playground. The world of early childhood in post war New Zealand.* Wellington, New Zealand: Bridget Williams Books Limited and New Zealand Council for Educational Research.

May, H. (2009). *Politics in the playground. The world of early childhood education in New Zealand* (2nd ed.). Dunedin, New Zealand: Otago University Press.

May, H. (2013). *The discovery of early childhood* (2nd ed.). Wellington, New Zealand: Auckland University Press with Bridget Williams Books.

May, H. (2014). New Zealand: A narrative of shifting policy directions for education and care. In L. Gambaro, K. Stewart, & J. Waldfogel (Eds.), *An equal start? Providing quality early childhood education and care for disadvantaged children* (pp. 147–170). Bristol, England: Policy Press.

McDonald, G. (1981). The story of a recommendation about care and education. In M. Clark (Ed.), *The politics of education in New Zealand* (pp. 160–173). Wellington, New Zealand: New Zealand Council for Educational Research.

Meade, A. (1990). Women and children gain a foot in the door. *New Zealand Women's Studies Journal, 6*(1/2), 96–111.

Meade, A., & Podmore, V. (2002). Early childhood policy administration under the auspices of the Department/ Ministry of Education. A case study of New Zealand. In UNESCO (Ed.), *Early Childhood and Family Policy Series No 1.* Paris: UNESCO.

Ministry of Education. (1992). *Circular 1992/17.* Wellington, New Zealand: Ministry of Education.

Ministry of Education. (1995). *Report on the direct (bulk funding) of kindergartens to the Education and Science Select Committee, 10 October.*

Ministry of Education. (1996). *Te Whāriki.* Wellington, New Zealand: Learning Media.

Ministry of Education. (2002). *Pathways to the future: Ngā Huarahi Arataki.* Wellington, New Zealand: Ministry of Education.

Ministry of Education. (2014). *Public expenditure on early childhood education (ECE).* Retrieved from http://www.educationcounts.govt.nz/indicators/main/resource/public-expenditure-on-early-childhood-education-ece

Ministry of Education. (2016). ECE services. Number of licensed ECE services, by service type, operating structure, ownership and year. Retrieved November 7, 2017, from https://www.educationcounts.govt.nz/statistics/early-childhood-education/services

Ministry of Education. (2017). Te Whāriki. He Whāriki mātauranga mō ngā mokopuna o Aotearoa Early childhood curriculum. Retrieved from https://www.education.govt.nz/assets/Documents/Early-Childhood/ELS-Te-Whariki-Early-Childhood-Curriculum-ENG-Web.pdf

Mitchell, L. (1996). Crossroads - Early childhood education in the mid-1990s. *New Zealand Annual Review of Education, 5*, 75–92.

Mitchell, L. (2002). *Differences between community owned and privately owned early childhood education and care centres: A review of evidence.* Wellington, New Zealand: New Zealand Council for Educational Research www.nzcer.org.nz.

Mitchell, L. (2005). Policy shifts in early childhood education: Past lessons, new directions. In J. Codd & K. Sullivan (Eds.), *Education policy directions in Aotearoa New Zealand* (pp. 175–198). Southbank, England: Thomson Learning.

Mitchell, L. (2011). Enquiring teachers and democratic politics: transformations in New Zealand's early childhood landscape. *Early Years. International Journal of Research and Development.* Retrieved from doi:https://doi.org/10.1080/09575146.2011.588787.

Mitchell, L. (2014, December 2). Put children's education before shareholders. *New Zealand Herald.*

Mitchell, L., & Brooking, K. (2007). *First NZCER national survey of early childhood education services.* Retrieved from http://www.nzcer.org.nz/default.php?products_id=1858

Mitchell, L., & Davison, C. (2010). Early childhood education as sites for children's citizenship: Tensions, challenges and possibilities in New Zealand's policy framing. *International Journal of Equity and Innovation in Early Childhood, 8*(1), 12–23.

Mitchell, L., Meagher-Lundberg, P., Caulcutt, T., Taylor, M., Archard, S., Kara, H., & Paki, V. (2014). *ECE Participation Programme evaluation. Delivery of the ECE participation initiatives: Stage 2.* Retrieved from http://www.educationcounts.govt.nz/publications/ECE/148513

Mitchell, L., Meagher-Lundberg, P., Davison, C., Kara, H., & Kalavite, T. (2016). *ECE Participation Programme Evaluation. Stage 3.* Retrieved from https://www.educationcounts.govt.nz/publications/ECE/ece-participation-programme-evaluation-delivery-of-ece-participation-initiatives-stage-3

Mitchell, L., Meagher Lundberg, P., Mara, D., Cubey, P., & Whitford, M. (2011). *Locality-based evaluation of Pathways to the Future - Nga Huarahi Arataki. Integrated report 2004, 2006 and 2009.* Retrieved from http://www.educationcounts.govt.nz/publications/ece/locality-based-evaluation-of-pathways-to-the-future-ng-huarahi-arataki

Mitchell, L., Meagher Lundberg, P., Taylor, M., Caulcutt, T., Kalavite, T., Kara, H., & Paki, V. (2013). *ECE participation programme evaluation. Baseline report.* Retrieved from http://www.educationcounts.govt.nz/publications/ECE/ece-participation-programme-evaluation

Mitchell, L., Royal Tangaere, A., Mara, D., & Wylie, C. (2006). *Quality in parent/whanau-led services.* Retrieved from http://www.educationcounts.govt.nz/publications/ece/36086/36087

Mitchell, L., & Wells, C. (1997). Negotiating pay parity in the early childhood sector. In New Zealand Council of Trade Unions (Ed.), *Closing the gap. Forum on equal pay* (pp. 163–172). Wellington, New Zealand: New Zealand Council of Trade Unions.

Moss, P., & Petrie, P. (1997). *Children's services: Time for a new approach.* London: Institute of Education, University of London.

Moss, P., & Petrie, P. (2002). *From children's services to children's spaces.* London: Routledge Falmer.

New Zealand Government. (1991). The Employment Contracts Act. Retrieved November 7, 2017, from http://www.nzlii.org/nz/legis/hist_act/eca19911991n22280/

New Zealand Government. (2013). Social Security (Benefit Categories and Work Focus) Amendment Act 2013. Retrieved November 7, 2017, from http://www.legislation.govt.nz/act/public/2013/0013/latest/DLM4542304.html

OECD. (2001). *Starting strong. Early childhood education and care.* Paris: Organisation for Economic Cooperation and Development.

OECD. (2006). *Starting strong 11: Early childhood education and care.* Paris: Organisation for Economic Cooperation and Development.

OECD. (2016). International Early learning and Child Wellbeing Study (IELS). Retrieved from: http://www.oecd.org/edu/school/international-early-learning-and-child-well-being-study.htm

OECD. (2017). The international early learning and child Well-being study – The study Retrieved from http://www.oecd.org/edu/school/theinternational-early-learning-and-child-well-being-study-the-study.htm

Penn, H. (2011). Policy rationales for early childhood services. *Korean Institute of Child Care and Education, 5*(1), 1–16.

Poutu, P. (2004). *Mana Tamariki. Paper presented at the 8th early childhood convention.* Palmerston North, New Zealand.

Randall, J. (2015). *Impacts of early childhood education social obligations on families and whānau.* (MEd Thesis), The University of Waikato, Hamilton, New Zealand. http://research-commons.waikato.ac.nz/handle/10289/9262

Reedy, T. (2003). Toku rangatiratanga na te mana-matauranga. "Knowledge and power set me free . . . ". In J. Nuttall (Ed.), *Weaving Te Whariki: Aotearoa New Zealand's early childhood curriculum document in theory and practice* (pp. 51–77). Wellington, New Zealand: New Zealand Council for Educational Research.

Royal-Tangaere, A. (1997). Kōhanga Reo: More than a language nest *Early Childhood Folio, 3,* 41–47.

Royal Commission on Social Policy. (1988). *The April report, Future directions* (Vol. 111). Wellington, New Zealand: The Royal Commission on Social Policy.

Smith, A. B. (2016). *Children's rights. Towards social justice.* New York: Momentum Press.

Smith, A. B., & May, H. (2006). Early childhood care and education in Aotearoa-New Zealand. In E. Melhuish (Ed.), *Preschool care and education: International perspectives* (pp. 95–114). London: Routledge.

State Services Commission. (1980). *Early Childhood Care and Education: A report of the State Services Commission Working Group.* Wellington, New Zealand: State Services Commission.

Stover, S. (Ed.). (1998). *Good Clean Fun: New Zealand's Playcentre Movement.* Auckland, New Zealand: Playcentre Publications.

Te One, S. (2003). The context for *Te Whāriki*: Contemporary issues of influence. In J. Nuttall (Ed.), *Weaving Te Whāriki* (pp. 17–49). Wellington, New Zealand: New Zealand Council for Educational Research.

The Treasury. (2008). *Briefing to the Incoming Minister of Finance 2008: Economic and fiscal strategies – Responding to your challenges.* Retrieved from http://www.treasury.govt.nz/publications/briefings/2008efs/17.htm

United Nations. (1990). *Convention on the rights of the child.* Retrieved from http://www2.ohchr.org/english/law/crc.htm

Waitangi Tribunal. (2012a). *Meaning of the treaty.* Retrieved from http://www.waitangi-tribunal.govt.nz/treaty/principles.asp.

Waitangi Tribunal. (2012b). *The principles of the treaty .*Retrieved from http://www.waitangi-tribunal.govt.nz/treaty/principles.asp.

Waitangi Tribunal. (2013). *Matua Rautia: The report on the Kōhanga Reo Claim.* Retrieved from www.waitangitribunal.govt.nz

Wikinson, R., & Pickett, K. (2010). *Spirit level: why equality is better for everyone.* London: Penguin Books.

Wikinson, R., & Pickett, K. (Producer). (2014). The Human Cost of Inequality. Lecture 1. Evidence of damage. *Sir Douglas Robb Lectures 2014.*

Wilson, M. (1997). Women and politics. In R. Miller (Ed.), *New Zealand politics in transition* (pp. 418–427). Oxford: Oxford University Press.

Woodhams, M. (2010, 19–21 November). Recognising mothering as real work: The role of playcentre in challenging public discourse. Proceedings of Women's Studies Association of New Zealand Conference 'Connecting Women, Respecting Difference', University of Waikato, Hamilton (pp 264–268).

Wylie, C. (1998). *Can vouchers deliver better education? A review of the literature with special reference to New Zealand.* Wellington, New Zealand: New Zealand Council for Educational Research.

Traditions of Democracy in Education

A central claim in this book is that over the last three decades, a dominant economic and market discourse has shaped ECEC policy and practice both in Aotearoa New Zealand and internationally. Problems and inequities emerging from this approach have run directly counter to aims for a socially just society where educational opportunities for all children and families are equitably realised. Helen Penn (2009, 2012, 2013) has been a constant and vociferous critic of education markets and for-profit ECEC and the problems when a quest for profits collides with the best interests of children and families. Following writers (e.g., Carr & Hartnett, 1996; Dahlberg, Moss & Pence, 1999; Moss & Petrie, 1997; Penn, 2012; Prout 2003) who ask critical questions about the kind of society these discourses sustain, this book turns to an alternative vision of a democratic society and the role that ECEC policy and practice might possibly play in promoting democratic values. Ideas for an alternative vision are analysed within an overarching frame of democracy, going back to Athenian origins of democracy and including recent writers on meanings and traditions of democracy in education. I take core ideas from John Dewey (1915) that democracy is something that has to be made and remade by each generation and of the capacity of education to build democratic society rather than reproduce society. Henri Giroux (1992) takes these ideas further in emphasising social criticism and struggle in his definition of democracy, while Michael Apple (2005) emphasises a commitment to "thick" collective forms of democracy. A section on democracy in Aotearoa New Zealand's educational traditions and history harks back to 1939, after the great depression, when Aotearoa New Zealand's Prime Minister Peter Fraser in a speech penned by Clarence Beeby the future Director General of Education famously pronounced on a vision of education as a public good and a right of the child citizen, of schools as public institutions and a public responsibility (May, 2003). Not encompassed within this vision was ECEC, which has never in Aotearoa New Zealand been treated as a public responsibility or child's right. I use these arguments to discuss core characteristics of policy and practice for an ECEC system founded on democratic values and to set a framing for analysis in subsequent

© Springer Nature Singapore Pte Ltd. 2019
L. Mitchell, *Democratic Policies and Practices in Early Childhood Education*,
International Perspectives on Early Childhood Education and Development 24,
https://doi.org/10.1007/978-981-13-1793-4_3

chapters. These set a scene for the book's conclusion, which examines what conditions might be needed for an integrated and democratic ECEC system in Aotearoa New Zealand and countries that share a market approach to ECEC provision.

1   The Case for Democracy in Education

The case for democracy in education and a new form of public ECEC is an ethical response to the expansion of ECEC that is occurring globally, the increasing institutionalisation of childhood, as more children spend long hours in ECEC settings, and the emphasis on standardised outcomes that is occurring in ECEC systems in countries that rely extensively on neoliberal ideology. Democracy in education raises possibilities for debating and generating new thinking and understandings about the purpose of education, children and childhood and the roles and responsibilities of the major players in children's lives. This will enable the creation within educational institutions, conditions that are responsive to children's lived experiences; a pedagogy of listening and relationships lays a foundation for these conditions.

Market reforms in education are a feature in Aotearoa New Zealand and other English-speaking liberal countries and have potential to undermine democracy in education. According to the US academic, Michael Apple (2005), educational reforms that have centred around a commitment to the market have "marked a dangerous shift in our very idea of democracy – always a contested subject – from 'thick' collective forms to 'thin' consumer-driven and overly individualistic forms" (p. 11). He saw one potential danger to be for employees to change from an allegiance to collective understanding and public service to an allegiance to working for profits for owners and investors. Pressure to align with profit motives is happening in private corporate ECEC centres in Aotearoa New Zealand where some teachers see themselves as having to juggle between the "business" side of their job, which is the "need to make profit", and "social" side, which is children's learning and development (Karmenerac, 2017). The "consumer", usually the parent in ECEC, must want to buy the service and is required to make decisions about the ECEC provision, but parents are often not knowledgeable about "quality" indicators, and their decisions may be based on misleading advertising information and short-term incentives, such as the first month at a reduced rate of fees. The practices of advertising to appeal to parents and offering short-term incentives are commonplace in private corporate centres in Aotearoa New Zealand and in other liberal countries. In Australia, Press (2016) has written of the "evocative, expensive and alluring advertising campaign using the Beatle's tune 'All you need is love', no doubt tapping into parents' desire for reassurance that their children were loved and nurtured when at (ABC) childcare centres" (Press, 2016, p. 12). ABC Learning was the large corporate childcare chain that collapsed in 2007, costing the Australian government millions in tax payer funding as it kept centres going while finding other providers (Brennan, 2007; Press & Woodrow, 2009; Sumsion, 2012). Helen Penn (2009,

2012, 2013) with Eva Lloyd (Lloyd and Penn, 2012) established and was co-director of the International Centre for the Study of the Mixed Economy of Childcare (ICMEC) at the University of East London's Cass School of Education and Community. Her focus is on policy in ECEC, and she is a rigorous analyst and critic of childcare markets and the growth of for-profit entrepreneurship. She argues that "for-profit care is often exploitative, and distorts or damages quality and equity of access" and notes the "unquestioning acceptance of economic simplification, and *absence* of debate or questioning in those countries [where the reach of the market paradigm is extensive], and the relatively unconditional acceptance, even amongst early childhood parent professionals, or by parents, of the use of for-profit childcare provided by entrepreneurs, is striking" (Penn, 2012, p. 20). Penn explores the position that for-profit provision is questionable, reversible and a matter of political choice. Likewise, Moss (2012) in the same volume, argues that the neoliberal approach to ECEC is but one possibility in many alternatives.

Cleveland and Krashinsky, in an OECD-commissioned report on funding mechanisms for early childhood education and care, state that "for-profit firms have an incentive to provide childcare that seems of high quality but is not. Because parents can be fooled into buying low quality care, low-quality providers will be able to underprice higher-quality producers and drive them out of business" (Cleveland & Krashinsky, 2002, p. 40). According to Apple, "In the process [of marketisation] as well, there is a very strong tendency for needs and values that were originally generated out of collective deliberations, struggles and compromises, and which led to the creation of state services, to be marginalised and ultimately abandoned" (Apple, 2005, p. 13).

Associated with marketisation and globalisation, has been a trend towards focusing educational policy on instrumental outcomes and measurement of student achievement, and to portray ECEC as preparation for academic success at school and productive life in the economy, at the expense of the child's holistic learning and development at the time. The *International Early Learning Study* (IELS) being developed by the OECD (2017) is a recent attempt to develop common tools with internationally standardised outcomes to assess 5–5.5-year-old children in four domains: emerging literacy/language skills, emerging numeracy/mathematics, self-regulation and social and emotional skills. The work, initiated in 2012, will be implemented in three to six countries in the late 2018 and early 2019. The rationale for the study is argued to be improving children's learning and the performance of education systems:

> Improving children's early learning will provide countries with immense gains in outcomes for individual children, as well as an effective and cost-efficient means to lift the overall performance of their education systems. To achieve such improvements, countries need valid and comparable data on what is possible and where improvements may be made in children's early learning. Information from this new OECD study on children's early learning will provide insights on the relative effectiveness, equity and efficiency of ECEC systems and also on the focus needed in early primary schooling. The study will also include a focus on the impacts of children's home learning environments. . . .
>
> Data from the study will also enable countries to map children's early capabilities to education performance at age 15, through PISA. Such cohort analysis will give countries a

better understanding of the strengths and improvements that could be made in their own systems as well as in other countries, and enable countries to see the value-add that their schooling systems really provide. (OECD, 2016)

Significant international concern about the study has been voiced by leading early years scholars and educators around the world for the potential of narrowly defined internationally standardised outcome assessment to shrink democratic possibilities for education. In a united statement, early childhood professors from nine countries – the UK, Sweden, Australia, Italy, Aotearoa New Zealand, Canada, France, the USA and Belgium – opened a colloquium in the *Contemporary Issues in Early Childhood* journal (Moss et al., 2016) to highlight concerns about the proposed study's assumptions, practices and possible negative effects. In its documentation for the IELS, the OECD positions "early childhood education and the proposed study as if they are purely technical exercises" (Moss et al., 2016, p. 346) while failing to acknowledge the political nature of education and argue for the political choices on which it is based. It makes assumptions that what it recommends is objective; it assumes "learning outcomes" can be observed internationally; and it makes no reference to environmental problems facing the world. Moss et al. also point to the critiques of the international PISA study, with which the IELS fails to engage. They discuss the failure of the IELS testing regime to accommodate and welcome diversity and the likelihood one effect will be "a growing standardisation and narrowing of early childhood education" (p. 349). Carr, Mitchell and Rameka (2016) have critiqued the IELS in relation to Aotearoa New Zealand, setting out the following implications:

(1) New Zealand's ECE curriculum takes a sociocultural perspective on learning; the OECD measures provide a 'one-world' view, in an internationally standardized context, (2) an unwarranted international reputation can be established, (3) low income communities may be especially vulnerable, (4) follow-on interventions, teaching to the OECD measures, are likely to encourage a pedagogy of compliance, and (5) we have already established more important issues to focus on. (p. 451)

Writing in an open letter and statement to Germany's Federal Minister of Family Affairs about Germany's potential participation in the study, representatives of five education organisations warned that measuring and standardising ECEC will decontextualise the processes of early childhood education, marginalise children and neglect diversity and difference (Wagner, Heise, Goller, Hocke, & Bender, 2016). Furthermore, the OECD information about the study, now a contractor has been secured for the work, indicates that countries wishing to contribute will need to provide a financial contribution to the work. Far from enhancing multiple possibilities and opportunities for children's wellbeing and learning, the OECD study risks narrowing the curriculum and widening inequalities to advantage children from families with high social and cultural capital.

By contrast to the OECD approach, Carr, Davis and Cowie (2015) in their literature scan of learning progress and outcomes in the early years point to the value of competencies/dispositional outcomes, which were highlighted by the Gordon

Commission (Gordon Commission on the Future of Assessment in Early Education, 2013), as twenty-first-century outcomes:

> Increasingly the goals of education reflect the growing concern with encouraging and enabling students to learn how to learn and to learn to continue learning; to become enquiring persons who not only use knowledge but persons who produce and interpret knowledge....
>
> The three Rs of Reading wRiting and aRithmetic will continue to be essential skills, but thought leaders in education ... increasingly point to varying combinations of Cs as essential processes in education. They are: Creativity and innovation, Conceptualization and problem-solving, Communication and collaboration, and Computer literacy....
>
> The new century places high value on communication as reading and speaking, but also as listening and collaborating, and processing information from multiple perspectives.... (p. 37) (Carr et al., 2015, p. 17)

These authors highlight quality participation as a key construct, described as aspects of engagement with activities and people that include an emphasis on collaboration and communication. The research, policies and programmes reviewed in their literature scan emphasise the situated nature of learning and that it is through participation that dispositional knowledge is integrated with the teaching of skills and knowledge. "This is an ecological and participative viewpoint about learners and learning, in contrast to a psychometric and behavioural viewpoint which tends to construe learning as an individual acquisition" (p. 12). The literature scan emphasises the importance of students having some responsibility for assessment and a programme that enables participation by all students. The authors link participation to belonging, a strand in *Te Whāriki*. Smith (2016) links participation and belonging to democracy when she writes:

> Within societies where adult power and authority is absolute, the concept of participation rights acknowledges children's role as citizens who can and do play an important part in democratic processes. Recognizing children's participation rights can therefore nurture children's sense of belonging and inclusion, and give them opportunity to bring about change themselves (Smith, 2007). These qualities are essential both for individuals and for democratic societies. (Smith, 2016, p. 12)

Underpinning and connected with democracy in education, then, is the international emphasis on human rights. In particular, the human rights expressed in key international instruments have prompted interest in citizenry rights as a goal for policy development in ECEC. While children are biologically immature, cultures decide how childhood is understood, and these understandings have repercussions for many spheres. Images of the child are associated with views about the value, purposes and outcomes of ECEC and the roles of children, teachers, families, communities and government (Mitchell, 2010; OECD, 2001, 2006; Rigby, Tarrant, & Neuman, 2007). Images of the child are reflected in policy design and also in curriculum and pedagogy. Drawing on Urie Bronfenbrenner (1979), cultural and national views about child development are accompanied by practices, beliefs and expectations that influence the nature of pedagogical practices.

The UN *Convention on the Rights of the Child (UNCROC)* (United Nations, 1990) is a useful framework for considering children's rights and agency. UNCROC has been ratified by all countries except South Sudan and the USA and is legally binding on those countries that have ratified it. Rights apply in different settings in which the child engages, including the home and the early childhood setting.

Lansdown (1994, p. 36) summarised the rights in the UNCROC as follows:

The provision Articles recognize the social rights of children to minimum standards of health, education, social security, physical care, family life, play, recreation, culture and leisure.

The protection Articles identify the rights of children to be safe from discrimination, physical and sexual abuse, exploitation, substance abuse, injustice and conflict.

The participation Articles are to do with civil and political rights. They acknowledge the rights of children to a name and identity, to be consulted and to be taken account of, to physical integrity, to access to information, to freedom of speech and opinion, and to challenge decisions made on their behalf.

A major shift in thinking embedded in UNCROC is that children are not only to be protected but also to be empowered to participate in society. The participation articles are particularly relevant because they have been only partially realised in many countries and contest a common way of thinking about children as predominantly vulnerable and dependent. Instead the focus is on children as citizens and active contributors.

Although participation rights theorisations have been critiqued for "privileging autonomy and individuals over relationships, communities and interdependence" (Tisdall, 2015, p. 83), Alderson (2012) regards rights principles as being open to local interpretation and implementation:

Broad, universal, intransitive principles in UN rights treaties are open to transitive local negotiation and application, to which sociologists could vitally contribute (Freeman, 2011) to help to reverse the present great shifts of resources and power away from younger and towards older generations. Rather than belittling human rights, future research about younger generations may increase interdisciplinary understanding of the political and embodied nature and purpose of inalienable human rights. (Alderson, 2012, p. 197)

The UNCROC has played a crucial role in foregrounding an image of the child as a citizen, giving visibility to the concept of participation and contribution and highlighting the need to find out about the views and perspectives of the child. The right to participate connects with a raft of participatory methods currently used in research and pedagogy to communicate with children and find out their views. A frequently cited and influential example is the "mosaic approach" for listening to young children's perspectives on their daily lives (Clark & Moss, 2011). The approach integrates verbal and visual methods and acknowledges children and adults as co-constructors of meaning. It draws from Reggio Emilia centres in Northern Italy on pedagogical documentation and ideas about a pedagogy of listening and relationships. Multi-methods enable children to express themselves in different ways. The approach is based on explicit views about childhood:

- Young children as 'experts in their own lives'
- Young children as skilful communicators

- Young children as rights holders
- Young children as meaning makers (Clark & Moss, 2011, p. 6)

Einarsdottir (2007) draws on a study with 2–6-year-old children in a playschool in Iceland and makes reference to a number of research studies carried out in the late 1990s and early 2000s to examine methodological and ethical issues related to informed consent, confidentiality, protection and interactions in researching with young children. One conclusion is:

> Researchers who conduct research with children have to be creative and use methods that fit the circumstances and the children they are working with each time. Since there is not one single method that fits all children and all circumstances it is important to master a variety of methods for gaining insight into children's perspectives. Different methods can shed light on different aspects and give a new breadth of understanding. Different children also have different ways of communicating, and therefore they prefer different methods to express their views. Children at different ages also prefer different methods. (Einarsdottir, 2007, p. 207)

Arguably, opportunities for participation and contribution from all players in ECEC are a hallmark of democracy in education.

2 Athenian Origins of Democracy

The tradition of democracy in education is inspired by a line of thinkers, activists, politicians and practitioners, stretching back to Athenian times. The concept of democracy derives from the Greek words "demos" (the people) and "kratos" (rule), so a democratic society is a society that is ruled by the people. Meanings and traditions of democracy in education have shifted over time and are contested, but the historical origins are useful for understanding core concepts today.

Athens in the fifth and fourth centuries BC was far from being a modern democracy. Nevertheless, Athenian democracy offers insights for thinking critically about democracy and its relevance for education because of embedded principles that encourage analysis of citizenship and power and debate about the "good life" and the active role of citizens in political decision-making. Raaflaub (2007) describes the democracy that existed in Athens from the middle of the fifth century as "a remarkable system, unprecedented, . . . capable of mobilising extraordinary citizen involvement, enthusiasm and achievement, enormously productive and at the same time potentially destructive" (p. 4).

Revision of laws between 410 and 399 BC extended the concept of citizenship and opened up Athenian society for greater citizen involvement. An overarching principle was that democracy is a form of participation in the common life of a political community and on the basis of a common good. Through free and equal participation, and through making and obeying laws within this political community, citizens are enabled to develop and realise their own human capacities (Ober,

2008). Thus a feature of Athenian democracy was the idea that democracy requires active participation of the citizenry and a collective vision of the common good.

In this time, the meaning of "citizen" was redefined and broadened from an elite male citizenry who had status and property to all male citizens regardless of their background, education or abilities. The definition of citizen did not include women, foreigners, slaves or children, but the Athenian redefinition is helpful in highlighting that status and power are "political rather than social attributes" (Farrar, 2007, p. 173). Aristotle defined a citizen as "someone who participates in public affairs" (Aristotle, 1981, p.19). This definition highlights both rights and obligations and the new idea that a citizen is a "political animal" (Aristotle, 1981, p. 43).

A crucial element in Athenian democracy was the creation of institutions and systems that functioned in a more democratic way and enabled a wider citizenry to be involved in decision-making. The roles and functioning of the institutions were made transparent through legally determined rules somewhat akin to a constitution. Democratic selection processes ensured opportunities for participation for those defined as "citizens". A fixed term of appointment allowed roles to be rotated. Through undertaking roles in the assembly, council and law courts, "Several thousand citizens thus were politically active every year – and many of them quite regularly for years on end" (Raaflaub, 2007, p. 5). The involvement in decision-making was more than consultation; the citizens on the assembly, council and law courts had power to decide and control policies and processes and oversee their implementation. So the institutions and systems enabled participation and equity for the adult males who were part of the defined citizenry.

These ideas can inform possibilities for democracies and constructions of citizenship currently, including incorporating democracy in education. As Raaflaub (2007, p. 14) notes:

> Directly or indirectly, Athenian democracy as an extraordinary experiment in social history, thus stimulates our own thinking about crucial issues of our own democracy and society, incomparably more complex though they are. The point is precisely the ancients help us focus on the essentials.

The mechanisms set up to enable knowledge to be shared were valuable practices. Ober (2008) argues that the Athenian democratic state was able to develop democratic institutions and cultural practices by addressing issues related to the organisation of knowledge. Networks were established and connected to enable knowledge to be dispersed widely. The process of aggregating knowledge or the "wisdom of the crowds" produced results superior to those of the decision-makers who were experts or were part of a small group. Aristotle described this process as democratic "summation", an aggregation of a variety of expertise within a group where members are mindful of the common good. Both these conditions, relevant and diverse expertise and an eye to the common good, need to be present. Ober (2008, p. 111) writes, "Aristotle acknowledges the role played by intergroup diversity in respect to knowledge and thus to the group's judgement capacity". Athenian democracy was effective because the different expertise of the diverse "hoi polloi" was combined to enhance social knowledge.

While there was much injustice within Athenian democracy, some principles for democracy in education are relevant today. One such principle is the value of collaborative sharing of expertise and knowledge to come to new, contextually relevant and creative ways to promote a common vision. As in the Athenian democratic state, this is supported by structures and practices to enable knowledge to be widely dispersed and co-produced. In later chapters, I will show how this can happen in early childhood policy at a national level, in policy advocacy through collective organisation and in pedagogy in local ECEC settings.

A second principle emerges from the opening of citizenship to a diversity of groups, the value of embracing diversity, being open to learn from others and to hear and practice home languages. Gundara (2011) makes links between principles of Athenian democracy and philosophical principles of intercultural education. He argues that ancient Greece was profoundly shaped by the Mediterranean multicultural environment in which it was located and therefore drew on interactions of varied cultural knowledge from different sources. One of the challenges in education today, he stated, is for educators to ensure that a:

> characterisation of difference and diversity in modern multicultural societies and institutions as a deficit and deficiency is rejected. If this legacy in democratic societies can be reversed, then at the public level diversity can lead to developing shared intercultural meanings and values. (p. 236)

Similarly, the *UN Convention on the Rights of the Child* (United Nations, 1990) places enormous emphasis on intercultural understanding and respect. Article 29c provides that the education of the child shall be directed to:

> The development of respect for the child's parents, his or her own cultural identity, language and values, for the national values of the country in which the child is living, the country from which he or she may originate, and for civilisations different from his or her own....

Article 30 states the right of the child to "enjoy his or her own culture, to profess and practice his or her own religion or to use his or her own language".

Early childhood education and care has a crucial role to play in intercultural education by developing theories, concepts and strategies that lead to inclusion and participation and that challenge deficit and ethnocentric beliefs. This is a pressing challenge worldwide as the number of immigrants and refugees is growing exponentially (United Nations High Commissioner for Refugees (UNCHR), 2014).

3 Transformations in the Meaning of Democracy and Citizenship

Wilfred Carr (1991) has argued that "the history of the concept of citizenship is a history of social struggle and political conflict in which, and through which its original Greek meaning has been gradually transformed and changed" (p. 375). He turns to the writings of T.H. Marshall as "offering the most authoritative formulation of the meaning of citizenship in modern industrial democracies" (p. 376).

Marshall (1950) claims that citizenship entails "a kind of basic human equality associated with the concept of full membership of a community" (Marshall, 1950, p. 8). He describes the history of the development of the concept of citizenship as differentiating into three parts or elements by the end of the nineteenth century – civil, political and social. The civil element incorporates the rights for freedom – liberty of the person, of speech and of thought – to own property and justice. The political element incorporates the right to vote and be elected. The social element means "the right to a modicum of economic welfare and security to the right to share to the full in the social heritage and to live the life of a civilised being according to the standards prevailing in the society" (p.11). Each element is associated with civil institutions – courts of justice, parliament and the educational system and social services, respectively. It was not until the twentieth century that the three rights attained equal status. Marshall argues that being a "citizen" endows both "rights and duties". Significantly "rights and duties" and who is defined as a citizen are not prescribed; societies create their own ideal of citizenship within a move towards greater equality. This then is an evolving process that needs to be responsive to people, time and place and seeks greater equality and participation.

The evolution of the status of citizenship towards inclusion of wider social groups has been influenced by organised rights movements. Concepts of democracy and citizenship have direct relevance to education because it is through education that participative roles can be understood and encouraged; that knowledge, skills and dispositions for participation can be enhanced; and a vision constructed of what education might possibly be. Clarity about what is meant by these concepts is critical for thinking about education provision and the kind of curriculum that is entailed.

Wilfred Carr (Carr, 1991; Carr & Hartnett, 1996) shows useful distinctions between two models of democracy that construct the meaning of democracy and democratic processes very differently. These models in turn have implications for the role of education, the nature of pedagogy and the way educational institutions are constructed and run. So there is a need to be clear about how the construct of democracy is understood.

A "moral model of democracy" derives from classical theory of ancient Greece and is informed by participatory theories of democracy. Carr sets out the core principles as:

> Democracy is an intrinsically justified form of social life constituted by the core value of political equality. It is the way of life in which individuals are able to realise their human capacities by participating in the life of their society. A democratic society is thus a society whose citizens enjoy equal opportunities for self-development, self-fulfilment and self-determination. (Carr & Hartnett, 1996, p.41)

A feature of classical democracy is the expansion of opportunities for participation of all citizens in public decision-making in economic, social and political spheres. In respect to education, democratic processes require "a knowledgeable and informed citizenry capable of participating in public decision-making and political debate on equal terms" (Carr & Hartnett, 1996, p. 41). In his earlier article, Carr (1991, p. 378) calls this a "moral model of democracy" – moral because of its basis in fundamental human values and its prescription of moral principles to which a democratic society must conform.

A second model of democracy is termed a "market model of democracy":

> Democracy is justified as the political system which is most instrumentally effective in securing the core principle of 'negative' liberty. By providing a method for selecting political leaders which curtails an excess or abuse of political power, it helps to protect the freedom of individuals to pursue their private interests with minimal state interference. (Carr & Hartnett, 1996, p. 43)

Carr and Hartnett (1996) label this construction of democracy "a value-neutral descriptive concept", based on assumptions that humans are private self-interested individuals with most having no desire to take part in political decision-making.

The construction of democracy adopted in this book as a framework for advancing ideas about early childhood education is an understanding derived from the concept of a moral model of democracy.

4 Recent Traditions of Democracy in Education

John Dewey's (Dewey, 1916, 1944) ideas and especially his book *Education and Democracy* comprise a relevant, influential and thorough consideration of the tradition of democracy in education. Consistent with the moral view of democracy delineated by Carr and Hartnett (1996), Dewey argues that democracy is primarily fostered in social contexts through social relationships. "A democracy is more than a form of government; it is primarily a mode of associated living, a conjoint communicated experience" (Dewey 1916, p. 87). Participation in all aspects of social life is emphasised as a key construct. Following from Dewey, "democracy is not confined to the sphere of political decision-making but extends to participation in the 'construction, maintenance and transformation' of all forms of social and political life" (Biesta & Lawy, 2006, p. 65). Dewey argues that for a society to develop as a democratic society, education must also operate as a democratic community that creates dispositions and interest in formulating and addressing shared concerns. This is powerfully encapsulated in his statement "Democracy has to be born anew every generation and education is its midwife" (Dewey, 1916, 1944). In these respects, at local levels, educational institutions including ECEC centres can be conceived as sites for democratic practice involving all players – children, families, teachers, educators and community, as participants in the education process. The process of policy formulation can likewise be developed through participation of the citizenry rather than an elite group of officials and politicians, and is made richer through democratic participation, as later chapters will show.

Interactions with a diverse group of people participating in a common interest and taking heed of each other are essential in promoting an inclusive and democratic society:

> The extension in space of the number of individuals who participate in an interest so that each has to refer his own action to that of others, and to consider the action of others to give point and direction to his own, is equivalent to the breaking down of those barriers of class, race and national territory which keep men from perceiving the full import of their activity. These more numerous and more varied points of contact denote a greater diversity of stimuli to which an individual has to respond; they consequently put a premium on variation in his action. They secure a liberation of powers which remain suppressed as long as the incitations to action are partial, as they must be in a group which in its exclusiveness shuts out many interests. (Dewey, 1916, 1944, p. 87)

These ideas of opening out citizenship to an ever-wider variety of groups and freer interactions between groups echo those that originated in Athenian times (though extremely limited then) and have been extended recently through rights movements. Within these interactions, concerns of mutual interest need to be recognised, and constant adaptations made. Differences of opinion and conflict can produce new thinking. Dewey writes of "continuous readjustment through meeting the new situation produced by varied intercourse" (p. 87).

Different approaches may be taken to dealing with conflict and differences of opinion. Hughes and MacNaughton (2000) have examined relationships between staff and parents in ECEC, finding that in the literature, often parent knowledge of the child is subordinated to the expert professional knowledge of staff through a process they call "othering" (parent knowledge is inadequate, parent knowledge is supplementary, parent knowledge is unimportant). They argue that where "othering" occurs, "communication cannot improve relationships between staff and parents unless it addresses the politics of knowledge underpinning them" (p. 247). They then draw on the work of Jürgen Habermas and Jean-François Lyotard to examine different ways of using communication "to create a new politics of professional knowledge". Informed by the work of Habermas, one approach relates to deliberative democracy and involves an attempt to reach consensus through negotiation of difference. A second approach from Lyotard is to seek the many diverse views of the child and to open up to exploring the knowledge-power relationships around each one. They argue, "Hope for change lies not in our agreements but in our disagreements, because in our disagreements (dissensus) we argue about what is 'the truth' and we question the dominant norms and values and seek to change them (Bertens, 1995)" (Hughes & MacNaughton, 2000, p. 255). Taking either approach, the benefit of parent involvement "would be a boost to local democracy by informed citizens who create local, collective knowledge about what is in children's best interests" (p. 256).

Likewise Giroux (1992) has proposed that democracy is a "celebration of difference, the politics of difference" (p. 11). In this thinking, schools are social forms within which the capacities of individuals to think and act critically are developed to the fullest. This occurs within a social justice aim; individual development is always linked to democracy and "social betterment". The purpose of education is "to prepare young people to be socially responsible, critically engaged citizens in a democratic society". Consequently, the individual will critically interrogate the social forms of schools rather than just adapt to the forms. Giroux argues for schools to be defined as democratic public spheres and for links to be made between schooling and the reconstruction of public life. In these ways, schools must develop and advance the democratic imperatives of society. He takes these ideas further in emphasising social criticism and struggle in his definition of democracy, which he defines as "an ongoing contest within every aspect of daily life" (Giroux, 1992, p. 155). In a similar way, Dewey raised a distinction between "education as a function of society" and "society as a function of education". In other words, does education simply echo societal values and practices or play a critical role in challenging, leading and formulating them? In a democratic education system, education strengthens democratic participation.

Democracy in education is linked to a theme of empowerment, agency and possibilities. Dewey described democracy as "a way of life controlled by a working faith in the possibilities of human nature . . . and faith in the possibilities of intelligent judgement and action" (Dewey, 1939, p. 2). In turn, this belief brings with it the need to provide conditions to enable capacities and possibilities to flourish.

Giroux depicts the role of teachers as "public intellectuals", arguing "If teachers are to take an active role in raising serious questions of what they are to teach, how they teach and the goals to which they are striving, it means they must take a more critical and political role in defining the nature of their work and the conditions under which they work" (Giroux, 1992, pp. 108–109). Likewise conditions need to strengthen teachers in their capacities to understand and question what forms of knowledge count; to think and act critically about individuals, groups and society; and to produce locally relevant curricula. If education performs a democratic role in shaping society, then it cannot simply be used to impart knowledge and beliefs but needs to offer opportunities to develop attitudes, skills and dispositions to formulate and achieve collective ends. At a national level, policy needs to abolish structures that perpetuate hierarchical divisions and inequalities. In an education with democracy in mind, educational institutions are public places; they are open and accessible to all within that local community, not a selected group where those outside the selection criteria miss out.

In conclusion, democratic values are foundational to a response to the problems and inequities that have emerged from a system that relies extensively on neoliberal ideology and markets for provision of ECEC. Many writers (Moss, 2009; Moss & Petrie, 1997, 2002; Prout, 2005), and including myself (Mitchell, 2007), have argued that we need to debate values about children and childhood as a basis for ECE provision. As Giroux writes:

> We have to ask what the purposes of education are, what kind of citizens we hope to produce. (p. 12). .. I think schools should be about ways of life. They are not simply instruction sites. They are cultures which legitimise certain forms of knowledge and disclaim others. The language for understanding this phenomenon in some pretty sophisticated ways is now starting to emerge. (Giroux, 1992, p. 14)

Citizenry rights and living in a democracy is a good place to start the debate. A new debate could enable different voices to be heard and new possibilities constructed for early childhood services as sites for democratic participation.

5 Democracy in Aotearoa New Zealand's Education Traditions and History

Clarence Beeby was the first director of the New Zealand Council for Educational Research from 1934 to 1938. He became Assistant Director of Education in 1938 and Director of Education from 1940, remaining as chief education adviser to the government until his retirement in 1960. When New Zealand elected a Labour government in 1935, the Minister of Education Peter Fraser, who became prime minister of New Zealand in 1940, initiated a comprehensive reform of the national education system, and, "under his leadership, New Zealand can claim to be the first country to reconstruct public education with the objective of providing equality of education opportunity" (Renwick, 1998. p. 337). According to Renwick, it was the combination of Fraser's political leadership and Beeby's professional leadership that enabled the educational reconstruction to succeed.

The vision on which the reforms were based was drafted in 1939 by Clarence Beeby, future Director General of Education, for the then Prime Minister Peter Fraser, and is set out in this famous quotation:

> The Government's objective, broadly expressed, is that every person, whatever his level of academic ability, whether he be rich or poor, whether he live in town or country, has a right as a citizen, to a free education of the kind for which he is best fitted and to the fullest extent of his powers. (McDonald, 2002, p. 26)

While its language is a little outdated, its vision is highly relevant today. Helen May rephrased the quotation in 2003 concerning the role of ECEC for young children:

> The Government's objective, should broadly speaking be, that every child: whatever their family circumstances, whether their parents are solo, separated, married or de facto, at work or at home, whether they be rich or poor, whether they live in town or country, are Māori or Pākehā, should have a right as a citizen to a free early childhood education that meets their family needs, recognizes their cultural heritage and provides a rich learning environment in a community of learning that empowers both adults and children to learn and grow as equal participants in a democratic society. (May, 2003)

At the heart of the vision is a view of education as a public good and a right of the child citizen, of schools as public institutions and a public responsibility. Apple (2005, p. 18) regards public institutions as "defining features of a caring and democratic society".

Democracy figured in Aotearoa New Zealand primary and secondary education through state provision and aspirations such as these, but this government vision did not apply to ECEC. Aotearoa New Zealand has never had a system of early childhood education that offers every child a right to free early childhood education that best fits "the fullest extent of their powers". The closest Aotearoa New Zealand has come to a vision for democratic provision was in the policy *Pathways to the Future Ngā Hurahi Arataki*, the 10-year strategic plan for early childhood education discussed in chapter "Aotearoa New Zealand Within Global Trends in ECEC Policy". The vision for the strategic plan was "for all children to participate in early childhood education no matter their circumstances" – a vision that lacked the imagination and breadth of the earlier Beeby/Fraser statement, needing perhaps a government official of the likes of Beeby who could pen a more eloquent statement. Or was it purposely restricted to participation? However, a significant shift in policy thinking occurred through integrated policies around quality, participation and collaboration that were "universally available and coherently organised around an understanding of children, families and communities as participants" (Mitchell, 2011, p. 10). These measures in combination started to weave principles of democracy within this particular reform.

The burgeoning dominance in Aotearoa New Zealand of corporate private education and care and home-based services has been actively encouraged through funding policies, and the result is a radically unequal patchwork of provision and cost structures that largely favour those with the social and cultural capital of the dominant class. The corporate world constructs early childhood services as places of commercial exchange, where the first duty of directors is to shareholders who expect a financial return on their investment and where parents are positioned as consumers purchasing a product. The business expertise expected of corporate providers requires financial and managerial expertise but no prior knowledge of professional issues of childcare, as Penn (2009) points out. With a focus on business and profit, corporate childcare will limit the potential for what an early childhood service might be. The predominant concern of owners is financial, and there is often a high level of standardisation. Corporate childcare does not operate as a community facility, and there is usually no opportunity for parents, teachers and children to take responsibility in deciding the shape and direction of the services. For-profit services "are situated in the economic sphere; they cannot also be forums within civil society" (Dahlberg et al., 1999, pp. 74–75). The ideas behind the UN committee's support for holistic and multiservice provision that coordinates services for families and is responsive to family and community contexts cannot be realised in an approach that imports practices from an unrelated context, as corporate chains have done in Aotearoa New Zealand.

It is not possible to prescribe an ECEC system that is founded on democratic values, since following Dewey, democracy is learned by doing and a democratic system is necessarily open to contribution and possibilities. However, some of the characteristics of policy and practice for an ECEC system founded on democratic values are suggested here.

As a foundation, there will be explicit social justice aims that operate at a national policy level and at a local level within ECEC settings. In respect to ECEC provision, every child should be able to access public and community early childhood education that suits their family context and cultural aspirations and enables child and family to flourish. Here the UNCROC Article 12 is relevant:

... that the education of the child shall be directed to:
(a) The development of the child's personality, talents and mental and physical abilities to their fullest potential
(b) The development of respect for human rights and fundamental freedoms and for the principles enshrined in the Charter of the United Nations
(c) The development of respect for the child's parents, his or her own cultural identity, language and values, for the national values of the country in which the child is living, the country from which he or she may originate, and for civilizations different from his or her own
(d) The preparation of the child for responsible life in a free society, in the spirit of understanding, peace, tolerance, equality of sexes, and friendship among all peoples, ethnic, national and religious groups and persons of indigenous origin
(e) The development of respect for the natural environment

A commitment to supporting families is another aspect; as Noonan said: "Early childhood services in some respects are the urbanised communities alternative to the fast disappearing extended family. Early childhood centres can play a crucial role in breaking down the isolation that is a feature of so many young parents" (Noonan, 2001, p. 71). Accessibility for all children and families and a commitment to opportunities for their development is a feature of a democratic ECEC system.

6   Conclusion

Traditions of democracy in education were analysed in this chapter in order to make a case for democratic principles to be used as a valuable framework for analysing policies and practices in ECEC that can address challenges of today's world. In the early years, these challenges include inequities in access to education, health care and economic resources that have emerged from systems that rely extensively on neoliberal ideology. There have been transformations in the meaning of "democracy" since Athenian times. Nevertheless, the value of articulating and progressing a common good through combining expertise and knowledge, and of opening up to diverse groups, are two principles emerging from early democratic experimentation. Democracy in education has been conveyed as holding out new possibilities for reimagining education as a participative process in which all parties exercise agency, which encourage critical thinking and which upholds human rights and intercultural understanding.

References

Alderson, P. (2012). Young children's human rights: A sociological analysis. *International Journal of Children's Rights, 20*, 177–198.

Apple, M. (2005). Education, markets, and an audit culture. *Critical Quarterly, 47*(1–2), 11–29.

Aristotle. (1981). *Politics*. Harmondsworth, England: Penguin.

Bertens, H. (1995). *The idea of the postmodern: A history*. London, UK: Routledge.

Biesta, G., & Lawy, R. (2006). From teaching citizenship to learning democracy: Overcoming individualism in research, policy and practice. *Cambridge Journal of Education, 36*(1), 63–79.

Brennan, D. (2007). The ABC of child care politics. *Australian Journal of Social Issues, 42*(2), 212–225.

Bronfenbrenner, U. (1979). *The ecology of human development*. Cambridge, MA: Harvard University Press.

Carr, M., Davis, K., & Cowie, B. (2015). *Continuity of early learning: Learning progress and outcomes in the early years. Report on the literature scan*. Retrieved from https://www.educationcounts.govt.nz/publications/ECE/continuity-of-early-learning-literature-scan

Carr, M., Mitchell, L., & Rameka, L. (2016). Some thoughts about the value of an OECD international assessment framework for early childhood services in Aotearoa New Zealand. *Contemporary Issues in Early Childhood, 17*(4), 450–454.

Carr, W. (1991). Education for citizenship. *British Journal of Educational Studies, 39*(4), 373–385.

Carr, W., & Hartnett, A. (1996). *Education and the struggle for democracy*. Buckingham, PA: Open University Press.

Clark, A., & Moss, P. (2011). *Listening to young children: The mosaic approach* (2nd ed.). London: National Children's Bureau.

Cleveland, G., & Krashinsky, M. (2002). *Financing ECEC services in OECD countries. OECD Occasional Papers*. Paris: OECD.

Dahlberg, G., Moss, P., & Pence, A. (1999). *Beyond quality in early childhood education and care: Post modern perspectives* (1st ed.). London: Falmer Press.

Dewey, J. (1915). *School and society*. Chicago: The University of Chicago Press.

Dewey, J. (1916, 1944). *Democracy and education*. New York: The Free Press, Macmillan

Dewey, J. (1939). *Creative democracy. The task before us*. Retrieved from http://www.beloit.edu/~pbk/dewey.html

Einarsdottir, J. (2007). Research with children: methodological and ethical challenges. *Early Childhood Education Research Journal, 15*(2), 197–211.

Farrar, C. (2007). Power to the people. In Raaflaub, K., Ober, J., Wallace, R., Cartledge, P., & Farrar, C. *Origins of Democracy in Ancient Greece*. Berkeley; Los Angeles; London: University of California Press. Retrieved from http://www.jstor.org/stable/10.1525/j.ctt1pp9pt

Freeman, M. (2011). *Human Rights*. Cambridge, UK: Polity.

Giroux, H. (1992). *Border crossings. Cultural workers and the politics of education*. London: Routledge.

Gordon Commission on the Future of Assessment in Early Education. (2013). *To assess, to teach, to learn: A vision for the future of assessment*. [Technical Report]. Retrieved from www.gordoncommission.org

Gundara, J. S. (2011). Ancient Athenian democratic knowledge and citizenship: Connectivity and intercultural implications. *Intercultural Education, 22*(4), 231–241. https://doi.org/10.1080/14675986.2011.617416.

Hughes, P., & MacNaughton, G. (2000). Consensus, dissensus or community: The politics of parent involvement in early childhood education. *Contemporary Issues in Early Childhood, 1*(3), 241–258.

Karmenerac, O. (2017). Doctoral thesis under examination. Constructions of teachers' professional identities in early childhood policies and practice in Aotearoa New Zealand.

Lansdown, G. (1994). Children's rights. In B. Mayall (Ed.), *Children's childhoods: Observed and experienced* (pp. 33–44). London: The Falmer Press.

Marshall, T. H. (1950). *Citizenship and social class and other essays.* Cambridge, UK: The Syndics of the Cambridge University Press.

McDonald, G. (2002). Dr CE Beeby. The quality of education. *SET, 2,* 25–27.

Mitchell, L. (2007). *A new debate about children and childhood. Could it make a difference to early childhood pedagogy and policy?* (Doctoral thesis, Victoria University of Wellington, Wellington, New Zealand. Retrieved from http://researcharchive.vuw.ac.nz/handle/10063/347

Mitchell, L. (2010). Constructions of childhood in early childhood education policy in New Zealand. *Contemporary Issues in Early Childhood Education, 11*(4), 328–341.

Mitchell, L. (2011). Enquiring teachers and democratic politics: Transformations in New Zealand's early childhood landscape. *Early Years. International Journal of Research and Development.* https://doi.org/10.1080/09575146.2011.588787.

Moss, P. (2009). *There are alternatives! Markets and democratic experimentalism in early childhood education and care.* [Working Paper No. 53]. The Netherlands: Bernard Van Leer Foundation and the Bertelsmann Stiftung.

Moss, P. (2012). Need markets be the only show in town? In E. LLoyd & H. Penn (Eds.), *Childcare markets. Can they deliver an equitable service?* (pp. 191–207). Bristol, UK: The Policy Press.

Moss, P., Dahlberg, G., Grieshaber, S., Mantovani, S., May, H., Pence, A., et al. (2016). The Organisation for Economic Co-operation and Development's International early learning study: Opening for debate and contestation. *Contemporary Issues in Early Childhood, 17*(3), 343–351.

Moss, P., & Petrie, P. (1997). *Children's services: Time for a new approach.* London: Institute of Education, University of London.

Moss, P., & Petrie, P. (2002). *From children's services to children's spaces.* London: RoutledgeFalmer.

Noonan, R. (2001). Early childhood education - A child's right? In B. Webber & L. Mitchell (Eds.), *Early childhood education for a democratic society. New Zealand Council for Educational Research Annual Conference October 2001* (pp. 61–68). Wellington, New Zealand: New Zealand Council for Educational Research.

Ober, J. (2008). *Democracy and knowledge: Innovation and learning in classical Athens.* Princeton, NJ: Princeton University Press.

OECD. (2001). *Starting strong. Early childhood education and care.* Paris: Organisation for Economic Cooperation and Development.

OECD. (2006). *Starting strong 11: Early childhood education and care.* Paris: Organisation for Economic Cooperation and Development.

OECD. (2016). International Early Learning and Child Wellbeing Study (IELS). Retrieved from: http://www.oecd.org/edu/school/international-early-learning-and-child-well-being-study.htm

OECD. (2017). The International Early Learning and Child Well-being Study (IELS) – The study. Retrieved from http://www.oecd.org/edu/school/the-international-early-learning-and-child-well-being-study-the-study.htm

Penn, H. (2009). International perspectives on quality in mixed economies of childcare. *National Institute Economic Review, 207*(7), 83–89.

Penn, H. (2012). Childcare markets. Do they work? In E. LLoyd & H. Penn (Eds.), *Childcare markets. Can they deliver an equitable service?* (pp. 18–42). Bristol, UK: Policy Press.

Penn, H. (2013). The business of childcare in Europe. *European Early Childhood Education Research Journal, 22*(4), 432–456. https://doi.org/10.1080/1350293X.2013.7883300.

Press, F. (2016). Premium services. At what cost? *Rattler, 119,* 11–13.

Press, F., & Woodrow, C. (2009). The giant in the playground: Investigating the reach and implications of the corporatisation of child care provision. In D. King & G. Meagher (Eds.), *Paid care in Australia: Politics, profits, practices.* Sydney, Australia: Sydney University Press.

Prout, A. (2003, September 3–6). *Children, representation and social change.* Paper presented at the European Early Childhood Education Research Association 13th Annual Conference on Quality in Early Childhood Education, "Possible childhoods: relationships and choices", Strathclyde University, Glasgow.

Prout, A. (2005). *The future of childhood*. London: RoutledgeFalmer.

Raaflaub, K. (2007). Introduction. In K. Raaflaub, J. Ober, & R. Wallace (Eds.), *Origins of democracy in ancient Greece* (pp. 1–21). California: University of California Press.

Renwick, W. (1998). Clarence Edward Beeby (1902–98). *Prospects, XXVIII, 2*, 335–348.

Rigby, E., Tarrant, K., & Neuman, M. J. (2007). Alternative policy designs and the socio-political construction of childcare. *Contemporary Issues in Early Childhood, 8*(2), 98–108. https://doi.org/10.2304/ciec.2007.8.2.98.

Smith, A. (2007). Children and young People's participation rights in education. *The International Journal of Children's Rights, 15*(1), 147–164.

Smith, A. B. (2016). *Children's rights. Towards social justice*. New York: Momentum Press.

Sumsion, J. (2012). ABC Learning and Australian early education and care. In E. LLoyd & H. Penn (Eds.), *Childcare markets. Can they deliver an equitable service?* (pp. 209–225). Bristol, England: The Policy Press.

Tisdall, K. (2015). Participation, rights and 'participatory' methods. In A. Farrell, S. Kagan, & K. Tisdall (Eds.), *The SAGE handbook of early childhood research* (pp. 73–88). Los Angeles: Sage.

United Nations. (1990). *Convention on the Rights of the Child*. Retrieved from http://www2.ohchr.org/english/law/crc.htm

United Nations High Commissioner for Refugees (UNCHR). (2014). *Mid year trends 2014*. Retrieved from http://www.unhcr.org/54aa91d89.html

Wagner, P., Heise, N., Goller, M., Hocke, N., & Bender, N. (2016, personal communication). [The OECD's International Early Learning Assessment: A statement on Germany's participation in the OECD survey].

Weaving a Curriculum

Te Whāriki (Ministry of Education, 1996), Aotearoa New Zealand's early childhood curriculum, developed in the early 1990s, was heralded by practitioners, trainers and experts in ECEC as a radical and exciting advancement that stood in stark contrast to traditional technicist notions of curriculum. Yet at the time, development of a national curriculum for ECEC had been regarded by those in the sector as a risky undertaking. On the one hand, there was a fear that a curriculum might constrain the freedom and play-based philosophy that characterised ECEC; on the other hand, there was a fear of a "trickle-down" effect from a prescriptive Aotearoa New Zealand school curriculum if opportunity to develop an ECEC curriculum was not taken up (Carr & May, 1993). What was unique in its development was the very close regard for and genuine consultation with more than 20 diverse sector groups over a lengthy period, the partnership with Te Kōhanga Reo National Trust (the national body representing Māori immersion language kōhanga reo) which "meant that the ideal of a document that would provide a bicultural and bilingual framework for early childhood curriculum in Aotearoa-New Zealand could become a reality" (Carr & May, 1993, p. 11) and the inclusion of all ages, birth to school starting age within an integrated curriculum framework. The aspiration statement for all children emphasised children's competence and agency; and the curriculum principles of family and community, holistic development, relationships and empowerment offered a strong platform for collective democracy to flourish. The sociocultural theoretical frame gave weight to social and cultural contexts; its aims were framed under the theme of mana, empowerment, and elaborated within five strands: mana atua, wellbeing; mana whenua, belonging; mana tangata, contribution; mana reo, communication; and mana aoturoa, exploration. The launch of the draft curriculum framework was marked by the Combined Early Childhood Union of Aotearoa (the trade union representing teacher/educators in kindergartens and childcare centres) with a national conference held in Christchurch in 1993, where the curriculum ideals were celebrated in the writers' keynote speeches. So highly valued by the sector are the aspirational statement for children, the principles and the strands, that, despite the

© Springer Nature Singapore Pte Ltd. 2019   65
L. Mitchell, *Democratic Policies and Practices in Early Childhood Education*,
International Perspectives on Early Childhood Education and Development 24,
https://doi.org/10.1007/978-981-13-1793-4_4

swings of policy, these have remained in the updated curriculum published in 2017 (Ministry of Education, 2017), which has as the title and central metaphor, *Te Whāriki*.

The title of *Te Whāriki*, or a woven mat, portrays the curriculum as a weaving in which each centre weaves their own curriculum mat according to their context, children and community. In this chapter, two case studies illustrate curriculum in action in Aotearoa New Zealand, where curriculum strands and valued learning are woven into the curriculum whāriki through democratic discussion and contribution. The first is of a rural kindergarten, where children plan a project to make a concrete path in their kindergarten and elicit support from families and local community to enable them to do this. The second is of an iwi-based ECEC centre where local whānau/hapū/iwi decides what knowledge should be available and how it should be made accessible. (Whānau is the Māori word for extended family; hapū is a clan or subgroup; and iwi is a tribe.) In these examples can be seen ways in which *Te Whāriki* offered scope for democratic participation by conceptualising children as competent and active participants, by being open to the content of learning being chosen through a process of co-production and by recognising the powerful potential contribution of families and community to curriculum.

1 Te Whāriki

Te Whāriki is a bicultural curriculum for children aged birth to school starting age. The commitment to the Treaty of Waitangi, Aotearoa New Zealand's founding document that was intended to be a partnership between Māori and the British Crown (see Chap. 2), was reflected in the development process for *Te Whāriki*. Tilly and Tamati Reedy worked in partnership with Margaret Carr and Helen May to construct the curriculum framework and widespread collaboration through working groups and consultation. A "central metaphor" for the curriculum derives from its title *Te Whāriki*; in Māori this translates as a woven floor mat. It is described in the curriculum document as follows:

> The early childhood curriculum has been envisaged as a whāriki, or mat, woven from the principles, strands and goals defined in this document. The whāriki concept recognises the diversity of early childhood education in New Zealand. Different programmes, structures, philosophies and environments will contribute to the distinctive patterns of the whāriki. (Ministry of Education, 1996, p. 11).

Tilly and Tamati Reedy, speaking about the development of *Te Whāriki*, conveyed its real strength to be the "capacity [of *Te Whāriki*] to establish strong and durable foundations for every culture in Aotearoa-New Zealand, and in the world" (Reedy & Reedy, 2013, p. 2). This was through a framework that emphasised children and families having agency in their own lives and cultural and contextual relevance.

In the formulation of Te Whāriki, Tamati and I worked to develop a theoretical framework that would recognise **the right of groups to choose the content of their learning, and the process by which this would be transmitted.** We were very aware of **tribal pride and sensitivity, of tribal histories and traditions, particular to, and peculiar to, each group.** So that was another major consideration for us. As a consequence we created a curriculum which we felt was not only answerable to the requirements of the Ministry of Education and its government, but was also multi-tribal and multi-cultural in its execution. With the translations we provided, we believe Te Whāriki is appropriate for all groups, with core elements that can cross cultures with respect, and still allow for individual developments specific to each person, each group, each tribe and each culture. (Reedy & Reedy, 2013, p. 2).

The original curriculum was published in 1996; in 2017 the curriculum was updated. In the updated curriculum (Ministry of Education, 2017), the metaphor of a whāriki or woven mat was again adopted, to show the interweaving of the four curriculum principles and five curriculum strands which together "give expression to the vision that children are "competent and confident learners and communicators, healthy in mind, body and spirit, secure in their sense of belonging and that they make a valued contribution to society" (Ministry of Education, 1996, p. 9; Ministry of Education, 2017, p. 6). The 2017 curriculum update explicitly emphasises collaboration with children, parents, whānau and community to create a local curriculum and the symbolic and spiritual meaning for Māori. It discusses symbolism within coloured depictions of the weaving as "the start of a journey that will take the traveller beyond the horizon" (p.11). Despite the policy turns and pressures in the period 2009–2017 (see Chap. 2), the core aspirations, values and framing survived in the updated *Te Whāriki*, and the Māori foundations were highlighted.

Te Whāriki links directly to principles of democracy in its framing; this in turn has a pervasive influence within the principles and strands. Most important, *Te Whāriki* moved away from a position that treats early childhood education and care (ECEC) settings as producing only that knowledge that is valued by a dominant culture; it actively encourages the co-production of knowledge within local settings, communities and cultures. Reedy and Reedy described as a real strength the "capacity of *Te Whāriki* to establish strong and durable foundations for every culture in Aotearoa-New Zealand, and in the world" (Reedy & Reedy, 2013, p. 2).

Penetito (2001), talking about the major problems in Māori education at a conference on ECEC for a democratic society, spoke of the boredom and alienation experienced by Māori children in schools with a curriculum that denies who they are, rules in which they have little or no say, teachers focused on ethnocentric subject expertise and teachers who have minimal tolerance for things Māori. He appealed to teachers "to 'know' the Māori children we teach, as individuals, as members of whānau, as tangata whenua, as manuwhiri, as members of hapū and iwi, as New Zealanders, as thinking and feeling human beings" (p. 18). He argued that local whānau/hapū/iwi must decide what knowledge should be available and how it should be made accessible. In his discussion of possibilities for Māori education, he highlighted the purpose of knowledge creation:

A holistic approach to education will require that questions about 'what counts as knowledge' (mātauranga), 'what counts as pedagogy' (whakakoranga), and 'what it mean to be

Māori' (mana Māori) are the key components of an educational praxis as well as being the primary purpose of the process of knowledge construction. (Penetito, 2001, p. 18).

This spirit of knowledge co-production is encapsulated within the framing of *Te Whāriki* as Tilly and Tamati Reedy have pinpointed. Penetito recommends that Māori has control over the process of researching for knowledge production and educational planning.

> . . . whānau/hapu/iwi have and retain control over the whole process. They decide what they want to know, who should do the searching, how the search will be conducted, what will be distributed and what will not, and who will have access to it. They are the owners of this local knowledge in terms of intellectual property and it is they who should decide the private-public differentiation of it. (Penetito, 2001, p. 27).

The curriculum authors for *Te Whāriki* drew on several theorists, most strongly Piaget, Bruner, Bronfenbrenner and Vygotsky, and a wide range of literature. Fleer (2013), noting the many theoretical voices present in *Te Whāriki*, conveys this to be both a strength and weakness. According to her, the new theoretical discourses enabled a move away from universal ideas about developmentalism, but on the other hand, the variety of positions had potential to generate confusion or misinterpretation. Nevertheless, *Te Whāriki* is largely based on a sociocultural view of learning and development (Lee, Carr, Soutar, & Mitchell, 2013) and makes explicit links to Bronfenbrenner's ecological theoretical framework. This theoretical basis draws attention to the settings in which the child participates and the interrelationships amongst these settings, for example, the ECEC setting and the home. It also highlights as influential, settings in which the child does not participate, but in which events occur that affect the child, for example, a parent's workplace and a parent's social network. The outer system includes the nation's beliefs and values about children and early childhood care and education. Hence the child's learning and development is always seen as occurring within a context that goes far beyond the immediate settings in which the child takes part.

The curriculum begins with an aspiration statement for children and four principles:

> The curriculum is founded on the following aspirations for children to grow up as competent and confident learners and communicators, healthy in mind, body and spirit, secure in their sense of belonging and in the knowledge that they make a valued contribution to society. (Ministry of Education, 1996, p. 9).

A vision of a democratic society is reflected in the emphasis within this statement on equitable opportunities for all children and belonging and participation.

Its four principles emphasise empowerment, holistic development, relationships and family and community.

> Empowerment – Whakamana. The early childhood curriculum empowers the child to learn and grow.
> Holistic development – Kotahitanga. The early childhood curriculum reflects the holistic way children learn and grow.
> Family and community – Whānau tangata. The wider world of family and community is an integral part of the early childhood curriculum.

Relationships – Ngā hononga. Children learn through responsive and reciprocal relationships with people, places and things (Ministry of Education, 1996, p. 14).

May (2005) writes that the concept of "child as citizen" is embedded in the foundation principle concerning the "empowerment" of children in Aotearoa New Zealand's early childhood education curriculum, *Te Whāriki* (Ministry of Education, 1996). "*Te Whāriki* positioned the consideration of rights, interests and culture as a crucial foundation for delivering 'quality outcomes'" (May, 2005, p. 23). *Te Whāriki* portrays children as active participants in learning, contributing with others to the co-construction of knowledge, a view consistent also with sociocultural views of learning associated with Vygotsky's theory.

Five strands of learning outcomes, each with goals for children, are woven within the principles in both the original and updated *Te Whāriki*. These are set out in Table 1.

Table 1 *Te Whāriki* strands and goals

Wellbeing – Mana atua	Belonging – Mana whenua	Contribution – Mana tangata	Communication – Mana reo	Exploration – Mana aotūroa
Children will experience an environment where:	Children and their families will experience an environment where:	Children will experience an environment where:	Children will experience an environment where:	Children will experience an environment where:
Goal 1: Their health is promoted	Goal 1: Connecting links with wider world are affirmed and extended	Goal 1: There are equitable opportunities for learning irrespective of gender, ability, age, ethnicity or background	Goal 1: They develop non-verbal communication skills for a range of purposes	Goal 1: Their play is valued as meaningful learning and the importance of spontaneous play is recognised
Goal 2: Their emotional wellbeing is nurtured	Goal 2: They know that they have a place	Goal 2: They are affirmed as individuals	Goal 2: They develop verbal communication skills for as range of purposes	Goal 2: They gain confidence in and control of their bodies
Goal 3: They are kept safe from harm	Goal 3: They feel comfortable with the routines, customs and regular events	Goal 3: They are encouraged to learn with and alongside others	Goal 3: They experience the stories and symbols of their own and other cultures	Goal 3: They learn strategies for active exploration, thinking and reasoning
	Goal 4: They know the limits and boundaries of acceptable behaviour		Goal 4: They discover and develop different ways to be creative and expressive	Goal 4: They develop working theories for making sense of the natural, social, physical and material world

Each strand lists a number of indicative learning outcomes; in total there were 117 across all the strands in the original. The labelling of these as "indicative" rather than prescribed reinforces that the curriculum is intended to be woven within each ECEC service and to be responsive to context, goals and values. The 2017 update reduced the learning outcomes to 20, referring to these as developing capabilities rather than fixed end points. The following stem accompanies each outcome in the update: "Over time and with guidance and encouragement, children become increasingly capable of…" (Ministry of Education, 2017, pp. 24–25). The emphasis within the curriculum on mana and empowerment and a holistic and relational understanding of participation offers a set of values for a democratic tradition in ECEC to flourish; *Te Whāriki* as a curriculum framework offers a basis for democratising ECEC, and it is a facilitating condition.

Democracy is not an explicit value in *Te Whāriki* as it is in curriculum documents in Nordic countries. For example, the Danish Act, where the general aims have been translated by Brostrom (2013, p. 243), emphasises both participation and taking responsibility for democratic undertakings within the preschool.

> [P]reschools must provide children with the possibility to participate in decision making and joint responsibility and understanding for democracy, and to contribute to children's autonomy and abilities to participate in binding social communities.

Critiquing *Te Whāriki* from a Danish perspective, Brostrom argued that curricula are needed to help children "act in a future society as critical-democratic subjects" and that such curricula is "much more powerful than curricula that only focus on children's comprehensive development – although this is of course a necessary component" (Brostrom, 2013, p. 254). He highlighted criteria from his analysis of a German Bildung-oriented approach that he considered necessary to realise democratic participation – "an emphasis on children's own activity and dialogue with others; a feeling of mutual obligation and commitment between children and teachers; and participation, action and democratic practices" (p. 246). In particular, Brostrom argued that the aims and content for education need to meet the challenges of problems that are typical of our epoch and that have a future orientation. He referenced Klafki's outline of "epoch-typical" problems that include "questions about war and peace, North-South conflict, problems of nationalism, ecological problems and sustainability, socially produced disparity, and the dangers and possibilities of new communications media" (Brostrom, 2013, p. 247). Brostrom argues that these problems are evident in preschools, that adults need to help children come to terms with them and that curricula needs to "[help] children to act in a future society as critical-democratic subjects" (p. 254). It is not that *Te Whāriki* does not enable these goals, but that because they are not explicit, it is over to the ECEC centre to determine its own values.

Similarly, Joy Cullen (2003) noted that there is little specification in *Te Whāriki* in moving from strands and goals to curriculum content. More recently, she argued that "practitioners cannot meet the principles of *Te Whāriki* if they are unresponsive to societal issues that impact on the daily lives of the children in their care. Nor can they engage with children as co-learners without respecting the funds of knowledge that children bring with them from diverse backgrounds" (Cullen, 2008, p. 12). Jenny Ritchie (2018, in press), writing of the 2017 *Te Whāriki* update, is critical that the updated curriculum does not adequately address challenges of honouring the commitments to Māori made in Te Tiriti o Waitangi and of cultural and linguistic "superdiversity", the climate change crisis and the associated need for education to address ways of living sustainably on a finite planet. Over many years, Ritchie has been a staunch advocate for realising the bicultural aspirations of *Te Whāriki*, and her research with teachers and in collaboration with Māori researcher Cheryl Rau has highlighted exemplars (e.g. Ritchie & Rau, 2008).

In the Aoteroa New Zealand case study outlined below, teachers' aims to build community through a co-constructive teaching and learning process were evident within their actual practice, including how they carried out their roles, and their expectations of children. These expectations included responsibility by children for environmental issues within their context. Discussion of beliefs and practices that gave emphasis to their commitment to biculturalism, community, human potential and worth was central to their pedagogical practice. This discussion seemed to be a way for teachers to deepen their understanding of the values they held for children and their community, to critique the meaning of values for practice and to offer a foundation for exploring how children and community can contribute to creating a democratic environment for learning and participation.

2 Case Study: Nurturing the Mana of the Child

The case study was drawn from data gathered in a professional network of 16 teachers from six kindergartens who met once a month over a period of 1 year with me as researcher and a professional development facilitator (Mitchell, 2007). Teachers brought examples of pedagogical documentation in order to analyse, reflect on and critique their pedagogical practice from their understanding of the "child as citizen". The aspiration statement for children from *Te Whariki* (Ministry of Education, 1996) and a perspective of a child as "rich in potential, strong, powerful, competent, and most of all connected to adults" (Malaguzzi, 1993, p. 10) were guiding principles. Opportunities were created within the network for teachers to think about and discuss their assumptions, values and the purpose of education, explore reciprocal influences of adults' and children's interactions and deepen opportunities for children, whānau and community to contribute to the curriculum. Some teachers wrote in a journal during the time; all teachers also took part in individual interviews at the start and end of the project.

The case study derives from data gathered with two teachers who worked within a kindergarten that was described like this.

Totara Kindergarten (fictitious name) is a three teacher kindergarten in a predominantly farming community. Forty-four children attend morning sessions (three hours on three days a week, and four hours on two days), and a different 44 children attend afternoon sessions

(2½ hours on three days a week). Younger children, mainly three-year-olds, attend in the afternoon, and then move on to the morning sessions when they turn four. Sixty-five percent of the children are Pākehā[1] New Zealanders, 24 percent are Māori and 11 percent are of other ethnicities. The families have a range of income levels. The kindergarten teachers have formed working relationships with a wānanga[2] and local marae,[3] as part of their interest in developing their kindergarten as a bicultural community. They are also trying to develop close relationships with the local school which adjoins the kindergarten, and think it important to build relationships with people, community groups and businesses in the community. Within the local community are a host of people and 'identities', all of whom had been involved in the kindergarten and hold significance: children, teachers/kaiako, a "carpentry tutor/builder/ interior designer," whānau, the local garden centre staff, cleaners, council workers, the local journalist, the teachers' families, neighbours and kindergarten "identities", Mrs. Heihei (the hen) and the guinea pigs. (Mitchell, 2007, p. 105).

2.1 Values and Beliefs

These teachers constructed democratic values and practices suitable to their context through thinking about and discussing new theories and ideas about childhood and critically examining them in relation to pedagogy and their own setting. The thinking and discussion itself was a form of democratic practice. There were consistencies between teachers' construction of statements of their values, their construction of their own roles and their documented examples of practice.

The teachers described their central focus as the mana (defined in the next paragraph below) of the child and emphasised the value of social relationships and belonging to a cooperative group where contributions of all players are welcomed. They described their main beliefs ("philosophy") about kindergartens as: "Whānau, tamariki, kaiako.[4] Working together to create an environment for learning, where the mana of each child is nurtured" (Teacher A and Teacher B, first interview, 1 June 2000).

Teacher A described teachers puzzling about the meaning of their original "philosophy" (held at the start of the network) of "empowerment" and why they wanted "to empower" children. The teachers decided that an empowered person can stand strong as a lone individual and thought this was inconsistent with their commitment to community building and biculturalism. Consequently they changed their stated "philosophy" to emphasising the "mana of the child", which they understood to be wider than empowerment, inclusive of biculturalism and of nurturing, never "trampling on" others. Their definition of mana came from an article by Soutar (2000) which Teacher A described as a light for them. The definition was typed out and put

---

[1] Pākehā is defined by Māori as meaning "extraordinary" or "white".

[2] Māori university

[3] Open space or plaza in front of meeting house

[4] Whānau means extended family, tamariki means children and kaiako means teacher/learner (akin to concept of pedagogue).

in the term book that documented ideas, children's projects, commentary and questions:

> Mana has several meanings in different contexts. Its definitions include power, status, prestige, authority, integrity and control. It is a key component of being Māori. In a Māori context when one's mana is acknowledged so too is one's potential. Because such an acknowledgement implies respect and trust and consequently freedom to develop further. When applied to young children, the nurturing of mana is vital to their wellbeing.
>
> . . . Making space for learning, for listening with eyes and ears and valuing children's knowledge and authority protects their personal tapu.[5] It conveys to children that their mana is heard, seen and felt by adults and peers. It also means that adults are able to guide meaningful learning situations for children. (Soutar, 2000, p. 8).

Much of the documentation Teacher A and Teacher B brought to the network, and the entries in Teacher A's journal, showed that both teachers were interested in finding out about new educational ideas and tried to *make sense* of them by asking questions about them. These teachers routinely spent time thinking and talking about ideas and values and questioning their meaning and consequences for their pedagogical practice. Both teachers had thought about deficit approaches to learning and consciously rejected these. Teacher B was influenced by her experiences as a primary school teacher in the 1970s and rejected a heavy emphasis on teacher-directed activities, such as art based on outlines drawn by teachers. She had lately read Freire's (1970/1996) *Pedagogy of the Oppressed* and was struck by his opposition to the "banking method" of teaching, of the teacher "depositing information" which the child absorbs. Teacher A described the key influences on her as a teacher as being *Te Whāriki* and reading about the early childhood programmes of Reggio Emilia (Edwards, Gandini, & Forman, 1998). These texts position teaching and learning as active co-constructions between parties.

After the second network meeting, where we discussed aspirations for children and the roles of kindergarten, Teacher A wrote in her journal: "Totara Kindy is a (forum) for engagement and dialogue enabling children to have the courage to think and act for themselves". She then asked the question, "What the heck is happening to enable this aspiration to be realised"? Asking what is happening raised questions for her about documentation, assessment and evaluation. She made linkages between these processes and "ensuring the programme/curriculum is relevant to children" and "informing whānau". The act of puzzling over theories and ideas and interpreting them within their kindergarten context seemed to help these teachers to become better able to base their practice on them. It was an ongoing process that enabled these teachers to incorporate their beliefs into the ways they worked with children, families and community.

The following project from Totara Kindergarten was discussed in the network. As the project was carried out, teachers photographed what was happening and put the photographs in the kindergarten term book. The term book is of happenings in

---

[5] "Tapu, like mana, is an essential element of being Māori. It demands respect and requires careful interactions. There is a notion of restriction, sometimes inaccessibility and caution surrounding tapu. Acknowledgement of tapu in relation to people is about respect of personal space and belongings, intellectual, physical or otherwise" (Soutar, 2000, p. 8).

the kindergarten, always of group projects and often involved children, parents, teachers and people from the Totara community. These term books were a source of reflection for teachers and children, a means for capturing family involvement and a celebration of the work of the kindergarten. The teachers' documentation and assessment were consistent with valuing group collaboration. The term book was not put together explicitly to show community, "but it was just full of it". Teacher A made the point that documentation shows what is valued: "Perhaps there are things others might see as more important.. ... The reality is that we see what we choose to document. And if someone was keen on maths [that's what they would document]" (Teacher A, tenth network meeting, March 2001).

The "Kindy books" that documented and celebrated group "term happenings" were portrayed as providing a window onto the kindergarten: "The material we choose tells us a story about ourselves and can help us see our own bias and thus help us broaden what we do" (Teacher A, journal excerpt).

The kindergarten participants often took part in projects that took place over a long time – months rather than days or hours – and the ideas and learning that occurred were built on subsequently. Not all project work was initiated by children; in many projects the teachers encouraged children to take responsibility and documented their efforts. In the example of an enduring project, teachers found out what the children were thinking about when they were working in the sandpit, so that they could help the children undertake work that would motivate and engage them and be useful. As a context, there is a concrete work in the locality where some parents are employed and a few children have experienced concrete-making at home.

2.2   A Project Extending Over Time and Place

The story began in 1998 when three boys in the sandpit were mixing water with sand, carting it in their trucks to dump it in another part of the sandpit and pat it down. The teachers asked and found out they were making concrete.

Teachers used this evident interest to talk with children about concrete—a dad making a concrete path and a nanny making concrete blocks for the barbeque. How did it hold together? Teachers and children discussed this idea. They decided to make real concrete. There was lots of talk about what they could make, and children contributed their ideas and came to decisions themselves to make a wall in the kindergarten.

It was a project that reached out into the community. Teachers and children went out looking at walls, photographing walls, drawing walls and asking their families about walls. Children discussed their ideas about the kind of wall they would like. They decided to make a low wall with a wooden top they could sit on at morning tea time. Children wrote lists of resources they needed for their project. They posted these on the noticeboard for parents and visitors to see and respond to.

A teacher offered a wheelbarrow for mixing concrete. A local garden centre donated tomato boxes as moulds for making concrete bricks. Children measured in buckets the water, sand and mortar after finding out the right quantities. Parents helped the children take the blocks out of the moulds and cement them in place. The local reporter visited and wrote a story. Her story headlines: "The great kiwi[6] tradition of 'do-it-yourself' is alive and well at Totara Kindergarten".

Since then, making concrete at the kindergarten has become a tradition. A concrete path being built by council workers outside the kindergarten offered opportunity for children to go out with their sketch books and pens, observe and draw what they were seeing and ask the workers questions.

Children have since used concrete to resolve a problem in the sandpit. There were gaps in the edging and the sand kept falling out. The children held a meeting and remembered the concrete. They took 2 days to dig a trench. One boy contributed a plan on how to make the boxing for concrete stand up: he had seen this done at home.

In the following year, another concrete project began to emerge. This project was instigated by the teachers. There were a lot of potholes in the roadway leading up to the kindergarten. As Teacher B said, "The children haven't talked about potholes or anything but we'll make them aware because it's part of the environment. Their cars pull up there every day. It's making the children responsible for their environment as well". Teacher B's comments show a process of the teachers selecting content that related to environmental issues in their own context and encouraging children to think about and respond to these issues themselves. This process is akin to that described by Stig Brostrom (2013, p. 247), who, writing of the Bildung ideal in ECEC in Denmark, argued that:

> … a critical-constructive Didaktik finds it necessary to formulate topics, problems and categories that give children necessary knowledge at the same time as they learn to handle the here and now of everyday life and of society in the long term.

In each project, children solved problems themselves and taught each other. The problem of making the boxing so that the sandpit edging would stand up was resolved by a 4-year-old who had seen concrete being made at home. He showed how to nail wooden struts at intervals between the two boxing edges to hold them apart and keep them rigid. Children were recollecting and going back over previous learning as they made plans and found ways to do things. This was a process of "metacognition" where children were thinking about their own thinking and using their thinking in a new situation. The photographic documentation of previous projects helped them do this because they could return to look at it. This is another reason why documentation is helpful – as something to return to – and why links between children's lives are valuable.

In doing this and other projects, there was a lovely sense of interdependence as children and adults worked together, collaborated and relied on each other. Children and adults listened and negotiated, coming to agreements, sharing and learning

---

[6] New Zealanders are sometimes referred to as "kiwis". A kiwi is a native bird of New Zealand.

skills. Roles were shared. Some children gave ideas on how to do things; others were doers – getting into the thick of concreting. Children's theories were respected. The kindergarten itself was a community operating on democratic principles. As well, it involved collaboration with the wider community: the council workers making the concrete path, a reporter who took a photo and wrote a story in the local paper, the garden shop that donated the tomato boxes for the boxing, the teacher who brought her wheelbarrow from home and the parents who came and helped.

At the 1998 international conference, *The City of the Possible*, held in Naples, Bruner (1998), spoke about the admiration in which he held Gian Battista Vico and Vico's recognition of ways in which human beings both live in reality and create the reality in which they live. Childhood is one arena, he argued, in which we can make it possible to create a world. He reflected on views coming through the conference that "having a sense of place, knowing where you are, somehow helps you develop a sense of your own personal identity, your uniqueness, as well as your place in the world". The children at Totara Kindergarten were creating their own local culture and building traditions that were to continue. Children were developing a "sense of agency" (Bruner, 1998, p.6), as they worked on meaningful projects that they had planned, developed themselves and succeeded in doing well.

Teachers worked from a social constructionist perspective, enabling children to have real influence over how the projects were conceived and progressed, and to create their own solutions when faced with difficulties, rather than telling children what to do, providing correct answers or doing things for them. There were opportunities for children to develop leadership roles. Children were encouraged to draw on their own "funds of knowledge" (Moll, 2000) from their homes and communities and were responsible for their own and others' learning processes. Children were valued for their contribution. In this way children had opportunities to experience democracy within the kindergarten.

Much of the content of the collective projects that were developed at Totara Kindergarten were environmental projects about caring for animals, making concrete, composting, collecting shellfish, growing vegetables and preparing and cooking food. In this respect, children were encouraged to understand and solve environmental problems, such as the pot holes in the driveway. Langsted has said "The game itself and the social relationships are the most important things. Skills and competence are by-products" (Langsted, 1994, p. 33). Within the concrete projects, learning of mathematical concepts was happening without being consciously taught, for example, mathematical problem-solving, dividing, measuring and estimating quantities. Writing tasks were undertaken for a purpose. The focus was the game and social relationships, which the Totara Kindergarten teachers said were of primary importance to them.

3 Case Study: Iwi Weaving a Curriculum

The United Nations Declaration on the Rights of Indigenous Peoples (UNDRIP) (United Nations, 2007) was adopted by the General Assembly on 13 September 2007 by a majority of 144 states in favour. At the time of the vote, Australia, Canada, Aotearoa New Zealand and the USA voted against the Declaration, and 11 countries abstained. "Essentially, the Declaration outlaws discrimination against indigenous peoples, promotes their full and effective participation in all matters that concern them, as well as their right to remain distinct and to pursue their own visions of economic and social development" (United Nations, 2007). Since then, Aotearoa New Zealand in 2010 and the other three countries voting against have supported the Declaration.

The debate against becoming a signatory to the Declaration in Aotearoa New Zealand was around Māori having rights and privileges not enjoyed by other New Zealanders, which some argued was not consistent with the idea of democratic citizenship. One shift in thinking about rights is from an understanding of human rights from an individual to a collective basis and to include indigenous rights to self-determination. Durie states that the Declaration defines indigenous rights in a more comprehensive way than Te Tiriti o Waitangi (discussed in Chap. 2), but Te Tiriti is unique in promising a "mutually beneficial relationship between Māori and the Crown, a partnership" (Durie, 2001, p. 7). He argues that since in New Zealand, many Māori have inadequate access to te ao Māori (the Māori world), facilitating such access needs to be a key educational role. This includes "access to language and knowledge, access to culture and cultural institutions such as marae[7] access to Māori economic resources such as land, forests, fisheries, access to customary foods, access to Māori networks especially whānau (extended family), and access to customary ways of exploring the world through time and space" (Durie, 2001, p. 4). Early childhood settings in Aotearoa New Zealand can make a contribution to at least some of these domains.

An Aotearoa New Zealand example of a Māori Trust Board (Maniapoto Trust) that is starting to construct Māori knowledge and develop its own curriculum within the framework of *Te Whāriki* is discussed next. This example draws data from a Ministry of Education-funded *Evaluation of the ECE Participation Programme* (Mitchell, Meagher-Lundberg, Davison, Kara, & Kalavite, 2016) which aimed to gather meaningful information about participation in ECEC of children from Māori, Pasifika, and low-income families and about the Ministry of Education initiatives that were designed to support participation. In this example, the Māori Trust Board was awarded a Targeted Assistance for Participation (TAP) funding grant to support them to establish a home-based service, an ECEC centre and a puna (Māori immersion playgroup). There is an "open door" policy, and parents in this centre are employed in many capacities and supported in training. The example is derived from interviews carried out by Helena Kara with parents, whānau, kaiako (teachers) and Trust mem-

---

[7] Open space or plaza in front of meeting house

bers and by further research undertaken by Vanessa Paki who wrote this section. Vanessa affiliates to Ngāti Mahuta and Te Atiawa and is a lecturer at the University of Waikato, Te Oranga School of Human Development and Movement Studies.

3.1   Iwi Curriculum: Mana Whenua

"A muri kia mau ki tēnā, kia mau ki te kawau mārō, whanake ake, whanake ake".
   (Forever hold fast to the spearhead flight formation of the kawau).
   The above saying is the vision of Maniapoto Trust that they interpret as being "our future well-being will be determined by the strength of our commitment to stand together united in spirit, mind and purpose". Their early childhood centre was funded through a Ministry of Education grant to develop services that reflect the language and culture of its community and attract Māori families to enrol. Maniapoto Trust drew on local knowledge and collaboratively developed its curriculum to make connections with their tribal identity and tribal lands. Maniapoto is the iwi (tribe).
   Maniapoto identity was conveyed as an important foundation in developing their curriculum framework. Maniapoto iwi takes an active approach to reclaiming and positioning indigenous cultural beliefs and knowledge at the heart of children's learning and whānau (extended family) development. In constructing their curriculum framework, they are conveying their own knowledges of what is in their interests, to design an education that upholds their mana as tangata whenua (people of the land). Iwi curriculum is what Wally Penetito describes as the space that "contextualizes the practices, questions, contradictions, representations, and effects that accompany the culture of education in their context" (Penetito, 2009, p. 291).
   Their curriculum reflects five pou or curriculum components of:

- Whānau ora (Whānau capacity – health and wellbeing of whānau).
- Whanaungatanga (relationships).
- Taonga tuku iho (treasures from the past).
- Te taiao (the natural world/environment).
- Anga whakamua (moving learners forward).

Connected with each pou is the transmission of traditional knowledge where the tamariki and whānau are surrounded by the traditional stories, practices, pedagogies and ways of being. One difference with Iwi curriculum is that their intergenerational transmission of language, identity and culture is embedded within rather than "added". Each pou draws from the tamariki of Rereahu as either dispositions for learning or kaupapa (themes) for transmission of knowledge. Rereahu who was a chief of Maniapoto was a direct descendant of Hoturoa, the captain of the Tainui canoe from Hawaiki to Aotearoa. The children of Rereahu were Te Ihingārangi, Maniapoto, Matakore, Tuwhakahekeao, Tūrongotapuarau, Te Io Wānanga, Kinohaku, Te Rongorito and Kahuariari. In an interview, one of the participants explained that:

We still have the framework of *Te Whāriki* but for us and the families/whānau the important issue was identity. Who, where, why Maniapoto? We've come to develop a curriculum about our pou. We've got eight of them out there who are Rereahu's tamariki (children). Maniapoto is out there and his sibling. Each pou has got an expertise and skill and that is what drives our curriculum here.. . .

Everything is done from a Maniapoto base. .. We use all our stories from Maniapoto to drive the learning and outcome. We are trying to get more of the mita of Maniapoto, the language, the words, and start using that way more. Our waiata [songs] we want to relate it to Maniapoto. For many of them they don't know those things. Even our staff thought they knew a lot about Maniapoto but they didn't.

3.2   Iwi Curriculum: Whakapapa

The term "curriculum" is used in [Te Whāriki] to describe "the sum total of the experiences, activities, and events, whether direct or indirect, which occur within an environment designed to foster children's learning and development" (Ministry of Education, 1996, p.10). The Maniapoto Trust curriculum also explores the totality of the child, whānau, hāpu and iwi through the metaphor of a harakeke (flax bush) which generates an understanding that for Māori, the child (the central flax shoot) is a crucial link between past and future, ensuring the future survival of the whānau (extended family). The metaphor identifies the connectivity between the child, the other and nature. From this place of origin and meaning, the harakeke represents the connectivity of the group so that the child is "protected, along with the nurturing, the teaching, and the training" (Reedy, 2003, p. 60). For the child, it represents the longevity and existence of the whānau. Further symbolic significance of the harakeke metaphor lies in its representation of the future of the whānau (Metge, 1996; Pere, 1984). In an interview, one participant related the metaphor to oranga (planning) where the curriculum is driven by the child's totality. Further, this participant conveyed the curriculum as a framework for kaupapa in regards to building whānau capacity.

3.3   Iwi Curriculum: Whanaungatanga

Iwi weaving their own curriculum is about relationships and is as much spiritual and intellectual as it is physical and political. These connections are central to the ways in which Maniapoto experience and make sense of their worlds and sense of place within them (Cheung, 2008; Mead, 2003). For Maniapoto iwi, the image of the child is surrounded, embraced and nurtured within a curriculum that acts and responds to a collective discourse through communal environments where the child's emotional, social, cultural, spiritual, physical and intellectual aspects are enhanced and nurtured for the future survival of their iwi. One interview participant discussed how the curriculum extends and reciprocates a curriculum where, in Maniapoto, the teachers and community groups play an active role in supporting and staying connected with each other. A kaumatua (elder) extended on the notion of relationships, explaining ways in which their curriculum sustains the interrelational bond between people and nature in promoting the revitalisation and dissemination of te reo Māori me ona tikanga (Māori language and culture) as a fight for all and as knowledge worth pursuing. He spoke of the way in which the three Maniapoto services, home-based (family daycare), early childhood education and care and puna (Māori immersion playgroup) work together in an integrated way.

> That programme is carried out in the other services as well and the staff meet and share ideas like in the three different services. We keep those relationships. Someone gets an idea and then shares it around so we are all working from the different tūpuna and are doing it at the same time so we can share ideas and extend the learning to food to gathering food to growing gardens. We have got gardens at our puna and gardens here for our children. There is a lot of sharing and working together. (Mitchell et al. 2016, p. 81).

The Māori word, "Whanaungatanga", refers to kinship, sense of family and belonging that ".....involves value processes that are interrelated" (McNatty & Roa, 2002, p. 91). For Maniapoto Trust, it carries expectations that relationships, roles and responsibilities are part of the cultural fabric and survival of their curriculum.

3.4   Iwi Curriculum: Sharing the Kaupapa

What does Iwi curriculum look like after early childhood? Returning to the vision of the Maniapoto Trust saying "A muri kia mau ki tēnā, kia mau ki te kawamārō, whanake ake, whanake ake" (Forever hold fast to the spearhead flight formation of the kawau), a question is how tamariki is supported to move from early childhood to school. Transition to school is a current policy and practice interest in Aotearoa New Zealand. Transition for Māori children was a goal in the first *Ka Hikitia* Managing for Success: The Māori Education Strategy 2008–2012 (Ministry of Education, 2008). By 2012, the Ministry of Education (2012) concluded:

> One of the main challenges of the first Ka Hikitia was that the strategy did not translate into real gains for many Māori learners and their whānau. Many members of the education community agreed with the intent behind the strategy, but didn't know what to do with it or how to put it into action. They were unsure where to go for help [bold in the original]. (p. 16).

For Maniapoto Trust, moving from one setting to another is not just the child transitioning by themselves but the transitioning of that culture (Macfarlane, Glynn, Cavanagh, & Bateman, 2007). Iwi curriculum can offer many opportunities for deepening understandings around cultural transitions and the implications. Aspirations for their people drive the Maniapoto Trust curriculum. One participant shared an experience of including Māori concepts and values as cultural tools for transitions. She explained the importance of maintaining their kaupapa during transitions.

> We went to one of the schools making sure that they realised that they're receiving a taonga (treasure) from us, our babies [are] a taonga, and you're not just taking a taonga you're taking a whānau. What is the Powhiri whakatau process (welcoming ceremony) when we take

them there? [We say] that we want to be a part of their life's journey in school. .. that we're going to be tracking them, that we want some. .. form of information coming from the schools to us about our babies.

In Reedy's (2003) view of the Māori child, an inherent essence of power, spirit, knowledge and meaning already exists within the child at the time of conception. The image of the child is of a taonga (treasure) that encompasses te uri o Papa-tū-ā-nuku (child belongs to the land), tūrangawaewae (tribal links), aroha (rule of reciprocity keeps the networks alive and functioning), kanohi ora (incarnation of the ancestors), te taura here tangata (living link with yesterday and the bridge to tomorrow), kawai tangata (genealogical links that strengthen whanaungatanga) and te ukaipō (the favoured, the special) (Reedy, 2003, pp. 57–58). This cultural discourse through the ceremony and rituals of a powhiri highlights the inextricable connectedness of spiritual and physical domains, dead and living and roles and responsibilities of those who are welcoming and those who are being welcomed (Barlow, 1991; Mead, 2003). Pōwhiri are essential for building and sustaining new and existing relationships with others.

4   Generating a Curriculum Whāriki and Democracy

Te Whāriki is theoretically complex (Nuttall, 2003), requiring teachers, children, parents, whānau and community to "weave" their own curriculum mat for all to stand on. Implementation of *Te Whāriki* is challenging, and education review office evaluation reports have shown there are considerable variations in teachers' understanding of *Te Whāriki* and practice (Education Review Office, 2013). In the two case studies in this chapter, different approaches to weaving a curriculum mat that upheld democratic principles were exemplified.

In Totara Kindergarten, teachers participated in a conscious and critical analysis of what and how their values might be progressed for their context, place and time. These teachers were members of a network, meeting with me, a professional development facilitator and other teachers to critique their pedagogical documentation from the vantage of "child as citizen" (Mitchell, 2003, 2007, 2010). This process was done with others and separately; it enabled a showcasing of documented exemplars from their kindergarten that were open to discussion and contributed to insights. The teachers' discussions in the network and their documentation showed the teachers had a long tradition of developing an articulated philosophy of values and beliefs and putting these into practice. These were consistent with democratic principles in their emphasis on agency of the child, community engagement and recognition of collective responsibility. The documentation highlighted these valued processes and outcomes. The network could be described as an enabling condition that allowed critical scrutiny of practice with others from a teachers' viewpoint.

Participants from Maniapoto Trust developed their curriculum framework from traditional stories and cultural values, beliefs and knowledge, advocating that these be carried though into school settings. Their image of the child was of a taonga (treasure) who was seen as crucially connected to the past, present and future. It was not the teachers (kaiako) who developed the Maniapoto curriculum framework in consultation with others but the collective body of iwi members (including kaiako) who drew from their cultural knowledge and understanding in its development. This process demonstrates the enactment of indigenous right to self-determination and collective democracy at work.

Internationally there has been emphasis on the creation of forums for diverse participants involved in early childhood education to enable democratic discussion and analysis about educational aims, children and childhood. Moss and Petrie (1997) advocated public debate about fundamental questions and issues concerning: aspirations for children; values about childhood and the place of children and childhood in society; and relationships between children, parents and society. They argued that early childhood education institutions as community institutions can provide opportunity for a wide group of participants to be engaged in debating these issues. Barsotti, Dahlberg, Göthson and Asen (1992) proposed that one condition for the renewal of early childhood education is that "the discussion of society's policies for children and youth takes a much more central position in public discussion and action" (p. 7). They suggested that one way for this to happen is through locally based forums with participation of local groups. Dahlberg, Moss and Pence (1999) explored these ideas further in relation to civil society and a new understanding of democracy which "calls for new forms of collective action and the proliferation of public spaces or forums in which collective action can take place" (p. 72). Early childhood institutions, they suggest, "can be understood as public forums situated in civil society in which children and adults participate together in projects of social, cultural, political and economic significance" (p. 73). Forums in civil society are based on features of social organisation such as trust, reciprocity and respect that offer a basis for benefit for all. Pence (Dahlberg et al., 1999) described the development of a partnership between First Nations Elders and the University of Victoria, Canada, where a "forum" for learning, involving elders, students, instructors, community members and written texts, enabled diverse views and voices to be heard.

In the two case studies in this chapter, different approaches to constructing educational goals and a locally woven curriculum have been illustrated. In Maniapoto Trust, a democratic tradition was supported by whānau, hapu and iwi (extended family, subtribe, tribe) making local Māori knowledge accessible and incorporating local knowledge within the curriculum. In exploring possibilities for Māori educational futures, Penetito argues that:

> In most cases whanau/hapu/iwi will need the assistance of researchers to document local knowledge as well as the guidance of professional educators to transform the knowledge into school curriculum. Of course, those same researchers and teachers might actually originate from those communities but they need not. (Penetito, 2001, p. 29).

In Totara Kindergarten, opportunities to develop and sustain a democratic tradition were supported by participants engaging with theory and in critique and debate, on their own and within a network.

5 Conclusion

Te Whāriki is a bicultural curriculum for children of all ages from birth to school starting age. It is characterised by an openness to contribution and inclusion of children, families, community and teachers. While democracy is not an explicit value, the curriculum links to democratic principles through reinforcing that what counts as knowledge in a curriculum is perspectival, wider than the "knowledge" favoured by a dominant group in society and must be inclusive of the language, culture and traditions of Māori, the indigenous peoples of Aotearoa New Zealand. Curriculum developers, Tilly and Tamati Reedy, described it as "multi-tribal and multi-cultural in its execution" (Reedy & Reedy, 2013, p. 2). An emphasis in *Te Whāriki* is on empowerment for all participants. In these ways, *Te Whāriki* affords opportunities for democratising education and for ECEC settings themselves to operate as democratic communities as Dewey has envisaged.

References

Barlow, C. (1991). *Tikanga whakaaro: Key concepts in Māori culture*. Auckland, New Zealand: Oxford University Press.

Barsotti, A., Dahlberg, G., Göthson, H., & Asen, G. (1992). *Early childhood education in a changing world*. Stockholm, Sweden: Stockholm Institute of Education.

Brostrom, S. (2013). Understanding *Te Whäriki* from a Danish perspective. In J. Nuttall (Ed.), *Weaving Te Whäriki. Aotearoa New Zealand's early childhood curriculum document in theory and practice* (2nd ed., pp. 239–257). Wellington, New Zealand: New Zealand Council for Educational Research.

Bruner, J. (1998). Each place has its own spirit and its own aspirations. *RE Child, 3*, 6.

Carr, M., & May, H. (1993). *Te Whäriki curriculum papers. Early childhood curriculum project*. Hamilton: Waikato University.

Cheung, M. (2008). The reductionist – Holistic worldview dilemma. *MAI Review, 2008, 3*, Research Note 5.

Cullen, J. (2003). The challenge of *Te Whariki*: Catalyst for change? In J. Nuttall (Ed.), *Weaving Te Whariki* (pp. 269–296). Wellington, New Zealand: NZCER.

Cullen, J. (2008). *Outcomes of early childhood education: Do we know, can we tell, and does it matter?* Jean Herbison lecture, New Zealand Association for Research in education (NZARE) Annual Conference, Palmerston North, New Zealand. http://www.nzare.org.nz/portals/306/images/Files/joy_cullen_herbison2008.pdf

Dahlberg, G., Moss, P., & Pence, A. (1999). *Beyond quality in early childhood education and care. Post modern perspectives* (1st ed.). London: Falmer Press.

Durie, M. (2001, February). *A framework for considering Maori educational advancement. [Opening address]*. Paper presented at the Hui Taumata Matauranga, Turangi/Taupo, New Zealand.

Education Review Office. (2013). *Working with Te Whāriki* Retrieved from http://www.ero.govt. nz/National-Reports/Working-with-Te-Whariki-May-2013

Edwards, C., Gandini, L., & Forman, G. (Eds.). (1998). *The hundred languages of children: He Reggio Emilia approach: Advanced reflections*. Norwood, MA: Ablex Publishing Corp.

Fleer, M. (2013). Theoretical plurality in curriculum design: The many voices of *Te Whāriki* and the *Early Years Learning Framework*. In J. Nuttall (Ed.), Weaving Te Whāriki. Aotearoa New Zealand's early childhood curriculum document in theory and practice (2nd ed., pp. 217-238). Wellington, New Zealand: NZCER Press.

Freire, P. (1970/1996). *Pedagogy of the oppressed*. New York: Continuum.

Langsted, O. (1994). Looking at quality from the child's perspective. In P. Moss & A. Pence (Eds.), *Valuing quality in early childhood services* (pp. 28–42). London: Paul Chapman.

Lee, W., Carr, M., Soutar, B., & Mitchell, L. (2013). *Understanding the Te Whāriki approach*. London: Routledge.

Malaguzzi, L. (1993). For an education based on relationships. *Young Children, 11*(93), 9–13.

Macfarlane, A., Glynn, T., Cavanagh, T., & Bateman, S. (2007). Creating culturally-safe schools for Maori students. *Australian Journal of Indigenous Education, 36*, 65–76.

May, H. (2005). A right as a citizen to a free [early childhood] education 1930s-2000s. Childrenz issues. *Journal of the Children's Issues Centre, 9*(2), 20–24.

McNatty, W., & Roa, T. (2002). Whanaungatanga: An illustration of the importance of cultural context. *He Puna Korero: Journal of Maori and Pacific Development, 3*(1), 88–96.

Mead, H. (2003). *Tikanga Māori: Living by Māori Values*. Wellington, New Zealand: Huia.

Metge, J. (1996). *New growth from old: The whānau in the modern world*. Wellington, New Zealand: Victoria University Press.

Ministry of Education. (1996). *Te Whāriki*. Wellington, New Zealand: Learning Media.

Ministry of Education. (2008). *Ka Hikitia – Managing for success. The Māori education strategy 2008–2012*. Wellington, New Zealand: Ministry of Education.

Ministry of Education. (2012). *Me korero—Let's talk: Ka hikitia—Accelerating success 2013– 2017*. Wellington, New Zealand: Author. Retrieved from http://www.minedu.govt.nz/theMinistry/PolicyAndStrategy/KaHikitia/MeKoreroLetsTalk.aspx

Ministry of Education. (2017). *Te Whāriki. He Whāriki mātauranga mō ngā mokopuna o Aotearoa*. In Early childhood curriculum. Retrieved from https://www.education.govt.nz/assets/ Documents/Early-Childhood/ELS-Te-Whariki-Early-Childhood-Curriculum-ENG-Web.pdf

Mitchell, L. (2003). Shifts in thinking through a teachers' network. *Early Years, 23*(1), 21–34.

Mitchell, L. (2007). A new debate about children and childhood. *Could it make a difference to early childhood pedagogy and policy?* Doctoral thesis, Victoria University of Wellington, Wellington, New Zealand. Retrieved from http://researcharchive.vuw.ac.nz/ handle/10063/347

Mitchell, L. (2010). Constructions of childhood in early childhood education policy in New Zealand. *Contemporary Issues in Early Childhood Education, 11*(4), 328–341.

Mitchell, L., Meagher-Lundberg, P., Davison, C., Kara, H., & Kalavite, T. (2016). *ECE Participation Programme Evaluation. Stage 3*. Retrieved from https://www.educationcounts. govt.nz/publications/ECE/ece-participation-programme-evaluation-delivery-of-ece-participation-initiatives-stage-3

Moll, L. (2000). Inspired by Vygotsky: Ethnographic experiments in education. In C. D. Lee & P. Smagorinsky (Eds.), *Vygotskian perspectives on literacy research: Constructing meaning through collaborative inquiry* (pp. 256–268). Cambridge, UK: Cambridge University Press.

Moss, P., & Petrie, P. (1997). *Children's services: Time for a new approach*. London, UK: Institute of Education, University of London.

Nuttall, J. (2003). Exploring the role of the teacher within *Te Whāriki*: Some possibilities and constraints. In J. Nuttall (Ed.), *Weaving Te Whāriki. Aotearoa New Zealand's early childhood curriculum document in theory and practice* (pp. 161–186). New Zealand Council for Educational Research: Wellington, New Zealand.

Penetito, W. (2001). If only we knew . . . Contextualising Maori knowledge. In B. Webber & L. Mitchell (Eds.), *Early childhood education for a democratic society*. Conference proceedings October 2001 (pp. 17–25). Wellington, New Zealand: New Zealand Council for Educational Research. Retrieved from http://www.nzcer.org.nz/system/files/ece-democratic-society.pdf

Penetito, W. (2009). The struggle to educate the Maori in New Zealand. In J. A. Banks (Ed.), *The Routledge international companion to multicultural education* (pp. 288–300). Routledge, New York.

Pere, R. (1984). *Ako: Concepts and learning in the Māori tradition*. Hamilton, New Zealand: Department of Sociology, University of Waikato.

Reedy, T. (2003). Toku rangatiratanga na te mana-matauranga. "Knowledge and power set me free . . . ". In J. Nuttall (Ed.), *Weaving Te Whariki: Aotearoa New Zealand's early childhood curriculum document in theory and practice* (pp. 51–77). Wellington, New Zealand: New Zealand Council for Educational Research.

Reedy, T., & Reedy, T. (2013). Te Whāriki: *A tapestry for life*. Paper presented at the New Zealand conference on early childhood education and care in co-operation with the OECD ECEC network, Wellington, New Zealand.

Ritchie, J. (2018). A fantastical journey: Reimagining Te Whāriki. *Early Childhood Folio, 20*(1), 9–14.

Ritchie, J., & Rau, C. (2008). *Whakawhanaungatanga – Partnerships in bicultural development*. Retrieved from http://www.tlri.org.nz/tlri-research/research-completed/ece-sector/whakawhanaungatanga%E2%80%94-partnerships-bicultural-development

Soutar, B. (2000). Nurturing mana and tapu - Italian style. *Early Education, 22*(Autumn), 7–10.

United Nations. (2007). *Indigenous peoples. Indigenous voices. Frequently asked questions*. Retrieved April 30, 2017., from http://www.un.org/esa/socdev/unpfii/documents/faq_drips_en.pdf

Assessment and Pedagogical Documentation

The purpose of assessment, what should be assessed and how it should be assessed in ECEC settings are hotly contested by academics, policy analysts and practitioners, with oppositional views about whether the predominant focus for assessment should be on measureable and standardised learning outcomes in a narrow range of domains or on formative assessment for learning that is socioculturally situated. Debate and contestation in ECEC (early childhood education and care) arenas internationally intensified when in 2016 the OECD announced its intention to pilot an International Early Learning Study (OECD, 2016), a cross-national assessment of early learning outcomes involving the testing of 5-year-old children in four domains. The study was rigorously criticised in academic journals (Moss et al. 2016; Carr, Mitchell & Rameka, 2016; Mackey, Hill, & De Vocht, 2016) and in statements issued by the Reconceptualising ECE group (Urban & Swadener, 2016) and by the New Zealand Association for Research in Education at its 2016 conference. Publications in national newspapers in Germany, Belgium, Canada, France and the UK have raised concerns. These concerns have sat alongside a fear of "schoolification" of ECEC and push down of standards applying to the schools sector to ECEC globally, including in Aotearoa New Zealand. However, a turning point in Aotearoa New Zealand has been the election of the 2017 Labour-led government, which is now overturning standards in the schools sector and whose policies hold out promise for the ECEC curriculum to influence schooling. A main argument in this chapter is that ideas about outcomes and how these should be assessed reflect ideas about what learning is valued and the nature of knowledge. Examples from Aotearoa New Zealand pedagogy and assessment are used to demonstrate an approach designed to emphasise and construct a democratic educational culture. Assessment practices that have democracy in mind will include the views of those being assessed, build a culture of success and be open to contribution from children, families and community. Valued outcomes will include learning dispositions and working theories to support democratic citizenship and lifelong learning.

© Springer Nature Singapore Pte Ltd. 2019
L. Mitchell, *Democratic Policies and Practices in Early Childhood Education*,
International Perspectives on Early Childhood Education and Development 24,
https://doi.org/10.1007/978-981-13-1793-4_5

1 Introduction

Analysis of debates about the image of the child, cultural priorities and desirable outcomes for children will contribute to understandings of how curriculum and assessment practices might support or hinder democratic practice. Assessment is not a neutral activity. Gordon Stobart (2008) in his book *Testing Times: The Uses and Abuses of Assessment* develops three main arguments about assessment:

- Assessment is a value-laden social activity, and there is no such thing as "culture-free" assessment.
- Assessment does not objectively measure what is already there but rather creates and shapes what is measured – it is capable of "making up people".
- Assessment impacts directly on what and how we learn and can undermine or encourage effective learning. (p. 1).

The title for his book points to the potential constructive and destructive consequences of assessment. Carol Dweck (2006) also identifies different consequences for learning orientations which are linked to different approaches to assessment: performance goals (the evaluation by others of students' achievement) or learning goals (in which students strive to increase their competence or master something new, to attempt hard tasks and to persist after failure or setback). Like Dweck, the literature contrasts two approaches to assessment. Assessment of learning focuses on what has been learned, such as tests of achievement in subject areas, and assessment of developmental skills on abilities and aptitudes, such as IQ scores. These are decontextualised assessments, undertaken for the purpose of highlighting a standard reached and measured against a norm or an "innate" ability. Assessment for learning places emphasis on "what is being learned and on the quality of classroom interactions and relationships" (Stobart, 2008, p. 145), the process of learning rather than a static "proof" of competence. A definition used by New Zealand's Assessment Reform Group emphasises gathering and analysis of data for the purpose of informing teaching and learning: "The process of seeking or interpreting evidence for use by learners and their teachers, to identify where the learners are in their learning, where they need to go to and how best to get there" (Assessment Reform Group, 2002, pp. 2–3). With this definition in mind, tests may play a part in assessment for learning if the responses are used to identify what has, and has not, been understood and if this leads to action to improve learning.

Stobart set out five "deceptively simple" key factors for assessment for learning (pp. 145–146) identified by the UK's Assessment Reform Group (1999): (i) the active involvement of pupils in their own learning, (ii) the provision of effective feedback to pupils, (iii) adjusting teaching to take account of the results of assessment, (iv) the need for pupils to be able to assess themselves and (v) a recognition of the profound influence that assessment has on the motivation and self-esteem of pupils, both of which are crucial influences on learning. Mitchell and Carr (2014) added a sixth factor (vi) a recognition of the profound influence that assessment has on the expectations and confidence of children's families. This addition was "in recognition of the understanding that family expectations and aspirations are a key factor for early childhood care and education provision and schooling (Siraj-Blatchford, 2010; Hattie, 2009), and assessment is a key influence on family expectations and aspirations" (p. 9).

The two models of assessment tend to link with different kinds of outcomes. Carr (Mitchell & Carr, 2014, p. 14) has summarised two kinds of outcomes and their associated models of assessment, from an adaptation of her earlier published model (Carr, 2001, p. 3). These are reproduced in Table 1. Arguably, Model Two links to democratic principles through its emphasis on a longer-term vision of citizenship, participatory assessment processes and a strength-based framework.

In Aotearoa New Zealand early childhood settings, Model Two is the main model of assessment used.

Before turning to Aotearoa New Zealand examples of assessment practices under Model Two, problems with the dominant "assessment of learning" approach are discussed. In chapter "Aotearoa New Zealand Within Global Trends in ECEC Policy", I argued that marketisation and globalisation have brought with it an emphasis on instrumental outcomes and measurement of achievement; alongside

Table 1 Two models of assessment and their associated outcomes

Assumptions about	Assessment Model One	Assessment Model Two
Outcomes of interest	A list of fragmented skills and items of knowledge that describe competence, often with a reference to school entry	A list of "lifelong learning" strategies and dispositions
		A longer-term vision of a citizen in a democratic society
Focus for intervention	Deficit-oriented. Gap-filling is emphasised	Strengths, disposition-enhancing, are emphasised
Units of analysis	Skills and items of knowledge	Episodes of learning as narratives
Validity	Objective observation	Interpreted observations and dialogue
Progress	Hierarchies of skills and knowledges, an accumulation of valued knowledge	Increasingly complex participation in a learning environment
Value to practitioners	Surveillance by external agencies	Communication with four audiences: Children, families, other staff and self (the practitioner writing the story, perhaps for or with the children)
	Planning for filling gaps in skill or knowledge	Planning for strengthening participation repertoires
Who does the assessing?	The practitioners	A democratic process. The *children* dictate stories and take photographs, the *families* contribute comments, and the *practitioners* add stories and revisit the collection with the child or children, enabling retelling, recognising and the collaborative construction of trajectories of learning

these trends comes a tendency to narrow the curriculum to the limited domains of those easily tested and able to be compared nationally and internationally. Hence the international benchmarking testing tools, such as Progress in International Reading Literacy Study (PIRLS), Trends in International Mathematics and Science Study (TIMSS) and the Programme for International Student Assessment (PISA), are used to rank countries' performance in different domains against norms and have taken on a status that leads to dominance of these curriculum areas in some countries. Likewise, the *OECD's International Early Learning Study*, being developed by the OECD (2017) and discussed in chapter "Aotearoa New Zealand Within Global Trends in ECEC Policy", will lead to country comparisons of internationally standardised outcomes that the OECD intends to link with PISA scores when the students are older.

Aotearoa New Zealand has experienced the consequences of accountability demands that focus on narrowly prescribed curriculum domains in the schools sector. National Standards were introduced into primary schools in 2010, requiring schools to make and report teacher judgements about children's levels of reading, writing and mathematics achievement at different times in the first 8 years of primary schooling. Teachers rate children's achievement against four standards – "above", "at", "below" or "well below" the standard. The aim set out on the Ministry of Education website is:

> To lift achievement in literacy and numeracy (reading, writing, and mathematics) by being clear about what students should achieve and by when. This will help students; their teachers and parents, families and whānau better understand what they are aiming for and what they need to do next. (Ministry of Education, 2017a).

The practice and impact of National Standards in Aotearoa New Zealand schools have been carefully documented, researched and publicised over almost a decade by Martin Thrupp, a Professor of Education at the University of Waikato. His findings and critique were recently brought together in his book about the National Standards, *The Search for Better Educational Standards: A Cautionary Tale* (Thrupp et al., 2017). The new Labour-led government soon after its election announced the removal of National Standards. However, lessons learned from the experiment with National Standards are salutary. In practice, Thrupp criticised the standards for the negative impact for children of labelling them below standard and a narrowing of the curriculum to literacy and numeracy. This has occurred in schools through decisions to take more time in the school day explicitly on literacy and numeracy, greater time required for teachers in assessing literacy and numeracy and a narrowing of the focus being taught within literacy and numeracy. Overall, a two-tier curriculum is being reinforced through the National Standards policy in some schools (Thrupp & White, 2013). Similarly, in the case studies of assessment practice in ECEC services and primary schools, Mitchell and Cowie et al. (2015b, p. 37) found that National Standards requirements were at odds with the valuing by principals, teachers and parents of a broad education and holistic assessment in context. The OECD review (Nusche, Laveault, MacBeath, & Santiago, 2012) of evaluation and assessment in Aotearoa New Zealand raised a similar warning and made a recommendation for "further work to ensure that the Standards' focus on literacy and numeracy does not marginalise other learning areas where measurement of performance and progress is more challenging" (p. 9).

These concerns that the breadth of learning will be reduced through measurement regimes are mirrored in Lingard's (2010) arguments that the purposes and effects of schooling are much broader than those reported in test scores. He is especially critical of the long-term damaging impact of high-stakes standardised testing:

> In particular, we need to distinguish between the short-term and long-term effects of high stakes accountability testing. While this kind of testing and the professional responses to itcan provide gains in the short term and a refocusing on the basics of literacy and numeracy, the long-term effects are degrading of schools and teachers' work, reductive in curriculaterms, and are ultimately counterproductive. (Stobart, 2008, p. 116).

Lingard points to successful schooling systems, such as in Finland, where there is no high-stakes, standardised testing but where teachers are well educated and have a high degree of professional autonomy and practice "intellectually demanding pedagogies for all students" (p. 137).

Interviews with parents in case studies of Continuity of Early Learning, which found out about how information was passed between ECEC settings, schools and home (Mitchell, Cowie, et al., 2015b), found parents in the study wanted information they could understand. Some found National Standards information hard to understand as did parents in the Research, Analysis and Insight into National Standards (*RAINS*) project (Thrupp & White, 2013). They wanted an idea of their own influence and how they might help their child.

A rationale for making standardised measurements is that they will be objective and valid across time and place. The framing ignores the context in which tests are undertaken and offers only a static representation of achievement at a point in time. To inform decisions about what to do next, teachers benefit from understanding more about contextual detail and having data from a variety of sources.

Dahlberg and Moss (2005) are highly critical of the social construction of preschools as "producers of predetermined outcomes" (p. 5), arguing that the construction is at the expense of other ways of thinking about ECEC, for example, the "moral-practical" and the "aesthetic-expressive". The assessment exercises used in the global testing regime constitute a "very partial view of education" (p. 10). Likewise, the Gordon Commission Technical Report (2013), *To Assess, to Teach, to Learn: A Vision for the Future of Assessment*, argues for assessment/curriculum goals that go beyond reading, writing and arithmetic, to stress problem solving, creativity and critical thinking. Assessment, it argues, needs "to be more sensitive to subjective phenomena, i.e., to affect, attribution, existential state, emotion, identity, situation, etc., as will also the teaching and learning transactions in which learners are engaged" (p. 38).

Doubtless, the careful research and writing by Thrupp and his associates and the advocacy by the teachers' union NZEI Te Riu Roa, which commissioned Thrupp's initial study, have influenced public and political understanding in Aotearoa New

Zealand. The 2017 Labour-led government had a grasp on the problems with National Standards and, within 1 month of its election, announced they would be removed. Chris Hipkins (2017), Minister of Education, in a media release announcing the introduction of the Education Amendment Bill 2018 that would remove National Standards, argued that they were "driven by ideology rather than evidence" and that "removing National Standards frees up schools to focus more on progress in subjects wider than just literacy and numeracy, to better prepare students for school and life".

Within Aotearoa New Zealand's ECEC sector, prior to the election of the 2017 Labour-led government, there has been a long-held fear that the linkages being made with National Standards (Alcock & Haggerty, 2013) would "trickle down" to the early childhood curriculum to emphasise those very specific numeracy and literacy skills. The removal of National Standards helps alleviate that particular fear, and indeed the Labour-led government's policy to allow *Te Whariki* to be used as the curriculum in the first 2 years of schooling opens new possibilities for ECEC to take a curriculum lead in schools.

2   Approaches to Assessment That Have Democracy in Mind

In a curriculum founded on democratic values, teachers will have an idea of a long-term aim of citizenship. Democracy is associated with ideals of educating citizens (Fielding & Moss, 2012; Giroux, 1992) who practice democracy as a "way of life" and for a radical educational practice that questions assumptions, what is counted as knowledge and power structures. In order for an approach to curriculum to be implemented as democratic, approaches to assessment need also to be congruent, able to respond to locally determined and collective values and with involvement of teachers, children, families and community as participants. In the early childhood context in Aotearoa New Zealand, Sweden and Italy's Reggio Emilia, pedagogical documentation has emphasised opportunities for participants to reflect and construct cultures of democracy and agency (Carr, 2008; Dahlberg, Moss, & Pence, 1999; Rinaldi, 2005).

Dahlberg et al. (1999) have argued for the use of pedagogical documentation as a tool for reflecting on pedagogical practice and for creating democratic pedagogical practice. Pedagogical documentation also enables those involved in the early childhood education setting to take responsibility for making meanings and decisions about what is going on there.

Dahlberg et al. (1999) differentiated between pedagogical documentation as a process and as content in that process:

> Pedagogical documentation' as *content* is material which records what the children are saying and doing, the work of the children, and how the pedagogue relates to the children and their work. This material can be produced in many ways and take many forms—for example, hand-written notes of what is said and done, audio recordings and video camera recordings, still photographs, computer graphics, children's work itself. ... This material makes

the pedagogical work concrete and visible (or audible), and as such is an essential ingredient for the process of pedagogical documentation.

The process of pedagogical documentation involves the use of that material as means to reflect upon the pedagogical work and to do so in a very rigorous, methodical and democratic way. That reflection will be done both by the pedagogue alone and the pedagogue in relation to others—other pedagogues, pedagogistas, the children themselves, their parents, politicians. (p. 148).

Documentation and dialogue enable processes of learning and teaching to be made visible so that they can be deconstructed. "Through documentation we can more easily see, and ask questions about which image of the child and which discourses we have embodied and produced, and what voice, rights and position the child has got in our early childhood institutions" (Dahlberg et al., p. 153). The role and operation of the early childhood education centre can be made visible through pedagogical documentation and afford a focus for debate (Dahlberg et al., 1999; Moss, 1999).

The emphasis in *Te Whāriki* on mana and empowerment and a relational and holistic understanding of participation offers a framework of democratic values. All four curriculum principles reflect an emphasis on agency, attending to the wider community, reciprocal relationships and cultural identity. It is also a bicultural curriculum statement, making reference to the 1840 *Treaty of Waitangi*, explained in chapter "Aotearoa New Zealand Within Global Trends in ECEC Policy". *Te Whāriki* was a leader within the education sector in efforts to ensure policy and practice are consistent with the principles of the *Treaty of Waitangi* (Lee, Carr, Soutar & Mitchell, 2013). The metaphor of a whāriki, as a woven mat, conveys the ways in which the four curriculum principles are interwoven with five curriculum strands. The weaving is done collaboratively with teachers, children, parents, whanau (extended family) and communities to create a contextually relevant local curriculum. The image of a whāriki portrays the curriculum as a "mat for all to stand on" (Ministry of Education, 2017b, p. 12).

Aotearoa New Zealand has responded to the ideas within its early childhood curriculum in its approach to assessment for learning. Documenting pedagogy through narrative assessment is commonly used by early childhood practitioners in Aotearoa New Zealand as a process in assessment, planning and evaluation. It has been made visible through the work of Margaret Carr and others (Carr, 2001; Carr, May, & Podmore, 1998; Carr et al., 2000) and through the use of a learning and teaching story framework. A learning story is:

a documented account of a child's learning event, structured around five key behaviours: taking an interest, being involved, persisting with difficulty, expressing a point of view or feeling, and taking responsibility (or taking another point of view)..... A Teaching Story, on the other hand, is about evaluating practice. (Carr et al., 2000, pp. 7–8).

Resource kits of exemplars of assessment, *Kei Tua o Te Pae: Assessment for Learning: Early Childhood Exemplars* (Ministry of Education, 2005, 2007, 2009a), and accompanying professional development were developed over the period 2005–2009, and a set of resources, *Te Whatu Pōkeka: Kaupapa Māori Assessment for Learning*, for assessment in Māori medium settings was published in 2009 (Ministry of Education, 2009b). Kit One explains that the framework emerged from the philosophy of *Te Whāriki*. The principles are also the principles of assessment and the strands are woven through. The title *Kei Tua o Te Pae* is a line from an oriori (lullaby) by Hirini Melbourne. It takes images from this oriori to apply to development, learning and assessment for learning.

> In an ever-changing world, we know that young children's horizons will expand and change in ways that cannot be foreseen. Children will travel beyond the current horizon, and early childhood education is part of that. It continues the shaping of a vision for children – that of their being "competent and confident learners and communicators, healthy in mind, body, and spirit, secure in their sense of belonging and in the knowledge that they make a valued contribution to society" (Te Whāriki, p. 9). Learning is a lifelong journey that will go beyond the current horizon. The details of the journey will change as the world changes, but this vision will remain the same. (Ministry of Education, 2005, Book 1, p. 5).

These ideas about uncertainty, change and possibility are evident in *Te Whāriki*'s description of learning outcomes as working theories and learning dispositions. Working theories are defined as:

> the evolving ideas and understandings that children develop as they use their existing knowledge to try to make sense of new experiences. Children are most likely to generate and refine working theories in learning environments where uncertainty is valued, inquiry is modelled, and making meaning is the goal. (Ministry of Education, 2017b, p. 23).

Learning dispositions as outcomes can be described as situated learning strategies plus motivation (Carr, 2001, p. 9). They are seen as combinations of ability, inclination and sensitivity to occasion by Perkins, Jay and Tishman (1993) and in *Te Whāriki* (Ministry of Education, 2017b, p.25). The idea of learning dispositions focuses on the development of identities that are positive about learning and able to support further learning, e.g. Dweck and Leggett's (1988) work on "mastery orientation". Siraj-Blatchford (2004) describes mastery orientation as children tending, after a setback, to "focus on effort and strategies instead of worrying that they are incompetent" (p. 11). She argues that in order to address the problem of orientations that can lead to lower outcomes, educators are required to "take an active role in planning for, supporting and developing individual children's identities as masterful learners of a broad and balanced curriculum" (p. 11).

> Learning dispositions necessarily incorporate a 'ready, willing and able' element. Being 'ready' means having the inclination, being 'willing' means having sensitivity to time and place, and being 'able' means having the necessary knowledge and skills. Learning dispositions enable children to construct learner identities that travel with them into new contexts and across time, in this way supporting lifelong learning.

Assessments "can be formative of democratic communities of teaching and learning" (Carr et al., 2001, p. 29). Four of these ways are:

- Assessments can construct and highlight valued outcomes for living in a democracy.
- Assessments can assist participants in the community to develop trajectories of learning.
- Assessments can provide opportunities for children to self-assess.

- Assessments can provide spaces for families and community to contribute to the curriculum.

The next sections provide Aotearoa New Zealand examples to illustrate some of these ways that assessment practices support and construct democracy in education.

3 Assessment to Construct and Highlight Valued Outcomes

Carr et al.'s literature scan on Continuity of Early Learning includes a section entitled "What Learning for the Mid-21st Century? Here the features of being an educated person that were set out in the Gordon Commission Technical Report were aligned with the key competencies in The New Zealand Curriculum, the strands in *Te Whāriki* and a similar set appearing in the 2015 *Early Years Learning Framework* (EYLF) for Australia" (Carr et al. 2015, p. 9). These are reproduced in Table 2.

This summary points to the value of dispositional outcomes for being an educated person; these are important outcomes for living in a democracy. When documented through assessment, features "of being an educated person" are given visibility and prominence and become open to critical discussion and understanding. In Sweden, where documentation of children's activities is a requirement, it is common to publicly display documentation panels including photographs, drawings, videos and written reflections. Liljestrand and Hammarberg (2017) analysed documentation panels in four preschools in Sweden in relation to national policy

Table 2 Alignments in curriculum of "features of being an educated person"

Gordon Commission Canada	NZC New Zealand	Te Whāriki New Zealand	EYLF Australia
Knowledge creation as participants in a knowledge creating society	(Creative, critical and metacognitive) thinking	Exploration	Children are confident and involved learners
Moving flexibly and rationally between concrete reality and abstractions from it	Using language, symbols and texts	Communication	Children are effective communicators
Living with increasing complexity and turning it to advantage whenever this is possible	Participating and contributing	Belonging	Children have a strong sense of identity
Cognitive persistence	Managing self	Wellbeing	Children have a strong sense of wellbeing
Collective cognitive responsibility: Engaging in collaborative activities that are rich in cognitively challenging activities	Relating to others	Contribution	Children are connected with and contribute to their world

goals, showing how the panels reflected curriculum goals of the competent and self-governed child. Nevertheless, these authors argue that such documentation may be linked to a culture of accountability, rather than being used as intended by practitioners at a local level.

Assessment can make visible outcomes that are valued in a particular context and co-produced within a local community rather than outcomes that are standardised and predefined. The example below is from the Continuity of Early Learning case studies (Mitchell et al. 2015a). This kindergarten was chosen to highlight its pathway towards bicultural assessment practice. The Totara kindergarten (fictitious name) kaiako (teachers) had clear ideas about outcomes that they valued and an underpinning philosophy of Te Ao Māori (the Māori world), sustainable/environmental education and whakamana, building mana (strength) (Fig. 1).

The kindergarten assessment documentation reinforces their values and illustrates how some values are put into practice:

Manaakitanga (hospitality) – looking after each other.
Kaitiakitanga (guardianship) – caring for Papatuanuku (In the Māori world view, land gives birth to all things, including humankind, and provides the physical and spiritual basis for life.)
Whanaungatanga (kinship) – valuing family and community.
Tuakana/teina – supporting each other [An older or more expert tuakana (brother, sister or cousin) helps and guides a younger or less expert teina (originally a younger sibling or cousin of the same gender).]

Assessments include community projects and contributions from children, parents and whānau. The teacher's documentation in Fig. 1, "Part of the worm sorting team", highlights the kindergarten values of sustainable environmental education and kaitiakitanga (guardianship and protection). Learning that occurs through such projects is made visible, not only about "the ways the world works" but also through children gaining "a sense of responsibility for the place". Caring for the worms was an evident concern ("worms don't like the light", "they had to go back under the soil quickly so their skin wasn't damaged by the sun", "put all the scraps in the special bucket so they don't go hungry"). Community contributions are mentioned in the story – "the wooden trough that Brian had made especially for the job" – and collaborative work of the "worm sorting team" is a focus. In these ways community, collectivism and collaboration are given value.

Assessment can highlight family values and beliefs. In a centre for refugee children and families, teachers made deliberate efforts to find out about family aspirations for their children and to reinforce these (Mitchell, Bateman, et al., 2015). Early literacy was especially significant for a Sudanese family, whose child Nyandie (fictitious name) attended the centre. A learning story "Nyandie Is a Writer" highlights Nyandie as "becoming an expert" in writing, thereby reinforcing Nyandie's identity as a writer with a "mastery orientation" – she practices and practices. The story is positive about the teaching role of Nyandie's mum and makes connections to how children learn within a social context, from learning that has interest and meaning for them.

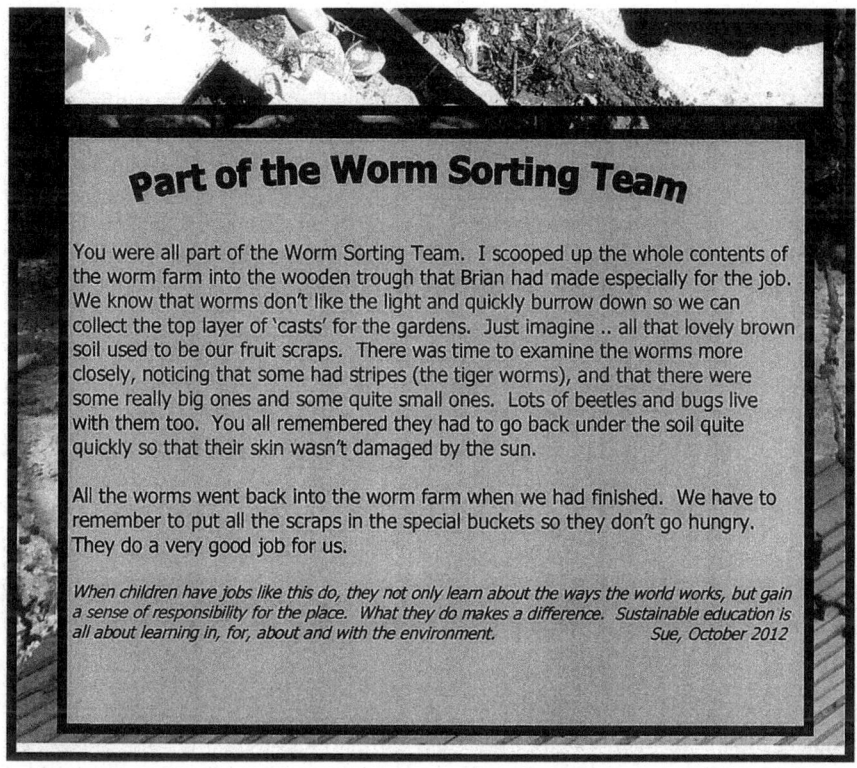

Part of the Worm Sorting Team

You were all part of the Worm Sorting Team. I scooped up the whole contents of the worm farm into the wooden trough that Brian had made especially for the job. We know that worms don't like the light and quickly burrow down so we can collect the top layer of 'casts' for the gardens. Just imagine .. all that lovely brown soil used to be our fruit scraps. There was time to examine the worms more closely, noticing that some had stripes (the tiger worms), and that there were some really big ones and some quite small ones. Lots of beetles and bugs live with them too. You all remembered they had to go back under the soil quite quickly so that their skin wasn't damaged by the sun.

All the worms went back into the worm farm when we had finished. We have to remember to put all the scraps in the special buckets so they don't go hungry. They do a very good job for us.

When children have jobs like this do, they not only learn about the ways the world works, but gain a sense of responsibility for the place. What they do makes a difference. Sustainable education is all about learning in, for, about and with the environment.   Sue, October 2012

Fig. 1 Totara Kindergarten assessment documentation. (With permissions from Whanau Manaaki Kindergartens)

Nyandie is a writer

March 2012.

Today as I find you at our writing table Nyandie, I notice you have written two letters as some letter Os and also some Cs. We have some letter N templates so we have a look at how capital letter N goes. You are writing very competently Nyandie, just three years old, you are a confident learner and today you showed me just what you can do. Your mum is a very good teacher and she helps you with all of your letters. You have become very interested in writing lately. This seems to be when you arrive and you and your mum spend some time together practising many letters. Every day you are practising and practising. Look aunty Robyn I can do C you tell me. C for cat. You are becoming an expert Nyandie.

I look forward to us working together and discovering more letters that interest you. We should try M for mummy and T for [Name] your mummy's name.

Te Whāriki reminds us that children enjoy their learning when it is in a social context, when they are interested and when their learning has meaning for them. Nyandie knows she is a writer and she knows A B C and now she is writing those letters. Love to you from Teacher Robyn. (Mitchell, Bateman, et al., 2015, p. 42).

More generally, Nyandie is developing an identity that is positive about learning and able to support further learning. Siraj-Blatchford (2004) describes mastery orientation as children tending, after a setback, to "focus on effort and strategies instead of worrying that they are incompetent" (p. 11) and also on problem solving.

4   Assessment to Show and Develop Trajectories of Learning

Assessment can contribute to democratic communities through assisting participants in the community to develop trajectories of learning (Carr et al., 2015). During
research on a Teaching and Learning Research Initiative (TLRI) project entitled *Key
learning competencies across place and time: Kimihia te ara tōtika, hei oranga mō
tō ao*, teachers at Aratupu Preschool and Nursery (a community-based ECEC centre
located in Christchurch) researched evidence for, and developed theories about,
"relating to others". "Relating to others" is a key competency in the NZ Curriculum
for schools (Ministry of Education, 2007) and links with Te Whariki strand contribution. The relationships between this concept and empowerment were important to
teachers who described a "favourite saying" as "We want children to be able to
leave this centre, knowing who they are and being confident in standing up for
themselves in future education systems and letting others know when their needs
are not being met" (Wilson-Tukaki & Davis, 2011, p. 21). Learning stories were a
starting point for analysis.

> The Learning Stories at Aratupu are designed to capture—in context—significant stories
> about the learning of children. They are written mostly by teachers and sometimes by par-
> ents. They are analysed largely by the teachers in terms of the social justice framework of
> the centre, Margaret Carr's (2001) dispositional framework and the principles of Te
> Whāriki. (Ministry of Education, 1996).

For this research project, the centre supervisor, Andrea Wilson-Tukaki, and other
teachers looked through existing documented learning stories to find stories that
were representative of "relating in action". These learning stories were discussed at
regular staff reflective meetings and between the research co-ordinator for the TLRI
project and the supervisor. There was "rigorous debate" about what these stories
"stood for" both at the centre and for the children featured in them. Through this
process the participants identified three layers of knowing:

> Knowing self – is about recognising who you are, where you have come from and what you
>   have to offer the wider world.. . .
> Knowing others – is about being able to transfer those knowing self dispositions to relating
>   with others. It is about children understanding one another, caring for each other,
>   respecting each other, supporting each other and working together to achieve common
>   goals.. . .
> Knowing this place – is about the children coming to understand these parts of the fabric
>   and their role in constructing and strengthening it. (Wilson-Tukaki & Davis, 2011,
>   p. 21).

These framed the perspective of relating to others and overlapped with other
competencies and dispositions to contribute to the "empowered child" who was at
the centre. These teachers were then able to pinpoint particular strategies they used
to encourage learning related to these ways of knowing.

In an exemplar in the Ministry of Education-funded *Continuity of Early Learning*
study, the teacher at an education and care centre used a learning story to show the
developing verbal language of an 18-month child, Louis, over a period of a few
weeks. In this story, ways in which teachers acknowledged and encouraged increas-

ingly complex verbal language for a range of purposes and contexts were highlighted (Mitchell, Cowie, et al., 2015a, pp. 34–35). The learning story was headed "Developing Language!" It traced exemplars of Louis expressing himself in a verbal way in interactions within the early learning centre. The first example showed Louis contributing to an invitation to suggest a song at "kai time" (time for food, in this case lunch time) and how teachers interpreted his suggested "pider" to be the children's song *Incy Wincy Spider*. They acted on his suggestion through making this the kai time song. Next, Louis was shown expressing his needs and wants when he asked for his bottle and his muzzy (a muslin cloth) – a request the teacher told Louis she was "more than happy to accommodate, as you now only have a bottle if you really want one". Another example showed teachers inquiring about a plaster on Louis' hand, to which he responded "Mama, plaster", a statement teachers interpreted as showing that Louis knew what this was and who put it there. Louis' mum added a handwritten comment here: 'I think this plaster story was a case of me having a plaster so Louis needed one – quite a common occurrence here now. Louis can say "Me too"'. Through this comment the child's language use at home and the context for the story were added. The learning story became a tool for the teacher and family to think together about Louis' verbal language. Final examples were of Louis incorporating language into play. A closing comment showed how teachers would encourage and support Louis and his language skills. In a script written to Louis and for his family, they explained this was: "by accepting and supporting these early words, by modelling new words and phrases, allowing you to initiate conversation and giving you time to respond and converse".

Much documentation in Aotearoa New Zealand ECEC settings is gathered together into a portfolio that children, teachers and family can use to understand progress and to celebrate it. In their research on children's transitions (Hartley, Rogers, Smith, & Lovatt, 2014), teachers from Mangere Bridge Kindergarten argued that the portfolios served two purposes. They were a resource for the school new entrant teacher to learn about the child's capabilities, interests and dispositions. Here, teachers would use the portfolio learning stories as a prompt to engage with the child about the learning. The portfolios were also the "vehicles for children to get to know each other in an easy, engaging, and interactive way" (Hartley et al., 2014, p. 3). The teachers in the school settings often noticed the children laughing and talking with each other about the stories and approaching adults to show them the stories.

5 Assessments to Provide Opportunities for Self–Assessment

The UN Committee on the Rights of the Child in *The right of the child to be heard. General Comment No 12.* (2009) describes the relational dynamics of participation and emphasises that the concept of participation applies in all relevant contexts of children's lives.

The term has evolved and is now widely used to describe ongoing processes, which include information-sharing and dialogue between children and adults based on mutual respect, and in which children can learn how their views and those of adults are taken into account and shape the outcome of such processes. (para 3).

It goes on to state that:

The concept of participation emphasizes that including children should not only be a momentary act, but the starting point for an intense exchange between children and adults on the development of policies, programmes and measures in all relevant contexts of children's lives. (para 13).

One of these contexts is assessment. There is now a body of literature about the value of self-assessment especially in the school context. Stobart (Stobart, 2008, p. 5) regards self-regulating approaches to assessment as valuable in encouraging skills for children to make decisions about themselves that will be important for an unknown future. The OECD review of evaluation and assessment in New Zealand schools regarded the encouragement for students to develop students' own capacity to regulate their own learning through self-assessment as one of the strengths of the Aotearoa New Zealand system. It claimed that assessment capability is fostered through student's active involvement in assessment. The review argued "This approach can foster student self-regulatory skills in two important ways: self-assessment can increase students' autonomy and meta-cognitive awareness and peer-assessment can help develop a team spirit of collaborative work in the classroom" (Nusche et al., 2012, p. 42).

While much of the literature on children's self-assessment is about school-aged children, a growing body of literature is about children's self-assessment in early childhood settings. Self-assessment is featured in the exemplars of thoughtful assessment practice in the Continuity of Early Learning case studies (Mitchell, Cowie, et al., 2015a) and is highlighted in some Aotearoa New Zealand studies where researchers and practitioners have worked together (e.g. Clarkin-Phillips & Carr, 2009; Mitchell, 2007; Peters, Hartley, Rogers, Smith, & Carr, 2009).

Nikau kindergarten in the *Continuity of Early Learning* case studies had the following vision for learning:

Children to be competent and confident, ask questions, problem solve – in keeping with *Te Whāriki* aspiration statement. To be respected, to respect each other. Know themselves as a learner, set their own goals for learning. Have pride in who they are and where they are from. (Mitchell, Cowie, et al., 2015a, p. 31).

These teachers purposely encouraged children to set their own goals for their work and then captured through photograph and exemplars what the child had worked on as a way to indicate progress and what the child valued. In taking the photographs and making the exemplars, the child had agency, being asked and saying what he/she wanted included in the portfolio. In these ways what was documented and the process of documentation indicated that adults valued children taking responsibility and determining their own learning. Going back to Stobart (2008), assessment links to identity and is capable of shaping how society, groups and individuals understand themselves. Children in this kindergarten were actively making their own choices and being reinforced for this in the content and process of documentation.

Mangere Bridge Kindergarten was a designated Centre of Innovation, funded over 3 years from 2006 to 2008 to research practices on the transition to school and to investigate effective ways to support children and families at this time (Hartley, et al., 2012). Teachers said that early in the research, they realised the importance of children's portfolios (containing learning stories, examples of work, photographs, etc.) in supporting a positive transition (Hartley et al., 2014). They described roles it could play in fostering a child's sense of belonging in the new classroom; in offering opportunity for the teacher to learn about the child's capabilities, interests, and dispositions; and as a tool for the child to use to get to know peers in the classroom. In 2013, teachers decided to trial a separate transition portfolio to "make visible the learning journey from early childhood education to school" (Carr, Clarkin-Phillips, Resink, Anderson, & Jack, 2013, pp. 36). The transition portfolio is a shortened version so that the primary teachers have time to read it and is intended to include information useful for teachers when beginning to build a relationship with the child. It includes both individual and group stories in context. Children chose their own three learning stories from their time at kindergarten for their transition – to – school portfolios. The choice was made with the teachers who took programmed time with the child to read the stories, find out about their favourites and the child's view of what was important learning for them. "Each transition portfolio thus contains a selection of learning stories chosen by children and teachers together—stories that illustrate competency and a sense of the child as a valuable contributor and learner in the early childhood centre and in their family life" (Hartley et al., 2014, p. 6).

Pedagogical documentation offers opportunities for children to revisit and build on previous activities and work. At Totara Kindergarten, teachers had photographed and documented a "wrestling match" where children had devised their own rules and laid out mats in a particular way. Six months later, when these same children wanted to organise a "wrestling match" again, they referred back to the documentation to remind themselves of the set-up and rules and replicated it in almost exactly the same way. In another kindergarten, a child remade a mobile construction in exactly the same way as a previous construction after examining a photo of it (Mitchell, 2003). These are indicators of the metacognitive awareness that Nusche et al. (2012) referred to.

6   Family and Community as Contributors to Assessment

Families and community can play a productive role in curriculum and assessment to support learning. A democratic community might be a place where all these participants are able to belong and make a contribution that makes a difference for learning, where they collectively "create a world" a term used by Bruner (1998). This requires teachers to establish productive partnerships with families and communities that facilitate, value and utilise children's and families' funds of knowledge. Assessment based on democratic principles requires a willingness to make practice visible through documentation and communication with families as well as others. Much of the literature on assessment for learning in the school sector does not discuss the influence of families and communities in assessment, although the importance of family expectations and family support for children's learning and development is well recognised. Within the early childhood sector in Aotearoa New Zealand, however, the role of families as both recipients of assessment information and contributors to assessment has been highlighted through the family and community principle of *Te Whāriki*. The follow-up resources on *Assessment for Learning: Kei Tua o te Pae*, devoted Book 5 to community: inviting the participation of children, families, whānau (extended family), teachers and beyond (Ministry of Education, 2005). Book 7 is about continuity. An earlier policy document (discontinued in 2009 under a different government), *Pathways to the Future: Ngā Huarahi Arataki*, strategic plan for early childhood education had as one of its goals "to promote collaborative relationships" (Ministry of Education, 2002). The goal recognises the importance of consistency and connectedness between the worlds of home and ECE setting. These ideas about the more active roles that families can play in curriculum and assessment are congruent with a sociocultural and funds of knowledge framing.

With Bronwen Cowie, I have argued that enabling family and whānau to play a productive role in assessment requires a reciprocal exchange of information focused on benefits for the child (Cowie & Mitchell, 2015). This section uses Aotearoa New Zealand research which has examined relationships with families in different types of ECEC setting to explore how this might be done.

Book 7 of *Assessment for Learning: Kei Tua o te Pae* (Ministry of Education, 2005) is entitled *Continuity*; it provides exemplars of family engagement in assessment. The story below shows Tane's family connecting activities in the kindergarten with activities at home.

> Tane has had an ongoing enthusiasm for sewing projects following a session at kindergarten where he used a needle and thread for the first time. With his mummum (grandmother), he made a bag with button decorations. Pictured above is the apron he made last week. The biggest challenge was coming to grips with having to finish each seam with some kind of knot to keep it all together. Tane's parent made connections with home and the past, thereby enriching the record of Tane's learning progress. His folder records the development of this enthusiasm and these skills at the early childhood centre over time, together with his involvement with other children. It describes him mastering the use of a sewing machine, drawing patterns, discussing the best fabric for the job, and sewing an outfit, which included a motorcycle helmet and a decorated jacket that he made with two other children. (p. 4).

In a playcentre setting, the educators working with the children are mainly the mothers and fathers or wider family members of the children enrolled. The families document assessment in the playcentre and, because of their intimate knowledge of their own children in both home and playcentre setting, are able to make the links visible and reinforce these.

Wilton Playcentre was a designated Centre of Innovation from 2003 to 2006. In the final report on their research project, several entries showed continuity of play and ideas explored between home and playcentre; between home, playcentre and crèche; and between home, playcentre and school. In the following example, Ainsley, a parent, records an entry demonstrating continuity between home and playcentre and across a number of sessions held on different days:

> "At morning tea, I usually sit with the guitar and encourage the children to suggest songs and sing them.
> Matthew's mother said Matthew had a song he had been singing at home "Baa baa blue sheep". We started off singing quietly so we could hear Matthew:
> "Baa baa blue sheep have you any jelly?
> Yes sir, yes sir, it's all gone smelly".
> That brought the house down.
> Matthew's mum explained to me later that Matthew's older brother had worked out the lines with Matthew. Matthew thinks the world of his big brother.
> Thereafter, the blue sheep/smelly jelly song became the central song of morning tea. Other children requested it including Matthew and everyone always thoroughly enjoyed it.

This entry shows continuity, initially for Matthew between his home and playcentre, leading to continuity across time, a sense of belonging and recognition of a well-received contribution from Matthew, and an enhanced sense of community through their shared joke for the children who were regularly part of that particular session" (van Wijk et al., 2006, pp. 93–94).

In teacher-led ECEC services where the connection with home is not as immediate as in playcentre, documentation and information need to be offered in forms that the family can access, understand and act on. Differences for parents in opportunities to contribute their understanding of their child to assessment practices is related to parental employment, cultural and linguistic background and the resources available to them. In our article *Equity as Family/Whanau Participation in Formative Assessment*, Bronwen Cowie and I argued that "Given the contribution parents have to make to their child's learning, overcoming obstacles that prevent some people from participating in the process of interaction and feedback is a matter of equity and social justice" (Cowie & Mitchell, 2015, p. 25). Consistent with thinking about democracy as participation, equity is also about the potential enjoyment for parents of involvement in their child's education.

Democratic principles and whānau (extended family) participation were exemplified in Lesley Rameka's study (Rameka, 2009) of a bilingual and bicultural Māori ECEC centre, Best of Both Worlds, which described the journey of the centre as it embedded "Māori epistemologies, ideas of valued learning and cultural norms and understandings" within its assessment philosophy and practices (Rameka, 2009, p. 32). The process of analysing assessment documentation was democratic: it involved monthly hui (meetings) with kaiako (teachers) to "discuss, document and feedback on assessment practices, philosophies and developing understandings" (p. 32). This was done in a rigorous and systematic way that reconnected and reconciled traditional Māori epistemologies and theories with centre philosophy and practice. Through this process, kaiako constructed centre principles for assessment. Based on narratives concerning the Māori ancestor hero, Māui-tikitiki-a-Taranga, the centre identified the following characteristics for their assessment framework:

- *Mana*: Identity, pride, inner strength, self-assurance, confidence.
- *Manaakitanga/aroha/tiaki*: Caring, sharing, kindness, friendship, love, nurturance.
- *Whānaungatanga*: Developing relationships, taking responsibility for oneself and others, tuakana/teina.
- *Whakatoi/whakakata*: Cheekiness, spiritedness, displaying and enjoying humour, having fun.
- *Rangatiratanga/arahina/maiatanga*: Confidence, self-reliance, leadership, standing up for oneself, perseverance, determination, working through difficulty.
- *Tinihanga/pātaitai*: Cunningness, trickery, deception, testing limits, challenging, questioning, curiosity, exploring, risk taking, lateral thinking (p. 35).

The ideas were already within the kaiako's philosophy and practice. "It was a matter of articulating and reifying the understandings in a way that they and others could understand" (p. 35). Rameka writes that an important part of the centre journey was writing assessment for whānau rather than for outside agencies and projects as the kaiako had done in the past. This entailed writing assessment as stories that would engage whānau and in language that was free of jargon. Furthermore, they had to capture the "essence of children – who the children were – rather than strive for clinical observations of unidentifiable subjects. They had to express an emotional connectedness, an open bias and passion that celebrated children's successes and achievements" (p. 35).

7   Conclusion

In conclusion, assessment can play a vital role in shaping a democratic education community within ECEC settings. The assessment approach matters very much and is highly relevant. The pathways taken by democratic and learning-oriented assessment practices are never prescribed or unidirectional. Assessment practices based on democratic principles require an ability and willingness to make practice visible through documentation and communication with children, families, other staff and oneself. The documentation itself is the subject of critical reflection, interpretation and discussion. In practice, it is difficult work for teachers to generate a critical attitude and bring to the surface stereotyped assumptions that limit participation. One policy challenge is how to offer all teachers opportunities for critical reflective discussion and access to resources and support that can help them develop professionally.

References

Alcock, S., & Haggerty, M. (2013). Recent policy developments and the "schoolification" of early childhood care and education in Aotearoa New Zealand. *Early Childhood Folio, 17*(2), 21–26.

Assessment Reform Group. (2002). *Assessment for learning: 10 principles*. University of Cambridge, England: Assessment Reform Group.

Bruner, J. (1998). Each place has its own spirit and its own aspirations. *RE Child, 3*(January), 6.

Carr, M. (2001). *Assessment in early childhood settings: Learning stories*. London: Paul Chapman.

Carr, M. (2008). Can assessment unlock and open the doors to resourcefulness and agency? In S. Swaffild (Ed.), *Unlocking assessment* (pp. 36–54). London: Routledge.

Carr, M., Clarkin-Phillips, J., Resink, C., Anderson, M., & Jack, T. (2013). Tōku mātauranga oranga: Making visible the learning journey from early childhood into school. *Early Childhood Folio, 17*(1), 36–40.

Carr, M., Cowie, B., Gerrity, R., Jones, C., Lee, W., & Pohio, L. (2001). Democratic learning and teaching communities in early childhood: Can assessment play a role? In B. Webber & L. Mitchell (Eds.), *Early childhood education for a democratic society* (pp. 27–36). Wellington, New Zealand: New Zealand Council for Educational Research.

Carr, M., Davis, K., & Cowie, B. (2015). *Continuity of early learning: Learning progress and outcomes in the early years. Report on the literature scan*. Retrieved from https://www.educationcounts.govt.nz/publications/ECE/continuity-of-early-learning-literature-scan

Carr, M., May, H., & Podmore, V. (1998). *Learning and teaching stories. New approaches to assessment and evaluation in relation to Te Whaariki*. Paper presented at the symposium for 8th European conference on quality in early childhood settings, Santiago de Compostela, Spain.

Carr, M., May, H., Podmore, V., Cubey, P., Hatherly, A., & Macartney, B. (2000). *Learning and teaching stories: Action research on evaluation in early childhood education*. Wellington, New Zealand: New Zealand Council for Educational Research.

Carr, M., Mitchell, L., & Rameka, L. (2016). Some thoughts about the value of an OECD international assessment framework for early childhood services in Aotearoa New Zealand. *Contemporary Issues in Early Childhood, 17*(4), 450–454.

Clarkin-Phillips, J., & Carr, M. (2009). *Strengthening responsive and reciprocal relationships in a whanau tangata Centre: An action research project*. Wellington, New Zealand: Teaching and Learning Research Initiative.

Cowie, B., & Mitchell, L. (2015). Equity as family/whānau opportunities to contribute to formative assessment. *Assessment Matters, 8*(Special Issue), 119–141.

Dahlberg, G., & Moss, P. (2005). *Ethics and politics in early childhood education*. London: RoutledgeFalmer.

Dahlberg, G., Moss, P., & Pence, A. (1999). *Beyond quality in early childhood education and care. Post modern perspectives* (1st ed.). London: Falmer Press.

Dweck, C. (2006). *Mindset: The new psychology of success*. New York: Random House.

Dweck, C., & Leggett, E. (1988). A social cognitive approach to motivation and personality. *Psychological Review, 95*(2), 256–273.

Fielding, M., & Moss, P. (2012). *Radical education and the common school. A democratic alternative*. London: Routledge.

Giroux, H. (1992). *Border crossings. Cultural workers and the politics of education*. London: Routledge.

Gordon Commission on the Future of Assessment in Early Education. (2013). *To assess, to teach, to learn: A vision for the future of assessment. Technical report*. Retrieved from www.gordon-commission.org

Hartley, C., Rogers, P., Smith, J., & Lovatt, D. (2014). Transition portfolios: Another tool in the transition kete. *Early Childhood Folio, 18*(2), 3–7.

Hartley, C., Rogers, P., Smith, J., Peters, S., & Carr, M. (2012). *Crossing the border: A community negotiates the transition from early childhood to primary school*. Wellington, New Zealand: NZCER Press.

Hattie, J. (2009). *Visible learning: A synthesis of over 800 meta-analyses relating to achievement.* London: Routledge.

Hipkins, C. (2017). Bill clears the way for education changes [Press release]. Retrieved from https://www.beehive.govt.nz/release/bill-clears-wayeducation-changes

Lee, W., Carr, M., Soutar, B., & Mitchell, L. (2013). *Understanding the Te Whāriki approach.* London: Routledge.

Liljestrand, J., & Hammarberg, A. (2017). The social construction of the competent, self-governed child in documentation: Panels in the Swedish preschool. *Contemporary Issues in Early Childhood, 18*(1), 39–54. https://doi.org/10.1177/1463949117692270.

Lingard, B. (2010). Policy borrowing, policy learning: Testing times in Australian schooling. *Critical Studies in Education, 5*(2), 129–147. https://doi.org/10.1080/17508481003731026.

Mackey, G., Hill, D., & De Vocht, L. (2016). Response to the colloquium 'the organisation for economic co-operation and Development's international early learning study: Opening for debate and contestation. *Contemporary Issues in Early Childhood, 17*(4), 447–449.

Ministry of Education. (1996). *Te Whāriki.* Wellington, New Zealand: Learning Media.

Ministry of Education. (2002). *Pathways to the future: Ngā huarahi arataki.* Wellington, New Zealand: Ministry of Education.

Ministry of Education. (2005). *Kei tua o te pae. Assessment for learning: Early childhood exemplars.* Books 1–10. Wellington, New Zealand: Learning Media.

Ministry of Education. (2007). *Kei tua o te pae. Assessment for learning: Early childhood exemplars.* Books 11–15. Wellington, New Zealand: Learning Media.

Ministry of Education. (2009a). *Kei tua o te pae. Assessment for learning: Early childhood exemplars.* Books 16–20. Wellington, New Zealand: Learning Media.

Ministry of Education. (2009b). *Te whatu pōkeka.* Wellington, New Zealand: Learning Media.

Ministry of Education. (2017a). *National standards.* Retrieved from http://www.education.govt.nz/ministry-of-education/specific-initiatives/national-standards

Ministry of Education. (2017b). *Te whāriki: He whāriki mātauranga mō ngā mokopuna o Aotearoa Early childhood curriculum.* Retrieved from https://www.education.govt.nz/assets/Documents/Early-Childhood/ELS-Te-Whariki-Early-Childhood-Curriculum-ENG-Web.pdf

Mitchell, L. (2003). Shifts in thinking through a teachers' network. *Early Years, 23*(1), 21–34.

Mitchell, L. (2007). *A new debate about children and childhood. Could it make a difference to early childhood pedagogy and policy?* Doctoral thesis, Victoria University of Wellington, Wellington. Retrieved from http://researcharchive.vuw.ac.nz/handle/10063/347

Mitchell, L., Bateman, A., Ouko, A., Gerrity, R., Lees, J., Matata, K., et al. (2015). *Teaching and learning in culturally diverse early childhood settings.* Retrieved from http://www.waikato.ac.nz/__data/assets/pdf_file/0008/257246/Teachers-and-Learning-for-website_2015-03-05pm.compressed.pdf

Mitchell, L., & Carr, M. (2014). *Democratic and learning oriented assessment practices in early childhood care and education* UNESCO (Ed.). Retrieved from http://unesdoc.unesco.org/images/0022/002265/226550e.pdf

Mitchell, L., Cowie, B., Clarkin-Phillips, J., Davis, K., Glasgow, A., Hatherly, A., et al (2015a). *Case studies of assessment practice. Examples from continuity of early learning: Learning progress and outcomes in the early years.* Retrieved from https://www.educationcounts.govt.nz/__data/assets/pdf_file/0005/163607/Continuity-of-Early-Learning-Case-Studies.pdf

Mitchell, L., Cowie, B., Clarkin-Phillips, J., Davis, K., Glasgow, A., Hatherly, A et al. (2015b). *Continuity of early learning: Learning progress and outcomes in the early years. Overview report and data findings.* Retrieved from https://www.educationcounts.govt.nz/publications/ECE/continuity-of-early-learning-data-findings

Moss, P. (1999). *Difference, dissensus and debate: Some possibilities of learning from Reggio.* Stockholm, Sweden: Reggio Emilia Institutet.

Moss, P., Dahlberg, G., Grieshaber, S., Mantovani, S., May, H., Pence, A., Rayna, S., Swadener, B. B., & Vandenbroeck, M. (2016). The organisation for economic co-operation and Development's international early learning study: Opening for debate and contestation. *Contemporary Issues in Early Childhood, 17*(3), 343–351.

Nusche, D., Laveault, D., MacBeath, J., & Santiago, P. (2012). *OECD reviews of evaluation and assessment in education: New Zealand 2011.* Retrieved from https://doi.org/10.1787/9789264116917-en

OECD. (2016). *International early learning and child wellbeing study (IELS).* Retrieved from http://www.oecd.org/edu/school/international-earlylearning-and-child-well-being-study.htm

OECD. (2017). The international early learning and child Well-being study – The study Retrieved from http://www.oecd.org/edu/school/theinternational-early-learning-and-child-well-being-study-the-study.htm

Perkins, D. N., Jay, E., & Tishman, S. (1993). Beyond abilities: A dispositional theory of thinking. *Merrill-Palmer Quarterly, 39*(1 January), 1–21.

Peters, S., Hartley, C., Rogers, P., Smith, J., & Carr, M. (2009). Supporting the transition from early childhood education to school: Insights from one centre of innovation project. *Early Childhood Folio, 13*, 2–6.

Rameka, L. (2009). Kaupapa Māori assessment: A journey of meaning making. *Early Childhood Folio, 13*, 32–36.

Rinaldi, C. (2005). Documentation and assessment: What is the relationship? In A. Clark, T. Kjorholt, & P. Moss (Eds.), *Beyond listening: Children's perspectives.* Bristol, UK: The Polity Press.

Siraj-Blatchford, I. (2004). Educational disadvantage in the early years: How do we overcome it? Some lessons from research. *European Early Childhood Education Research Journal, 12*(2), 5–19.

Siraj-Blatchford, I. (2010). A focus on pedagogy. In K. Sylva, E. Melhuish, P. Sammons, I. Siraj-Blatchford, & B. Taggart (Eds.), *Early childhood matters. Evidence from the effective preschool and primary education project* (pp. 149–165). London: Routledge.

Stobart, G. (2008). *Testing times: The uses and abuses of assessment.* Abingdon, Oxon: Routledge.

Thrupp, M. with Lingard, B., Maguire, M. & Hursh, D. (2017). *The search for better educational standards: A cautionary tale.* Dordrecht, The Netherlands: Springer. http://www.springer.com/gp/book/9783319619576

Thrupp, M., & White, M. (2013). *Research, analysis and insight into National Standards Project. Final report: National Standards and the damage done.* Hamilton, New Zealand: Wilf Malcolm Institute of Educational Research.

United Nations Committee on the Rights of the Child. (2009). *The right of the child to be heard* (General Comment No 12). Retrieved from http://www.refworld.org/docid/4ae562c52.html

Urban, M., & Swadener, B. B. (2016). Democratic accountability and contextualised systemic evaluation. *International Critical Childhood Policy Studies, 5*(1).

van Wijk, N., Simmonds, A., Cubey, P., Mitchell, L., with Bulman, R., Wilson, M., & Wilton Playcentre Members. (2006). Transforming learning at Wilton Playcentre. Wellington, New Zealand: New Zealand Council for Educational Research.

Wilson-Tukaki, A., & Davis, K. (2011). Relating to others. Three ways of knowing. *Early Childhood Folio, 15*(2), 20–24.

Influencing Policy Change through Collective Action

Aotearoa New Zealand academics, unionists and activists have a history of acting collectively to debate, formulate and progress their collectively desired early childhood education and care (ECEC) policy directions. Meade (1990) described the critical role played by the Campaign for Quality Education in giving women and children "a foot in the door" to increase funding for ECEC when a flank of new right politicians in 1988 were cutting back government expenditure. Advocates from the early childhood teachers' union harnessing support from families and community, and working with national early childhood organisations and academics, have been highly influential in influencing policy change through collective action. Wells (1991) has described policy change as happening "against the odds", during a period of harsh labour laws and punitive social and economic policies in the early 1990s. Three stories of collective action are told in this chapter. They occurred during the 1990s and early 2000s: a kindergarten story of collective strategising and action to achieve pay parity of kindergarten teachers' salaries with primary and secondary teachers, a story that started to be told by Mitchell and Wells (1997); the campaign to achieve pay parity for teachers in education and care centres and the reasons for its limited success; and the story of a collective group formed by the union for policy development that resulted in the publication and widespread endorsement of the report *Future Directions: Early Childhood Education in New Zealand* (Early Childhood Education Project, 1996; Wells, 1999). This report pointed the processes of consultation and direction for the subsequent government initiated ECEC strategic plan, *Pathways to the Future: Ngā Huarahi Arataki* (Ministry of Education, 2002). A main argument is that participatory decision-making processes that draw on a diverse range of expertise from committed individuals and organisations can generate a sound platform for ECEC policy that upholds democratic values of equity and inclusion. These Aotearoa New Zealand stories show ways in which through acting collectively in a common cause, ordinary people can have influence.

© Springer Nature Singapore Pte Ltd. 2019
L. Mitchell, *Democratic Policies and Practices in Early Childhood Education*,
International Perspectives on Early Childhood Education and Development 24,
https://doi.org/10.1007/978-981-13-1793-4_6

1 Introduction

Participative processes in decision-making were a hallmark of Athenian democracy that "had the beneficial effect of promoting a dynamically productive relationship between knowledge and governance" (Ober, 2008, p. 266). Although participatory political processes were costly, Ober argues that costs were more than compensated for by the social co-operation that came from the useful knowledge produced and used within the contexts of democratic institutions and culture. These contexts were described as both "innovation-promoting" and "learning-based". The Totara Kindergarten and Maniapoto Trust examples of weaving a co-produced curriculum, described in chapter "Traditions of Democracy in Education", showed participative processes happening at a local and community level. This chapter is concerned with national policy-making and distinct ways in which participatory processes have influenced ECEC policy development in Aotearoa New Zealand. The participative processes described here were founded in a stated vision of equity and social inclusion and drew on expertise from a diverse group of committed individuals and organisations. Through harnessing the expertise and strengths of the group and using collective power in public and political persuasion, a platform for ECEC policy advances and their acceptance by government was laid.

In Aotearoa New Zealand, a participatory approach to policy formulation has happened in two quite distinct ways. One way has been where the government has seen the benefits of participatory approaches in achieving worthwhile proposals and has provided resources to enable participation in policy formulation. This happened in the development of the ECEC curriculum, *Te Whāriki*, ideas about principles for which were first discussed in a week-long residential course run by the then Department of Education (now the Ministry of Education) at Lopdell House in Auckland during the late 1980s (Te One, 2003). The curriculum development process involved academic leadership from Helen May and Margaret Carr, Māori leadership from Tilly Reedy and Tamati Reedy, establishment of expert working groups, discussion papers and a lengthy consultation period over a draft curriculum. This story is told elsewhere (Lee, Carr, Soutar, & Mitchell, 2013; May, 2009; Te One, 2003); an agreed vision for children was a basis, the commitment to equity and depth of understanding of the writers and a high degree of strategising lay behind the processes that were adopted. Always, alliances were built behind the scenes.

The second way in which participatory processes have succeeded is in spite of the government, with groups using a form of resistance politics, where they have opposed the ECEC policy status quo, organised alternative policy framings and advocated publicly and with opposition political parties for their adoption. Neither approach is pure, with elements from each discernible in the tactics taken.

In the next sections, three examples of participatory processes and collective organisation that had powerful influences on ECEC policy during the 1990s and early 2000s are told. I was an "insider" during these times of actions, so the story is told from my background as the national secretary of the Combined Early Childhood Union of Aotearoa and then, after amalgamation, my work with the NZEI Te Riu

Roa, the union for early childhood and primary school teachers and school support staff. The first example is of industrial employment campaigns to achieve parity of the pay of kindergarten teachers with the pay of teachers in primary and secondary schools (pay parity). The second, with only partial success, is the campaign and efforts to achieve parity of the pay of teachers in education and care centres with the pay of kindergarten, primary and secondary teachers. The third is of a broader-based and sector-wide campaign to develop policies to support high-quality ECEC.

2 The Pathways to Pay Parity

ECEC services are run, staffed and used predominantly by women. Ninety-eight percent of early childhood staff are women; a percentage that has changed little since ECEC services were established in Aotearoa New Zealand in the 1890s. Traditionally the rates of pay for teachers in the early childhood sector have been very low. It was not until 1982 that an industrial union for childcare workers (as they were termed at that time) was registered. The union, the Early Childhood Workers Union (ECWU), negotiated its first multi-party agreement with 15 "willing" employers in 1984. Despite the integration of childcare within an education administration in 1986, ECEC continued to be regarded by many as a "care" service, undertaken by women whose work is systematically undervalued. As May (1994, p. 148) writes "At a deeper level there are deep seated issues associated with society's negative perception of paying women to "work with – teach – care for" young children; a task that mothers do for love".

Equal pay was first recognised as a legal right in Aotearoa New Zealand's public sector in 1960, but it took a further 12 years for this right to be extended to the private sector in 1972. Equal employment opportunities were briefly recognised as a legal right in 1990; then under the State Sector Act, the provision was reduced from being an entitlement to obligations of employers to be "good employers", with a reference to equal pay. During the 1990s, equal pay for ECEC teachers was hard to achieve in a deregulated labour market and without legislated and enforceable backing. Pay rates were well below those of teachers in the schools sector. In 1999, experienced registered teachers with a degree on the best union negotiated collective agreements in the childcare sector (Consenting Parties Early Childhood Teachers' Collective Employment Contract) and kindergarten sector (Kindergarten Teachers' Collective Employment Contract) earned 52% and 46%, respectively, below comparable teaching positions in the school sector (Mitchell, 2005). Many early childhood teachers in the childcare sector earned considerably less than this. Smith, Ford, Hubbard and White's (1996) study of 100 childcare centres showed privately owned centres paid lower wages and provided poorer conditions than community-owned centres.

In this context, the union, NZEI Te Riu Roa, developed strategies for negotiating pay parity for teachers in the early childhood and schools sectors. Unlike equal pay arguments, which compare skills qualifications and experiences of a predominantly

female occupational group with skills, qualifications and experience of a predominantly male occupational group, the case for pay parity used internal comparisons
with the largely female primary teacher workforce.

This story of achieving pay parity examines the context and events of the 1990s
decade leading up to the pay parity settlement for kindergarten teachers of 2002 and
a partial pay parity settlement for a small percentage of teachers in education and
care centres in 2004. My argument is that pay parity required several things: an
understanding of the policy context; a thorough analysis of the legitimacy of the
case for pay equity for early childhood teachers; a persuasive collective campaign
that captured the imaginations and hearts of the public – the public did support ideas
because these were articulated well; strategic thinking – timing action around key
political events when there was greater effect; government politicians who supported the claim; and intervention by the state to enact pay parity. Persistence was
crucial. Kindergarten teachers challenged the perversion of the democratic process
that privatised kindergartens through the State Sector Amendment Act 1997. Their
campaigning ensured issues remained in political focus, and when the Labour-led
government was elected at the end of 1999, it moved quickly to return teachers to
the state sector and negotiate a single employment agreement. Pay parity followed
from this. The progress towards pay parity for teachers in the education and care
sector was much less spectacular and only partially achieved for a fraction of the
workforce. There was a low level of unionisation overall, many private employers
were antagonistic to collective bargaining, and these teachers had never had a foothold within the state sector. Yet, despite enormous obstacles, partial pay parity was
achieved with a group of willing employers. Drawing from both stories, a main
argument is that effective unions are crucial in a participatory democracy. In
Aotearoa New Zealand, the unions provided a means to organise, give voice to and
persist in a collective effort to progress pay equity for ECEC teachers.

3   The Context and Events of the 1990s

The National government in power during the early 1990s deregulated the labour
market, introducing the 1991 Employment Contracts Act (New Zealand Government,
1991), which privileged the principle of individual freedom in employment matters.
It was an extreme reform that tilted power away from workers in favour of employers, and undermined collective bargaining and the role of unions. A special investigation by the International Labour Organisation declared the Employment Contracts
Act to be in breach of international worker rights to freedom of association and to
bargain collectively. Margaret Wilson, law professor, speaking at the New Zealand
Council of Trade Unions *Closing the gap* forum on equal pay (New Zealand Council
of Trade Unions, 1997), argued that "equality has no role to play in the new market-
oriented workplace". Within this harsh industrial climate, the unions for early childhood workers and kindergarten teachers (CECUA, NZEI Te Riu Roa) had setbacks,
made progress, and against the odds, set the scene for negotiated pay parity

settlements – full pay parity for kindergarten teachers; a partial pay parity for a percentage of teachers in education and care centres.

3.1   A Kindergarten Story

During the 1950s to 1980s, kindergartens were described as the "flagship" of government support for the early childhood sector (Davison, 1998; Wylie, 1992). For a long time the kindergarten sector had aspired to be treated equitably with schools and from 1947, kindergartens were part of the state sector, along with primary and secondary school teachers. This relationship became fractured during the 1990s when the government of that time, adopting stringent new right ideologies, introduced measures to privatise kindergartens and sever state responsibility. The policy measures introduced in the early 1990s included removal of a regulation forbidding kindergartens from charging fees while at the same time freezing the amount of funding to kindergartens, making fee charging hard to resist as costs increased over time. The government removed itself from responsibility for paying teacher salaries, which it had done previously. Instead it provided kindergarten associations with a bulk grant of money from which it was expected to pay salaries and meet all other costs; and the funding was insufficient to cover everything.

Before 1992, kindergarten funding was tagged for particular operational costs (e.g. professional support, buildings, administration) and allocated to be spent on those costs. Because kindergarten teachers were then state employees, their salaries were paid directly through the government's central payroll system. Teachers' salaries, the biggest cost component for kindergartens, were therefore taken care of by the government.

Bulk funding of teachers' salaries was first proposed in 1988 in *Before Five* (Lange, 1988), the government's ECEC policy document. Bulk funding is a competitive funding mechanism based on amounts of funding calculated mainly on a per child capita basis and paid as a bulk grant directly to the employer. However, it was not until the National Party became the government at the end of 1990 that bulk funding was seriously on the agenda. The Combined Early Childhood Union of Aotearoa (1992) argued that bulk funding was a way for the government to distance itself from state responsibility for kindergartens and make it easier for the government to stop meeting the full costs of teachers' salaries and other items. If kindergarten associations – the employers – were responsible for deciding on spending and there was not enough governmental funding, they would most likely be forced to make cutbacks or charge parents fees. Neither option was desirable in a public system of education that prided itself on principles of being free to every child and on its qualified teaching workforce.

The Combined Early Childhood Union of Aotearoa and unions covering workers from other sectors united in a campaign to *hold on* to what we had. Direct salary funding was one thing we wanted to hold on to. Kindergarten teachers were very good at getting the issues that concerned them across to their parents, and during

1991 and 1992, parents, teachers and associations were united in opposition to bulk funding. Union members performed eye-catching and publicity-producing street theatre and songs, flooded the offices of members of parliament with artwork, called public meetings and talked to parents. We believed that if associations refused to accept bulk funding it would not be imposed on them. "Say No" was our message.

Against their formerly stated position, in November 1991 associations held a special meeting in Wellington and decided to accept bulk funding. We were told by an "insider" that four of the largest kindergarten associations, Wellington, Central North Island, Waikato and Auckland, had met with the Ministry of Education officials and been offered extra money if they were to accept bulk funding. These associations swayed the meeting. From then bulk funding was implemented in March 1992. Needless to say the extra funding was not forthcoming.

From 1992 to 1996, kindergarten funding was virtually frozen. Underfunding was part of the government's systematic drive to entirely privatise kindergartens. The intention was clearly for ECEC services to operate as much as possible like a business in a competitive market. Over this time, scandals emerged when private owners running childcare services as businesses made huge personal gains through spending government bulk funding on property upgrades. Staff and children did not benefit. Growth in private business ownership of ECE services was phenomenal and profit margins were high. Kindergartens and community-based education and care centres dwindled as a percentage of the ECEC sector.

This occurred in a wider context of cost-cutting and restraint, described by Prime Minister Jim Bolger:

> Short term sacrifices and some major long term sacrifices are both needed if we are to succeed in the battle for economic growth and the return to full employment. Everyone knows we have to adjust. My aim is that everyone plays their part in this process. (Bolger, 1990).

But as a group of union members sang in a protest song in Cuba Mall in Aotearoa New Zealand's capital city, Wellington stated: "It's hard to tighten your belt when you're wearing nappies".

In this climate, achieving pay increases let alone pay parity was formidable. The strategy of the unions was to hold together collectively to fend off the new right agenda. We saw the need for a united education union with a strong membership base, able to influence public opinion and policy. In 1990 the Kindergarten Teachers Association (the union covering kindergarten teachers) and the Early Childhood Workers Union (the union covering childcare workers) amalgamated to form the Combined Early Childhood Union of Aotearoa (CECUA). In 1994, CECUA amalgamated with the New Zealand Educational Institute (the union covering primary teachers and school support staff) to form NZEI Te Riu Roa. This is the union today for early childhood teachers, educators, primary school teachers and support staff in education.

Evidence supporting the case for pay parity was made in a written publication (NZEI Te Riu Roa, 1994a), with a section written by the Council of Trade Unions economist, Peter Harris, showing that the current fiscal policies were not assisting the reduction of debt. Harris's paper provided an economic argument for governments to spend on human and physical infrastructure. The union strategy was to address the inadequate funding levels as a first step to pay parity, first by campaigning for increased kindergarten funding and gaining public support so that money would be available for pay increases. The campaign lasted for 17 months, during which time the government was pressured to change its funding policy three times: the first was a conditional package with "strings attached" – the "strings" were kindergartens being forced to increase their hours – the second a modest funding increase and the third a funding increase and an additional one off payment for teachers. The union settled on this last option. The campaign was planned by the union national executive and officials and discussed in branch meetings, so everyone was behind it. Some actions were nationally decided; members also decided what they would do locally, giving a vibrant local flavour to what was done. For the first time in history, the employers' organisation, the NZFKU, agreed to combine in this joint campaign. One of the most successful tactics we used was a petition calling on the government to increase kindergarten funding. Rather than this being presented as a single national petition, many members signed the petition as chief petitioner and then went to their local MP with parents and whānau (extended family) and community supporters to present it and talk about the issues. When parliament was sitting, the local MP was then obliged to stand and read the petition out individually. In this way, 263 identical petitions were read aloud – more on this single issue than ever before.

This pressure resulted in a special hearing of the Government Education and Science Select Committee which recommended "favourable consideration" be given to the funding of kindergartens. These were days of action in every community where kindergarten teacher members of the union used innovative and eye-catching ways to get their messages into the public arena. "Kindergarten funding – no strings" was brought home on the day of a national strike, where 1400 kindergarten teachers nationwide (out of a total workforce of 1600) flew balloons and flags, decorated cars and double-decker buses, wrapped strings around statues in parliament grounds and rallied, marched and handed out leaflets. The most significant agreement of the settlement of the collective contract for pay parity was to undertake a job evaluation to compare the skills, experience and qualifications of kindergarten teachers relative to those of primary teachers. Wells (1991) has described policy change as happening "against the odds", during this period of harsh labour laws and punitive social and economic policies in the early 1990s.

This was the beginning of new troubles; in an undemocratic backlash against the successful campaign, the government passed under urgency legislation removing kindergarten teachers from the State Sector Act. Urgency stifled public debate by bypassing a select committee process where people could have their say. In a bizarre reversal of the notion of equity and an insult to organised collective action, Hon. Jenny Shipley, the Minister of State Services, argued that kindergarten funding should be brought down to the low common funding level of all ECE services.

> It is true that kindergarten teachers and, in particular, the New Zealand Educational Institute, have been able to use their industrial muscle. The time has come for that to stop.

In the past because of the State Services Commission involvement, the negotiations have been used by the New Zealand Educational Institute to secure additional funding for kindergarten associations over and above that allocated to the early childhood sector through the budget process. This is an avenue to secure extra funding for wage increases that is simply not available to other early childhood providers. The government is not prepared to allow this inequity to continue in the forthcoming contract negotiation. (Shipley, 29 April, 1997).

When the politicians debated the issue in the House of Parliament, kindergarten teachers from Wellington who were active union members rushed to sit in the galleries to carry placards and hear the debate: there was crying when the legislation was passed. The next day was the union's May first rally – "May day! May day! Red alert. Early childhood in crisis" – another publicity capturing slogan designed by the union and brought home through a picnic in parliament grounds with red balloons, children, families, teachers and political speeches. Union national secretary, Joanna Beresford, told the rally:

Early childhood is in crisis. The crisis has been deepened by the sleazy actions of the government and its ACT [a right wing political party] supporters in this building last night. Excluding kindergarten teachers and associations from coverage of the State Sector Act shows clearly the contempt for the early childhood sector and the ordinary workers of New Zealand.. .. Advocates of the bill from government ministers to ACT MPs indulged in a verbal feast of misinformation, and history rewriting in their futile attempts to justify the unjustifiable.

One of the trends over this time was in my view a shift from the Ministry of Education offering "free and frank advice" to becoming a politicised government department tendering advice in line with political viewpoints. And so, the Ministry of Education in supporting removal from the State Sector Act argued that "this would reduce the government's fiscal risk in the medium to longer term" – true but without any analysis of broader educational or equity considerations. Did these responses have the public interest at heart? Tangentially, David Fisher, working with *The New Zealand Herald* (a national newspaper), evidenced growing politicisation of the public service too in his commentary on the astounding differences in dealing with Official Information Act requests over his 25 years as a journalist to 2015. Where previously he would simply speak to government officials on the telephone to gather information, now interviews have fallen away, and instead written Official Information Act (OIA) requests are sent. "They require OIAs which are being sent to the media to be sent to the minister for sign off first. It astonishes me that any minister would think they have any business reviewing OIAs before they get sent out" (Fisher, 2015, p. 101).

The job evaluation to compare the skills, experience and qualifications of kindergarten teachers relative to those of primary teachers was commissioned by the employers and the union and undertaken by a researcher, Janice Burns, who had considerable expertise in the design and implementation of job measurement methodologies. A key finding was that:

The roles of kindergarten teachers and basic scale / senior primary teachers are similar in size, and there is an area of considerable overlap. There appears to be no justification for the

difference in salary at any time of the three levels of the pay scales, either in terms of qualifications required or the size of the job being undertaken. (Burns, 1999, p. 5).

A reverse take on equity again was put forward, this time by Education Minister
Nick Smith. "The union's proposition would unfairly discriminate against other
early childhood teachers" (cited in May, 2005, p. 12).

When a new and sympathetic Labour government was elected at the end of 1999,
it was willing to act. Kindergarten teachers were reinstated to the State Sector Act
in 2000. Pay parity was agreed in August 2002, with a 4-year phase in. It was especially significant that the Secretary for Education was a party to this agreement
since this bound the government into negotiating and paying costs of the kindergarten teachers' employment settlements.

Even so, public opinion was not fully won over. A headline in a national newspaper read "Preschool teachers win 61 percent pay rise – a job that's child's play?"
(Dominion, 17 August, 2002). And the national president of the secondary school
teachers' union, the PPTA, argued on national radio programme *Morning Report*
"Why should nappy changers be paid the same as secondary teachers?"

3.2 A Childcare (Education and Care) Story

These attitudes were one reason why teachers in the largely private education and
care sector had a less successful campaign and only a small percentage won a partial
pay parity settlement through a union agreement negotiated with the New Zealand
Childcare Association, an umbrella organisation representing some employers. The
negotiated agreement covered a small percentage of education and care centres in
the "Consenting Parties Agreement" – 2 years later. "At a deeper level there are deep
seated issues associated with society's negative perception of paying women to
'work with – teach – care for' young children; a task that mothers do for love" (May,
2005, p. 148).

Public attitudes were not the only reason for difficulties faced by the union and
teachers in the education and care sector in achieving pay parity. Teachers in this
sector came from a much more disadvantaged context compared with the context
for kindergarten teachers. Unlike kindergartens, childcare (education and care) centres had never been part of the state sector, and the government had never been
responsible for negotiating and paying teacher salaries. Reinstating that connection
with the state had been key to achieving an enduring pay parity settlement for kindergarten teachers in 2002. Teachers in education and care centres had a very low
level of unionisation, which dropped even further following the Employment
Contracts Act. The Employment Contracts Act had removed union rights of access
to worksites. Many for-profit private employers, resistant to union influence on
workers employed in their business, subsequently refused entry of union representatives to their centres. This made it much more difficult to recruit, retain and organise
education and care teachers as union members. The Employment Contracts Act had

a devastating effect in reducing the number of centres and teachers who were party to the five collective employment awards that covered education and care centres. Until 1991, the National Childcare Centres Award with minimum rates and conditions had applied to most education and care centres, and employers who were not party to other "better" awards were bound by it. It covered 350 centres. A regional award in Otago and Southland covered 48 centres; a collective award covered staff employed in three university centres; and the award with the "best" pay rates and conditions covered about 150 centres. This was called the "Consenting Parties Award" and was first negotiated in 1984 with employers who consented to be party to negotiations (May, 2005).

A good number of private employers were deeply antagonistic to union membership and to having to abide by collectively bargained awards. They wanted to set their own pay and conditions without involvement of the union. Some for-profit entrepreneurs had a vested interest in profit margins for their own gain; and staff salaries, as the biggest cost in an ECEC centre, cut into potential profits. The Employment Contracts Act 1991 gave these employers the sought after freedom in employment matters by discriminating against collective bargaining and removing recognition of unions.

> The Employment Contracts Act 1991 radically alters the system of labour law in New Zealand by moving its focus from the collective to the individual level, and the locus from the industry or occupation to the individual employing enterprise. At the same time, the Act significantly shifts the balance of bargaining power further towards employers. (Anderson, 1991, p. 127).

The first award to expire under the new industrial legislation of the Employment Contracts Act was the National Childcare Centres Award. Since this Act had removed provisions for "good faith bargaining", employers had no obligation to bargain collectively. Many employers simply refused to turn up to negotiations; only 6 of the original 350 employers signed up to 1 of 2 contracts that replaced the National Childcare Centres Award. Most of the other employers who had been covered by this award subsequently made their own individual employment agreements with their own staff, without union involvement. Many were intent on reducing pay and conditions; profit-making private owners resisted their profit margins going to teacher pay. The Otago and Southland Award fared slightly better, but coverage was more than halved: 18 of 48 employers became party to the new collective contract. The Universities Award split into three identical contracts, one for each university, and retained its coverage. The newly negotiated Consenting Parties Award retained most of its centres. The upshot was catastrophic. Union membership in this sector fell by around 20%, and the task for the union of negotiating many small contracts stretched resources. Another difficulty was the fact that there was no strong employers' organisation, making union communication with employers time-consuming and difficult.

In this context, a parallel pay parity campaign alongside the kindergarten campaign was held by the union, NZEI Te Riu Roa, with teachers in education and care centres, using the same message: "Secondary, primary, or early childhood. .. A teacher, is a teacher is a teacher. One teaching profession. One teaching pay scale. Pay parity for registered early childhood teachers". The same economic analysis, undertaken by NZCTU economist Peter Harris with information about pay rates written by the union, applied to teachers in education and care centres (NZEI Te Riu Roa, 1994b). Both kindergarten and education and care teachers campaigned to increase early childhood funding as a necessary precursor to pay increases. The difference in strategies for both groups was in the "road to pay parity for teachers in childcare centres", where the strategy formulated by the union's elected industrial committee was to bring teachers into one collective employment contract as a first step to achieving parity for all teachers in this sector.

The union and employers managed to negotiate a pay parity claim for only the Consenting Parties Collective Employment Contract (as it was then named) – 2 years after the Kindergarten Collective Employment Agreement was settled. Rates payable were conditional on funding. A new ECEC funding formula linked higher rates of funding for qualified teachers to the Consenting Parties Collective Employment Contract rates, but only at the first step of the scale. Hence pay parity for teachers in education and care centres was only ever partial. A statement in the current Early Childhood Education Collective Agreement (as it is now named) 2016–2017, which covers 106 employers (114 centres), states:

> The parties to the ECECA are committed to achieving pay parity with qualified and certificated teachers in kindergarten and in the primary and secondary education sectors for qualified and certificated teachers covered by this agreement. The parties acknowledge that adequate government funding is fundamental to achieving this vision and agree to meet during the term of this agreement to discuss how pay parity might be fully achieved. (NZEI Te Riu Roa, 2016).

In 2018, the Ministry of Education funding rules continue a linkage between higher funding rates and the entry level step of the collective agreement:

> Higher funding rates for education and care services are only available to services that agree to pay all primary and ECE qualified and certificated teachers employed by their service at least at the Q1, Q2, Q3 and Q3+ entry levels in the current Early Childhood Collective Agreement of Aotearoa New Zealand. (Ministry of Education, 2018).

These parallel stories highlight the power of collective organisation and action focused on strategic goals that are of importance to the collective membership and conveyed in ways to gather support from stakeholders. Kindergarten teachers had the advantage of high levels of union membership and were able to gain support from employers and families. Their foothold in the state sector, temporarily lost in the 1990s, was regained under a sympathetic government in 2001. Teachers in education and care centres had never been state servants and were a much less unionised workforce than kindergarten teachers, making collective organisation more difficult. Profit-making private owners resisted their profit margins going to teacher pay increases and obstructed union access. Without state commitment to pay parity and pay equity and to intervening in pay negotiations, winners and losers will continue to be created in a market-led system.

4   Future Directions

The mid-1980s and mid-1990s were times of sweeping social, economic and educational reform in Aotearoa New Zealand. Neo-liberal reforms emphasised self-sufficiency and market provision. Welfare benefits were cut to the extent that they were set at a level below the official poverty line, a move that even the New Zealand Treasury criticised. This was a time when new policy directions were announced and major reviews in the social and education sectors were undertaken. The government's Economic and Social Initiative Statement, setting the policy direction, emphasised four principles: fairness (targeting those most in need), self-reliance (taking care of yourself), efficiency (highest return for tax payer dollars) and greater personal choice (alternative providers). Reviews in the education sector followed and included four reviews in ECEC of the major areas of funding; staffing, qualifications and training; properties; and a support agency for ECEC, the Early Childhood Development Unit. The reviews were top down and undemocratic, written by government officials without sector involvement. While officials called for submissions, these were singularly disregarded in the harsh funding reductions, lessening of teacher qualification requirements and shifts from universal to greater targeting in funding (Wells, 1999). The so-called consultation was lip service and insulting.

In this same context as the pay parity campaign, the union (NZEI Te Riu Roa) undertook advocacy initiatives centring around the rights of young children to access good quality ECEC services. Unionists were tired of top-down reviews of ECE in which we were not consulted and the outcomes from which we did not agree.

The union decided that the sector needed to make its own review of ECEC and develop proposals for which members could then gain support and publicity. Our project, *Future Directions*, was initiated by the union and undertaken in collaboration with representatives of the seven largest national organisations representing the diverse ECEC service types. These were all community based. A well-regarded academic and advocate, Geraldine McDonald, chaired the review. Union president, Clare Wells, and I acted as secretariat. As Geraldine McDonald stated in the Foreword:

> In the last seven years, early childhood education has had its fair share of change. ... A feature of the early childhood policy development has been the carrying out of "top down" reviews.. ... There appears to have been an erosion of high quality publicly funded early childhood education. (Early Childhood Education Project, 1996, p. 1).

This story of *Future Directions* exemplifies the value of committed ECEC representatives using participatory practices to construct valuable and useful knowledge and to cooperate in its dissemination. The involvement of organisation representatives rather than individuals was central to the success of the project since it enabled widespread consultation to draw on the knowledge residing in diverse and grass roots ECEC services. As a result, the solutions and recommendations were both useful and innovative. These features were also argued to be benefits of participatory knowledge by Ober in relation to Athenian democracy (Ober, 2008, p. 265).

We set ourselves up as a review group (the *Early Childhood Education Project* group), writing overall terms of reference to "provide a rigorous and coherent review of the current situation of ECE in Aotearoa New Zealand and the access of children to it". Further terms of reference expressed values to "recognize and value diversity of organisations, cultures and communities" and "contribute towards a comprehensive policy for Māori education". We put government relationships and legislative frameworks under scrutiny with terms of reference to "examine the relationships between the work of various government agencies and the early childhood providers in order to establish their contribution to quality education for young children" and "examine the extent to which government legislations supports quality education for young children". A specific aim was to "develop proposals on the structures and funding required to ensure quality education for young children". An appreciation of participatory democracy was embedded in the approach. We aimed to "build widespread understanding and support for the proposals" (Early Childhood Education Project, 1996).

An interim report was based on our discussions, consultations and analysis and review of government policies, guidelines and demographic information. It was dispersed widely to ECEC services and organisations for comment and promoted through the media. We asked for written submissions on the interim report, in a similar way to what we had seen in government reviews – except we were the project leaders reading and taking on board the submissions. The feedback from this activity was included in the final report. The group ended with agreed proposals on the structures and funding needed for high-quality early childhood education and care – with one exception where agreement on a funding recommendation was split. In this instance, we published both recommendations and pointed out the differences.

The three main goals of our report were:

- That the long-term goal for early childhood education services is to be universally funded on a basis that is equitable with schools by the year 2000. Just as the government funds the schools sector, it should in the same way fund early childhood services.
- That the development of policy at national, regional and local levels be undertaken as a partnership between the government, practitioners and parents/caregivers.
- That the government develop a strategic plan for early childhood as a sector. The consultation process should include representative from health, social welfare, education, justice and parents. The strategic plan should include how society can offer holistic support for families/whanau raising young children (Early Childhood Education Project, 1996).

A reason for having a strategic plan was to move away from an approach where there were no long-term policy goals or overall vision, and we seemed to lurch from one policy position to another as governments changed. We did not know whether budgets would bring any funding increases or if they did how these would be delivered. In this respect, the group was influenced by the European Commission

Network on Childcare (1996) report *Quality Targets in Services for Young Children*, which set objectives and established conditions for achieving these. It proposed "targets" that the Network believed could be achieved by the European Union within 10 years. Likewise, our report presented specific and achievable recommendations or targets.

The timing of the project was crucial – the group had strategised to launch the final report in time for the 1996 general election in Aotearoa New Zealand. The launch was held at the Beehive – the seat of government – where the leaders of the main political parties and their education spokespersons responded to the group's report.

Two politicians praised the consultative processes very highly, affirming the solid basis for a credible report. The then leader of the opposition, Helen Clark, who became prime minister of Aotearoa New Zealand in 1999 said: "What makes the report highly credible is that the project team itself was broadly based, and there was very extensive consultation throughout the sector".

Margaret Austin, then education spokesperson of the United Future political party, said: "About the most significant document to emerge in the lead up to election 96. What you have shown very clearly is that you understand the meaning of participatory democracy and can use it to your advantage".

Early childhood organisations adopted the recommendations as their organisation policy. This was the beginning of a sustained campaign to keep the report and proposals in front of the public and politicians, through days of action, street theatre, media statements and a petition personally delivered to every member of parliament in their electorate office by teachers and parents.

A long-term strategic plan was developed after Labour became government in 1999, with Helen Clark as prime minister; it can be directly attributable to the *Future Directions* project. Analysis of government policies shows that subsequent policies adopted many of the recommendations of the *Future Directions* report too.

5   Conclusion

In 2006, speaking at the *Corporate Governance in the Public Sector Conference*, then New Zealand Council of Trade Unions vice president, Helen Kelly (2006), argued that alongside other core elements of good governance, such as transparency and accountability, was an overlooking, a disregard of the role and potential contribution of unions and workers in governance decisions. She argued that an under-utilisation of these contributions results in loss of productivity and reduction in democracy. Instead "promising" practice in public service governance from a union perspective needs to start from a recognition of the commitment of unions to public sector values and unions as social partners.

The stories discussed here show ways that through union leadership, many people participated in policy formulation that generated possibilities for new directions. These new directions were not based on individual self-interest but founded instead on ideals of "public good" (Borman, Danzig, Garcia, & Callan, 2012). As Giroux argues "a need for social movements to invoke stories as a form of public memory – stories that have the potential to move people to invest in their own sense of individual and collective agency, and stories that make knowledge meaningful in order to make it critical and transformative" (Giroux, 2014, p. 240). The stories can also be seen as a commitment to public good values that go beyond individual gain for the union members and the many others who took part. The proposals and campaigns were developed through participation in shared endeavours that had as their goal the construction of a more socially just ECEC system and that extended beyond the here and now into the future. They offer promise of what can be achieved through committed people acting collectively.

References

Anderson, G. (1991). The employment contracts act 1991: An employers charter? *New Zealand Journal of Industrial Relations, 16*(2), 127–142.

Bolger, J. (1990). *Economic and social initiative statement.* Wellington, New Zealand: Government Print.

Borman, K. M., Danzig, A. B., Garcia, D. R., & Callan, E. (2012). Introduction: Education, democracy, and the public good. *Review of Research in Education, 36*, vii–xxi.

Burns, J. (1999). *Kindergarten and primary teachers; A comparison of their work.* Wellington, New Zealand: Top Drawer Consultants.

Combined Early Childhood Union of Aotearoa. (1992). *Annual Report.* Wellington, New Zealand: Author.

Davison, C. (1998). Kindergartens and their removal from the State Sector Act. *New Zealand Annual Review of Education, 7*, 151–167.

Early Childhood Education Project. (1996). *Future directions: Early childhood education in New Zealand.* Wellington, New Zealand: New Zealand Educational Institute Te Riu Roa.

European Commission network on childcare and other measures to reconcile employment and family responsibilities. (1996). *Quality targets in services for young children.* Brussels, Belgium: European Commission Equal Opportunities Unit.

Fisher, D. (2015). The OIA arms race. In S. Andrew & J. Gracewood (Eds.), *Tell you what: Great New Zealand nonfiction 2016* (pp. 97–106). Auckland, New Zealand: Auckland University Press.

Giroux, H. (2014). America's descent into madness. *Policy Futures in Education, 12*(2), 237–241.

Kelly, H. (2006). *A union perspective on state sector governance.* Paper presented at the corporate governance in the public sector conference, Wellington, New Zealand.

Lange, D. (1988). *Before five.* Wellington, New Zealand: Government Print.

Lee, W., Carr, M., Soutar, B., & Mitchell, L. (2013). *Understanding the Te Whāriki approach.* London: Routledge.

May, H. (2005). *Twenty years of consenting parties: The 'politics of 'working' and 'teaching' in childcare 1985–2005.* Wellington, New Zealand: NZEI Te Riu Roa.

May, H. (2009). *Politics in the playground. The world of early childhood education in New Zealand* (2nd ed.). Dunedin, New Zealand: Otago University Press.

Meade, A. (1990). Women and children gain a foot in the door. *New Zealand Women's Studies Journal, 6*(1/2), 96–111.

Ministry of Education. (2002). *Pathways to the future: Ngā Huarahi Arataki.* Wellington, New Zealand: Author.

Ministry of Education. (2018). *ECE funding handbook*. Retrieved from https://www.education.govt.nz/early-childhood/running-an-ece-service/funding/ece-funding-handbook/completing-the-rs7-return/9-6-attestation-of-certificated-teachers-salaries/

Mitchell, L. (2005). Policy shifts in early childhood education: Past lessons, new directions. In J. Codd & K. Sullivan (Eds.), *Education policy directions in Aotearoa New Zealand* (pp. 175–198). Southbank VIC, Australia: Thomson Learning.

Mitchell, L., & Wells, C. (1997). Negotiating pay parity in the early childhood sector. In New Zealand Council of Trade Unions (Ed.), *Closing the gap: Forum on equal pay*. Wellington, New Zealand: Author.

New Zealand Council of Trade Unions. (1997). *Closing the gap. Forum on equal pay*. New Zealand Council of Trade Unions. Wellington, New Zealand: Council of Trade Unions.

New Zealand Government. (1991). Employment Contracts Act 1991 (1991 No 22) from http://www.nzlii.org/nz/legis/hist_act/eca19911991n22280/

NZEI Te Riu Roa. (1994a). *Kindergarten teachers. The case for pay parity. Government spending and public debt*. Wellington, New Zealand: New Zealand Educational Institute.

NZEI Te Riu Roa. (1994b). *Early childhood workers. The case for pay parity. Public spending and government debt*. Wellington, New Zealand: New Zealand Educational Institute.

NZEI Te Riu Roa. (2016). *The early childhood education collective agreement of Aotearoa New Zealand*. Retrieved from https://www.nzei.org.nz/AgreementDoc/ECEA.pdf

Ober, J. (2008). *Democracy and knowledge: Innovation and learning in classical Athens*. Princeton, NJ: Princeton University Press.

Shipley, J. (1997, April 29). *House of representatives parliamentary debates. State Sector Amendment Bill 1457*. Wellington, New Zealand: Hansard.

Smith, A. B., Ford, V. E., Hubbard, P. M., & White, E. J. (1996). *The quality of childcare centres for infants in New Zealand* (State of the art monograph, 0113–4442; no 4). Palmerston North, New Zealand: Massey University, New Zealand Association for Research in Education.

Te One, S. (2003). The context for Te Whāriki: Contemporary issues of influence. In J. Nuttall (Ed.), *Weaving Te Whāriki* (pp. 17–49). Wellington, New Zealand: New Zealand Council for Educational Research.

Wells, C. (1991). *The impact of change – Against the odds*. Paper presented at the Early Childhood Convention, Dunedin.

Wells, C. (1999). Future directions: Shaping early childhood policy for the 21st century – a personal perspective. In I. Livingstone (Ed.), *New Zealand Annual Review of Education* (Vol. 8:1998, pp. 45–60). Wellington, New Zealand: School of Education, Victoria University of Wellington.

Wylie, C. (1992). *First impressions: The initial impact of salary bulk funding on New Zealand kindergartens*. Wellington, New Zealand: New Zealand Council for Educational Research.

Policy Frameworks and Democratic Participation

1 Introduction

Considerable interest has emerged in policy approaches that work to sustain and encourage democratic participation and responsive pedagogy in ECEC (early childhood education and care). Teachers and educators who are in direct interaction with children and families are crucial players, but all the main participants in ECEC – children, families and practitioners – are influenced by opportunities and impediments afforded by policy. Oberhuemer, Schreyer and Neuman's (2010) analysis of professionals in 27 ECEC systems across Europe highlights many issues, including variable and often low pay rates, unsupportive conditions of employment, a gendered workforce, variable qualification levels and opportunities for professional development and recruitment and retention issues. Using findings from an evaluation of New Zealand's strategic plan for early childhood education (Mitchell et al., 2011), this chapter highlights ways in which policy initiatives interacted to support child and family participation through provision of ECEC and to address workforce issues. A range of initiatives aimed to enhance children's participation and develop collaborative relationships with families. Extensive support for improving teacher qualifications and professional capabilities helped teachers to think critically and develop teaching practice. In combination the initiatives encouraged the development of communities of learners and contributed to democratic practice. A key argument is that benefits came from policies that were universally available and coherently organised around an understanding of children, families and communities as participants.

© Springer Nature Singapore Pte Ltd. 2019   125
L. Mitchell, *Democratic Policies and Practices in Early Childhood Education*,
International Perspectives on Early Childhood Education and Development 24,
https://doi.org/10.1007/978-981-13-1793-4_7

2   Policy Frameworks to Support Democratic Participation and Pedagogy

A 2008 Ministry of Education commissioned literature review on outcomes of early childhood education (ECE) (Mitchell, Wylie, & Carr, 2008b) synthesised a body of research studies analysing the impact of ECE on outcomes for children (cognitive, learning dispositions, social emotional and health) and families (parenting and parent life course outcomes and maternal employment). The review report produced a diagram summarising the facilitating conditions that support the teaching and learning that in turn contributes to positive outcomes for children and families. It found that at the heart, an early childhood setting with positive outcomes is characterised by:

- Intentional teaching.[1]
- Family engagement with ECE teachers and programmes, where social/cultural capital and interests from home are included and both family and teachers can best support the child's learning.

A complex curriculum involving both cognitive and non-cognitive dimensions (p. 7).

The chapters on curriculum and assessment have exemplified that education with democracy at the heart includes these features. Participation in teaching and learning is shared with children, families and communities. Children have agency; they are perceived as competent and resourceful and are encouraged to be active in their own learning and the learning of others. The associations between these features and child outcomes are two-way, with linkages from child outcomes back to the ECE setting.

In this chapter, I discuss "facilitating environments" that provide conditions for the very important principles of access for every child, responsiveness to families, and democratic and learner-centred practice to flourish. I begin by discussing findings from an evaluation of New Zealand's strategic plan (2002–2009) which examined policy initiatives in relation to children's access and staffing. In the second part, I discuss teachers as researchers who added a research component to their everyday work of teaching, learning and formative documentation. This idea relates to Giroux's (1988) thinking of teachers as intellectuals, playing an active role in shaping the curriculum. They are aware of their own values and attitudes, investigate their pedagogy to bring about positive change and work out strategies to play a transformational role. This section includes examples from Aotearoa New Zealand ECEC settings of teachers who worked with research associates to analyse and develop their practice.

---

[1] Settings that provide opportunities for "sustained shared thinking", rich teacher-child interactions, engaging programmes, peers learning together and assessments with valued outcomes in mind

3 Strategic Plan for Early Childhood Education

Pathways to the Future: Ngā Huarahi Arataki (Ministry of Education, 2002) was the first ever long-term strategic plan for any education sector in Aotearoa New Zealand. The process of development was highly participative, with a *Working Group for the Development of the Strategic Plan for Early Childhood Education* (the Working Group) of 31 representatives brought together to draft proposals, undertake consultation and finalise a report. The chairperson was Dr. Anne Meade, a well-regarded academic who had chaired previous ECE policy working groups.

The Working Group, of which I was a member, did not always agree, particularly about funding and ownership yet, through consultation and some common values, finalised a report (Working Group for the Development of the Strategic Plan for Early Childhood Education, 2001). However, the government did not adopt this Working Group report as policy. Instead it appointed a Technical Working Group to develop more specific and fiscally responsible proposals. The "blue skies" thinking of the initial Working Group report was somewhat curtailed in the final government strategic plan, particularly its recommendation for "an entitlement to a reasonable amount of free early childhood education for all children before they start school", but the government report (Ministry of Education, 2002), published in 2002, was still largely aspirational. It had the following overarching vision: "Government's vision is for all New Zealand children to have the opportunity to participate in quality early childhood education no matter their circumstances" (Ministry of Education, 2002, p. 1). This vision statement connected the three strategic plan goals of (1) increasing children's participation in quality ECE; (2) improving quality and (3) promoting collaborative relationships between ECE services and parents, whānau (extended family), iwi (tribe) and health and social services and between ECE services and schools.

Specific actions to support implementation of the strategic plan goals were decided in 2002 and amended or developed as the plan progressed. Reviews of regulation and funding, research and a commitment to involve the ECE sector in ongoing policy development and implementation were intended to support implementation. Details of all the strategic plan actions and an evaluation over the years 2004, 2006 and 2009 are discussed in a locality-based evaluation of the strategic plan (Mitchell & Hodgen, 2008; Mitchell et al., 2011; Mitchell, Royal Tangaere, Mara, & Wylie, 2008a). The focus in this chapter is on findings from this locality-based evaluation and an evaluation of the sustainability of ECE services by Julian King (2008). It examines some of the strategic plan's major policy initiatives and ways in which they enabled democratic provision, as well as aspects of Aotearoa New Zealand that are in opposition. First, the chapter shows how the provision of "20 hours free ECE" for 3- and 4-year-olds substantially increased funding and an enhanced funding system made access to ECE possible for many children who might not otherwise have attended. Inequities in affordability associated with income levels were largely dispelled. Secondly, it discusses a range of initiatives aimed at improving teacher qualifications, professional capabilities and developing communities of learners and how these contributed to enhanced quality and democratic practice.

The evaluation of the strategic plan followed the same 32 ECE services through from 2004 and 2006 to 2009 (Mitchell et al., 2011). This provided opportunity to gather baseline data when the strategic plan had been announced, but only early stages of some actions were in place, data at a midpoint when further strategic plan actions had just started and earlier actions consolidated and data in 2009. The comparison enabled a mapping of the changes that occurred in ECE services and for parents on indicators of intended outcomes of the strategic plan and contextual information linking any change to take-up or not of policy initiatives. The 32 ECE services in which full data was gathered were 12 education and care centres, 8 kindergartens, 8 playcentres, 2 Pacific early childhood groups and 2 home-based (family daycare) services. Eight kohanga reo took part, but in 20s04 and 2006 only. They were in eight localities in Aotearoa New Zealand that had median incomes below the average for Aotearoa New Zealand. Mixed methods were used: observations by trained observers over two half days using a process quality rating scale developed and validated in Aotearoa New Zealand, teacher interviews about their pedagogical practice, parent questionnaires and a management survey and an ECE service profile.

Following steps for rubric development detailed by Davidson (2005), a set of rubrics were constructed to enable evaluative judgments to be made about levels of overall achievement for intended outcomes of the strategic plan. The rubric descriptions were based on prior research and developed in discussion with academic experts in the field and the Ministry of Education. For each outcome, levels of ratings (very good, good, fair and poor) and patterns of change were described across the three evaluation years. These patterns of change were analysed in relation to data from participants about supports and barriers to improvement and in relation to strategic plan policy initiatives and ECE service uptake of opportunities afforded by these. In this way, the impact of government policy initiatives was gauged.

3.1   Children's Access and Participation

UNCROC offers a useful conceptual tool for thinking about access to ECEC. The UNCROC principles can be used to uphold an argument that access to quality ECE for all children whose families wish them to participate in ECE is a child's right. Rosslyn Noonan, then New Zealand's Human Rights Commissioner, made this argument in 2001 in her speech to NZCER's *Early childhood education in a democratic society conference.*

> Article 29 of the UN Convention on the Rights of the Child states that the education of the child shall be directed to, amongst other things, 'the development of the child's personality, talents and mental and physical abilities to their fullest potential'. In the New Zealand context the results of the *Competent Children* longitudinal study and other research confirms the very significant impact of quality early childhood education on a child's achievements

at primary school. On that basis early childhood education can be viewed as an implicit element of the right to free primary education provided for in the international Conventions that New Zealand has ratified. And not to ensure universal access could, arguably, amount to discrimination or at least indirect discrimination. (Noonan, 2001, p. 65).

A child's right to access ECEC is incompletely realised in Aotearoa New Zealand. Access is dependent on whether ECEC services are affordable, whether provision is convenient for families, whether times suit the needs of families and whether the type of service "philosophy" is what suits the family. In 2007, Robertson's (2007) study of parent decision-making in relation to ECEC found limited choice for families in rural communities. In the same year, 31% of parents actually using ECEC in a New Zealand Council for Educational Research national survey (Mitchell, 2008) stated that times and days were unsuitable. More recently, a *National Evaluation of the ECE Participation Programme* (Mitchell, Meagher-Lundberg, Davison, Kara, and Kalavite 2016b) found the main barriers for priority of families[2] in participating in ECEC were structural features of ECEC, cost being the most common. Cost includes fees and indirect costs, such as food and transport to and from services. Inflexible hours and inaccessible location were the next most prominent barriers. An overriding concern for parents was whether their child would be safe and whether adults in the ECEC setting could be trusted. In other words, it is how ECEC services are funded, organised and located and whether they are a "good fit" and responsive to families that matter most.

The funding initiatives in the strategic plan had a direct impact on the cost of ECE, thereby encouraging access for many 3- and 4-year-old children who might not otherwise have attended ECE. Government expenditure on ECE increased almost fourfold over the years 2006 to 2009 (Ministry of Education, 2011). A new funding system, established in 2005, was calculated and differentiated between service types mainly on the basis of costs, particularly costs of employing qualified teachers in teacher-led services. This system paid higher rates for ECE services employing higher percentages of qualified and registered ECE teachers, according to differential funding bands. In 2007, 20 h free ECE (later renamed 20 h ECE) was funded for 3- and 4-year-olds who were attending teacher-led services. The proposal for 20 h free ECE was intended to "send a strong signal of the importance of ECE and the public benefits that accrue from ECE participation" (Cabinet Policy Committee, 31 March 2004, p. 9). Compulsory fees could not be charged although parents could be asked to pay optional charges. ECEC services had to "opt in" to the scheme. Within this universal funding system were two funding components: a new equity funding grant to offset additional costs in some communities and services and the continuing means tested childcare subsidy for parents in paid employment or study or having a child with special needs. The main form of support for capital works continued to be the discretionary grant payable to eligible community-based services in areas of low ECEC participation and in areas of high projected population growth.

---

[2] These include many Māori and Pacific learners, those from low socio-economic backgrounds and students with special education needs.

Early in the roll-out of the strategic plan, Julian King undertook a study of the sustainability of early childhood services. It was too early to offer definitive findings over time, but trends towards improved sustainability were positive.

> Analysis of the available national-level data suggests that the ECE sector as a whole is sustainable, and perhaps becoming gradually more so. The most striking observation is the stability in the indicators of occupancy, operating surplus/deficit, and working capital throughout a time period of several years pre and post introduction of the Strategic Plan. Some indicators also suggested a recent improvement in sustainability, but a longer time series is needed to establish whether this is a trend. (King, 2008, p. 79).

Ministry of Education indicators on affordability of ECE show that the affordability of early childhood education substantially improved with the introduction of 20 h free ECE in 2007. Fees paid by households fell 33.6% in the year from June 2007 to June 2008. Relative to the 5.2% rise in average ordinary-time earnings over the same period, affordability rose by 36.9% (Ministry of Education, 2014). From the perspectives of parents who responded to questionnaires in the strategic plan evaluation, 20 h free ECE eased family budgets, benefiting family life and children's learning and socialisation. It enabled some families to enrol children who would otherwise have missed out. In this way, the universal investment in ECE helped to diminish some inequalities in access linked to cost.

The policy also enabled more children to participate in ECE. Nationally, the percentage of children who had participated in ECE before they went to school increased from 92.9% in 2004 to 93.4% in 2006 and to 93.9% in 2009. Average weekly hours of attendance in an ECE service also increased from 16 h (2004) to 16.9 h (2006) and to 19.5 h (2009).

Funding mechanisms for ECEC in Aotearoa New Zealand have often changed as new governments take power. This happened following the election in 2009 of a new centre-right government (the National-led government). The 20 h free ECE policy was changed in name to "20 hours ECE", on the grounds that this was "…a more honest expression of the programme's intent" (Tolley, 31 January 2009). The removal of "free" made it clear that free education as an entitlement for children was not to be a policy priority and signalled a philosophical shift away from government taking greater responsibility for early childhood education for all children.

Affordability decreased following the National-led government funding reductions introduced in February 2011 which removed the top two additional bands of funding for teacher-led services employing 80% or more ECE-qualified and ECE-registered teachers. ECE services in this position would generally be unable to employ the higher percentage of qualified teaching staff (who cost more than unqualified teachers) on existing budgets unless they passed on costs to parents. Ministry of Education data analysis shows the financial impact on services of the cut to the funding bands as "an average funding per hour drop of 8% for those services impacted, and an estimated 5% decline in affordability for parents" (Ministry of Education, 2014).

According to Gordon Cleveland, an economist who, with others, constructed a childcare demand and affordability model for the City of Toronto (Cleveland, Krashinsky, Colley, & Avery-Nunez, 2016), the main policy lever to encourage ECE participation is affordability. This is consistent with findings from Aotearoa New Zealand studies (Mitchell, Meagher-Lundberg, Arndt, and Kara 2016a) that cost is the greatest barrier preventing families from enrolling their child in ECE.

A clear implication is that funding and provision policies need to be considered as a whole and in relation to objectives centred around the rights of all children to access good-quality ECE. The concept of a legal entitlement to ECE has been adopted in many European countries, with children having a right to access publicly funded ECE provision. The OECD *Starting Strong IV* report (OECD, 2015) of ECEC in 24 OECD jurisdictions reported that 18 of these offer a legal entitlement to a place for all or certain groups of children. A universal legal entitlement to a place refers to "a statutory duty for ECEC providers to secure (publicly subsidised) ECEC provision for all children living in a catchment area whose parents, regardless of employment, socio-economic or family status, require an ECEC place" (pp. 20–21). Aotearoa New Zealand is one of six jurisdictions which does not offer access to a place as an entitlement. In all countries except Kazakhstan, the starting age for a place coincides with the age that paid parental leave ends.

Free early childhood education is offered by 18 of these OECD jurisdictions, but not always in conjunction with an entitlement to a place. Countries vary in the number of hours of free ECEC (from 12.5 to 60) and whether it is targeted to certain families depending on variables such as income and employment or universally available. In Aotearoa New Zealand, the government funds 20 h ECE for all 3- and 4-year-olds to a level that should make it able to be offered free of charge. However, providers are able to ask for optional charges and set their own enrolment criteria. Some providers, who are mainly private and corporate business owners, demand that families enrol for more than the "free" hours and charge fees for extra time. Aotearoa New Zealand does nothing to cap fees or curtail business profits. One way to ensure accessibility to ECE is through forecasting and planning ECE provision, alongside guaranteeing children an entitlement to a free place.

3.2 A Qualified and Professionally Supported ECE Workforce

A range of strategic plan initiatives supported the ECE workforce to become qualified (in teacher-led services) and to support teachers professionally. The Ministry of Education published a series of assessment resources (Ministry of Education, 2005b, 2007, 2009), an ICT strategy (Ministry of Education, 2005a) and a self-review resource (Ministry of Education, 2006) congruent with the sociocultural framing of *Te Whāriki*. The resources featured exemplars of practice from the diverse range of ECE settings to support assessment in keeping with the empowerment principles and credit view of children and families expressed in *Te Whāriki*. Concurrent with their publication, the Ministry of Education funded professional development related to the assessment exemplars.

One of the most ambitious goals was that in 2012, 100% of regulated staff would be required to be registered teachers. Targets were set to increase the employment of registered teachers in teacher-led services in stages over time periods 2005, 2007, 2010 and 2012. Diverse incentives including grants, scholarships and allowances were offered to support reaching the targets. Unfortunately, the 2009 change in government brought the staged plan to an end and cut two funding bands that gave higher levels of funding to services with more than 80% registered teachers.

Over the period 2003 to 2009, the Ministry of Education designated 20 ECE services that had innovative approaches to teaching and learning as Centres of Innovation. They were funded for a period of 3 years to work with research associates to build their use of innovative approaches, facilitate action research and share their knowledge and models of excellent practice with others in the ECE sector.

Positive shifts, starting to be evident in 2006, continued to occur on the intermediate outcomes of the strategic plan that had been a specific focus for these MOE initiatives. Nationally, the percentage of registered teachers in ECE teacher-led services climbed spectacularly from 37.3% in 2004 to 56.4% in 2006 and to 64% in 2009. It has continued to rise, and in 2017, it is close to 80%. Teacher-led services in the evaluation study showed similar shifts in levels. The shifts were associated with widespread use of government incentives (64% of teacher-led services had used government incentives by 2006, and 67% had used them by 2009). These shifts would not have occurred without the government's firm resolve to establishing a qualified teaching profession. May (2009) comments on the staunch opposition from various players in the sector "including private operators, areas that had difficulty meeting the demand for qualified teachers, those experiencing the political and industrial effects of increased costs, and from parent-led services such as playcentre and Kōhanga Reo" (p. 269).

The take-up of qualified teachers and professional resources and development were linked positively to ratings of observed process quality and indicators of "good" assessment, planning, evaluation and self-review processes. These included an opening up of the curriculum to parents and whānau (extended family) through invitations for their involvement in assessment and planning. In 2004, 36% of parents surveyed were involved in these processes. This had risen to 47% in 2006 and 60% in 2009. Teachers' understanding of *Te Whāriki* was enhanced. Meade, who led the Centre of Innovation programme, argued that "Ideas that have come from teachers have a different impact from the ideas of academics. The audience sees the COI findings as more authentic and directly applicable to practice" (Meade, 2007, p. 6). This dissemination of exemplars from actual practice was a feature of the published professional resources too. The policy initiatives supported and reinforced each other. Services that had high ratings of process quality tended also to have high ratings on the four outcomes: teaching and learning processes, teacher qualifications, relationships with parents and teachers' understanding of *Te Whāriki*. Elsewhere I have argued that "Benefits came from policies that were universally available and coherently organised around an understanding of children, families and communities as participants" (Mitchell, 2011, p. 10) and that this emphasis on participation is in keeping with the curriculum framing of mana and empowerment.

4   Teachers as Critical Thinkers

Over 100 years ago, John Dewey (1915) made a distinction between education as a function of society and society as a function of education. If the role of education is to build society – a democratic society – teachers need to pay careful and critical attention to how they teach and why and to questions of value and perspectives of others, children and adults. Writing of radical education, Giroux (1992, p. 10) argues the need for "a language of critique, a questioning of presuppositions" and as well "a language of possibility...a positive language of human empowerment". By empowerment he means the ability to think and act critically with reference to the individual and society. Some of the attitudes, qualities and behaviours that are valued in a democratic community are "plurality, respect for difference, dialogue, listening, deliberation, shared enquiry, critical judgement, co-operation, collective decision-making, individual freedom, the common good, participation" (Moss, 2009, p. 1).

One of the main challenges in affording opportunity for democratic pedagogical practices are for early childhood teachers themselves to learn to problematise the ways in which they have constructed the image of the child and family. There is need for them to become aware of and question power imbalances and to think critically about the role of the teacher and the purpose of the early childhood institution. Analysis of debates about the image of the child, cultural priorities and desirable outcome for children will contribute to understanding how pedagogical practices might support democratic provision. Dahlberg, Moss and Pence (1999) argued for a learning process which challenges dominant discourses. They contended that the way pedagogues construct the child has consequences for relationships with children and families and the design of the early childhood environment. Changing the construction of the child contributes to the production of new practice.

The *Stockholm Project* discussed by Gunilla Dahlberg *in Beyond Quality in Early Childhood Education and Care* (Dahlberg, Moss, & Pence, 1999) used a process of networking of pedagogues and researchers combined with pedagogical documentation to foster critical analysis and reflection. These processes were key to enabling change to take place. The networking enabled multiple perspectives to be heard, and the pedagogical documentation made concrete examples of practice visible.

> Pedagogical documentation opens up a possibility for moving back and forth between conceptual tools and practice. As well as deconstruction, documentation has enabled the pedagogues to develop their practice through struggling with a new construction of the child and themselves as pedagogues, and in this way to take more control over their own practice. (p. 136).

Nevertheless this was challenging work and it took time for pedagogues to make changes in thinking.

Similarly, in an Aotearoa New Zealand study (Mitchell, 2007), the roles of a teachers' network and policy discussion forums as a means to create debate about early childhood education policies and pedagogy were explored. The research was committed to critiquing constructs of children and exploring implications for creation of early childhood centres that support democratic citizenship. The teachers' network was intended to provide opportunity for such investigation and critique. Pedagogical documentation offered concrete evidence of interactions and work within the setting: it went beyond teachers talking about what they thought they did. Exploring data from different perspectives sometimes affirmed teachers and on occasions "created surprise" when teachers' perceptions were different from those of others and from the data presented in the documentation. New Zealand researchers (Carr, 2000; Timperley & Robinson, 2001) investigating how teachers challenge assumptions and revise their understandings suggest that "creating surprise through exposure to discrepant data" (Timperley & Robinson, 2001, p. 283) is a key process.

Teachers also gained insights from discussing pedagogical documentation from other kindergartens that they applied in examining their own practice. There were some changes in the power relationships between teachers and children, and teachers and parents, and differing constructions of the roles of teacher and learner, child and parent, were formed. The shifts were towards seeing childhood, not as "an essentialised category" but as being produced within a set of relationships (Prout, 2005, p. 76) and towards greater participation of children, families and community in the teaching and learning community.

Beliefs about children influence how adults act towards children; they are often engrained, unanalysed and hard to change. Discussion of values and beliefs within a local ECE setting is one way for participants in a community to come together to weave a curriculum that enables the setting to meet locally negotiated goals and community aspirations. These locally negotiated goals will sit within the curriculum, with its democratic principles (empowerment, family and community, holistic development and relationships) and strands (belonging, wellbeing, contribution, exploration, communication) that lie at its heart.

In Aotearoa New Zealand, opportunities for critical analysis and exploration of pedagogical practice have been made possible through government funds and small university grants to enable teachers to work in partnerships with research associates.

The Teaching and Learning Research Initiative (TLRI) is a government fund for collaborative research between researchers and teacher researchers about teaching and learning in the early childhood, school and tertiary sectors. It aims to build research capability and to make a difference to teaching and learning in Aotearoa New Zealand. The issues chosen for research are those that are important to education institutions: teachers are partners in the research and research aims, and questions are constructed collaboratively. The fund was established in 2003 and has funded 23 early childhood projects since then. Research reports are available on the TLRI website.[3]

A recent example of critical analysis and exploration of pedagogical practice through a TLRI grant is a study carried out from 2015 to 2017 by researchers Keryn

---

[3] http://www.tlri.org.nz/home

Davis and Ruta McKenzie with teachers from two "sister" education and care centres, a full Samoan immersion centre and an English-medium centre with families from diverse cultures, the majority being Pākehā or Palagi (New Zealanders of European descent). The language and culture of the Samoan centre was "deeply rooted to Samoan ways of being doing and knowing" (Davis & McKenzie, 2016, p. 9), while the English-medium centre was shaped by Western world views. The project aimed to look for examples and find out about children's working theories about identity, language and culture in action. In their analysis of the first set of data, Davis and McKenzie concluded that the "sister" relationship between the two research sites, between the research leaders (teacher researchers) in each site and between the research associates (who are Pākehā and Samoan respectively) was particularly important in enabling cross-cultural analysis of data. This analysis also impacted on teaching practice.

> The process has also included analysis that explores multiple cultural viewpoints to make meaning of children's theories. This analysis is helping to shift what teachers are noticing about what children are making sense of, and how, and this is in turn is shifting how teachers are responding to children. (Davis & McKenzie, 2016, p. 13).

The Centre of Innovation programme was another government-funded early childhood initiative that encouraged teachers to take a critical view of their practice. To become a Centre of Innovation, early childhood services had to be already engaged in innovative, worthwhile practice that was able to be researched. Teacher researchers from the Centres of Innovation worked in partnership with research associates to research and develop their existing innovative practice. They were also required to disseminate information about their innovation and the outcomes of their research. At the end of each Centre of Innovation project, the teacher researchers and their research associates produced a final research report which was published on the Ministry of Education Education Counts website[4]. The idea for Centres of Innovation came from the initial strategic plan working group, whose members were interested in Centres of Excellence in the UK, but wanted centres to be designated for 3 years only so that a greater number of centres could benefit from researching their practice over time and disseminating information. The working group members preferred not to use the name "excellence" because of its connotations of uniform and measureable quality, rather than of local, situated constructions of quality. The initial Working Group proposed the name "Centre of Research and Development". This was changed to "Centre of Innovation" within government policy. Fifteen Centres of Innovation completed their projects over the period 2003 to 2009.

Robyn Gibbs and Jenny Poskitt (2009), who evaluated the Centre of Innovation programme concluded that:

> ...there were many good outcomes for teachers, including opportunities to engage in critical thinking that challenged their previously held assumptions about teaching and learning. As a result of their collaborative professional learning, many teachers reported that their

---

[4] https://www.educationcounts.govt.nz/publications/ECE/22551

planning, formative assessment processes, and increased use of ICT within the learning and teaching programme were of a higher quality. Teachers reported that RAs [Research Associates] played a significant role in exposing them to a range of theories that extended their content and pedagogical knowledge. These comments were confirmed by the Research Leader, RAs and in many of the COI milestone reports. (p. 15).

To the dismay of many participants in Aotearoa New Zealand's ECEC sector, the programme was cut by the National-led government in 2009, while four projects were still midway through their term. It has never been replaced; but the policy development planned by Aotearoa New Zealand's new Labour-led government offers opportunity for revisiting research and professional development priorities. The selection of a limited number of Centres of Innovation and TLRI projects in each year raises questions about fairness and the opportunity for all early childhood services to extend their ideas and practice through well-funded collaborations with research associates.

Not all projects in Aotearoa New Zealand have received government funding. In a number of educational research projects, universities have provided small grants to cover limited costs of university researchers working with teachers to research an aspect of teaching practice. The researchers and teachers work out a topic of mutual interest and agree on the roles and responsibilities of each party. Often, a form of participatory action research is chosen as a research method.

In one such project, funded by a small University of Waikato Faculty of Education Research grant, Kelly and White (2011) researched with teachers in six ECEC settings to consider two overarching research questions:

1. What might nature-based learning look like in diverse Aotearoa New Zealand ECE services that are committed to sustainability?
2. What are some of the pedagogical issues and provocations teachers face in this domain?

Each site also developed its own specific research questions.

Through their participation in the action research cycles in this project, the teachers extended their understanding of pedagogy informed by the curriculum *Te Whāriki* and its relationship to nature education and sustainability. "They revisioned *Te Whāriki* rather than seeing that a paradigm shift was needed to 'return to nature' in their pedagogy." (p. 6). The projects where nature-based education occurred were mainly outside the research settings ("beyond the gate") and took place regularly over several months. Learning was play-based, there was reasonable risk-taking, and teachers needed to know each child well and to develop trust in each other's professional judgements and in the environment as the context for learning. Knowing about land features from traditional Māori and non-Māori perspectives helped teachers become more "place responsive". Teachers' knowledge and knowledge of sustainability principles allied to tikanga Māori values was enriched and deepened through incorporation of the funds of knowledge of families and iwi. There were advantages in going "beyond the gate":

The luxuries of unhurried time, 'wild' open spaces, and fewer distractions including noise, supported teachers' mindfulness throughout this research project. Nature environments enabled them to slow down, 'be present', recognise more, and teach intentionally. These kinds of programmes do not exist for all children in Aotearoa New Zealand. (Kelly & White, 2011, p, 6).

The findings highlighted for the participants "the relationships and interconnections between nature and teachers, children and their families, as well as the sophisticated knowledge base that is required." (p. 7).

During another project (Mitchell et al., 2015) at Pakuranga Baptist Kindergarten, teacher researchers analysed the responsiveness of the kindergarten to the values and beliefs of their culturally and linguistically diverse community. Jacqui Lees, the supervisor, described the process of purposefully recruiting staff from the same cultural and linguistic backgrounds as their children to strengthen opportunities for cultural understanding and communication. Teachers engage with parents and children, as far as possible, in their own languages, so that families are able to experience that all languages are valued and used regularly in their daily practice.

In an initial workshop with teachers from two other ECEC centres in the research project, Jacqui said that over the past few years, a whakatauki by Kukupa Tirikatene, a Kaumatua of COMET (City of Manukau Education Trust), had become increasingly meaningful for the kindergarten teaching team:

> E kore e taea e te whenu kotahi ki te raranga i te whāriki kia mōhio tātou kiā tātou. Mā te mahi tahi ō ngā whenu, mā te mahi tahi ō ngā kairaranga, ka oti tēnei whāriki.
>
> The tapestry of understanding cannot be woven by one strand alone. Only by the working together of strands and the working together of us all will such a tapestry be completed.

She described the whakatauki as being especially significant in an environment of increasing cultural diversity, because the families, children and teachers create the community each day. In a presentation within the workshop, she said "We each bring who we are and in the daily process of being together we transform each other. In this way the identity of our place is constructed each day by everyone adding layers to who we are collectively". These teachers had read *Ethics and Politics in Early Childhood Education* (Dahlberg & Moss, 2005) and were influenced by ideas about a "pedagogy of listening" (pp. 98–102). Jacqui said the teachers worked to weave through their curriculum the value of respect by listening. Influenced by Rinaldi, they had come to see listening as being more than just hearing another's words but "as being open to the differences between us, listening being an openness to other points of view, an openness which requires that we let go of the idea that our way of doing things is the right way or the only way".

Teachers in this kindergarten set about to have daily conversations with families "to take a look at what is happening, to engage with any areas of difference or misinterpretation and to see if a different idea enriches us as a group or if it is diametrically opposed to what we believe and we need to challenge it. This process allows us to reflect on our taken for granted assumptions and to make changes in ways that will grow our learning community." (Interview). They also have discussions with groups of parents to talk about how they see their children, what values they hold in their families and what kind of people they want their children to grow to be. These teachers attributed the reason why the kindergarten attracted many Chinese families to a shared value base of respect, collaboration, wonder, responsibility and openness that flowed through their interactions with children, families and staff. These values are further intentionally foregrounded in children's learning stories and thereby given prominence and reinforced.

The discussions with families highlighted some areas of concern and values for particular families that were "diametrically opposed" to what teachers believed was sound educational practice. In these events, everyday conversations were held, and documented learning stories reinforced learning of value to the parent. Literacy learning is picked out in learning episodes to reinforce that although the kindergarten does not use worksheets and have formal writing time, children are learning writing through everyday activities that are fun. Writing about this practice of discussion and accommodation, kindergarten in the practitioner-focused publication *Early Childhood Folio*, Jacqui Lees stated:

> At times the understanding of differences in values has required extensive negotiation, particularly around the values of independence and interdependence. For many kiwi [New Zealand] families and teachers it is seen as important that children learn to be independent and to do things for themselves. However, for many of the cultural groups in our kindergarten there is a question about this value, because children are part of a family and have parents whose responsibility is to do things for them as part of their care for them, so it is seen as less necessary for them to be independent at this young age. Over the past few years the teachers at the Kindergarten have seen an increase in grandparents in primary caregiving roles, some of whom wanted to come each day to feed their grandchildren lunch. The teachers have accepted this as a cultural value but felt over time we could offer a middle ground that would enable our community to see that we offer support to children as learners, and that we would feed them if necessary while still encouraging them to become self-managing. However welcoming families' presence in the kindergarten whenever they have wanted to be there has also meant that families feel that the kindergarten is an environment that is theirs as well as their children's. (Lees, 2016, pp. 15–19).

In common, in the projects where academic researchers worked with teacher researchers, participants commented on seeing curriculum and pedagogy through other lenses, giving them new ways of thinking and seeing. These lenses included influences of theoretical and research publications.

During one of the Centre of Innovation projects at Wadestown Kindergarten (Simonsen et al., 2010, teachers as first authors), a pedagogical discussion group met to discuss research-based theoretical readings relevant to the research focus. The aim was to investigate the thinking about and use of concepts and approaches relevant to the project, keep up to date in understanding of relevant research and theory and develop a wider view and understanding through the process of discussing different perspectives on the same material. Each member of the discussion group (teacher researchers, research associates) came to the discussion session, having read two readings provided by a member of the team. Later this process was extended to each participant coming to the session having prepared a "one pager" of written comments on key points gained from the reading. The commentary was not prescribed, and over time it included new insights gained, questions raised by the reading, linkages to own experiences and ideas to think about in relation to the

Centre of Innovation research. Each person in turn presented their views from their written "one pager", and the group discussed the contributions. Yvette, the head teacher, remarked on the influence of Kress (2000) on her thinking about multimodal literacies which she had come to understand as more than expression and communication but also as ways of knowing and conceptualising. Both writing and discussion supported new understandings. "The act of writing the 'one pagers' seemed to encourage each person to thoughtfully process and synthesise the reading, and the social practice of having a turn to discuss their thinking within a larger group allowed points of difference and similarity to be uncovered, and new ideas and interpretations to be made" (Simonsen et al., 2010, p. 83). In this Centre of Innovation, the multimodal communications used for the purpose of critical enquiry (making, viewing and analysis of videorecorded learning episodes; finding out views from children and families; construction and discussion of learning stories; reading, writing about and discussion of theoretical writing; presentation to practitioner groups) all supported participants' shifts to more complex and deeper understanding and appreciation that knowledge is situated and perspectival. The link between theory and practice was conceived by participants as a two-way iterative dialogue, shown in Fig. 1 and described as follows:

> Central to our research process was the idea of facilitating dialogue between theory and practice in such a way that each serves to inform and deepen understanding of the other.

This is a very similar process to that described by Gunilla Dahlberg about the *Stockholm Project* where theoretical concepts were "tried out, discussed, negotiated and problematized in practice" (p. 142). In recent research in the schools sector, Hennessey and Deanney (2009) explained a process of "intermediate theory building" through researchers and teachers collaborating in critical scrutiny and discussion of digital video recordings of classroom activities. Through these processes, an "intermediate theory" was developed that acted as a bridge between key constructs in sociocultural theory and teacher strategies. An intermediate theory is located and contextualised, and highlights conditions in which theories apply. Like the Wadestown Kindergarten Centre of Innovation, their process of collaboration involved participants in a back and forth analysis and discussion between theory and practice.

Video and other forms of pedagogical documentation are powerful tools for this purpose because they offer rich texts of practice that can be viewed and analysed by more than one person and revisited over time. Video can make visible different modes of expression. In the Wadestown Kindergarten research, video captured sound, dance, movement, drama episodes, facial expression and gesture. In the *Stockholm Project*, the Wadestown Kindergarten project, and the intermediate theory building project, the power of using pedagogical documentation came from the

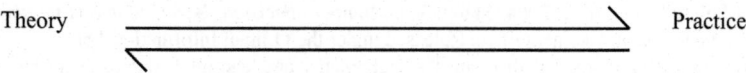

Theory   Practice

Fig. 1 Theory and practice dialogue. (Simonsen et al., 2010, p. 95)

interpretive framework co-constructed between researchers and teachers. The facilitating environments in these projects included access to researcher expertise and readings; tools for documentation, especially access to ICT, video cameras, photographic equipment, computers, printers and scanners; and time to experiment with different ways of documenting, getting together as a group, holding discussions, analysing the documentation and talking with parents and children. It was also a matter of teachers prioritising this work over other activities in their demanding working environments.

5 Conclusion

Aotearoa New Zealand's experiences over the period of the implementation of the strategic plan for ECE draw attention to the critical importance of policies, management practice and teacher practice to develop and sustain early childhood centres operating as democratic public spaces. However, a vision for public education has not been realised. Access for every child to ECEC depends on suitable ECEC services being available for families where they are needed and free ECEC being an entitlement. These conditions are not met in Aotearoa New Zealand's ECEC landscape, where a reliance on parent choice and privatised provision has led to continued inequities in access and quality.

Policy support to ensure structural conditions for quality needs to be provided. In Aotearoa New Zealand during the implementation of the strategic plan, the structural conditions supported through policy initiatives were teacher qualifications, ongoing professional development, professional resources and support for practitioner research and critically reflective practice. Underpinning these was a curriculum framework that emphasises empowerment, holistic development and responsive relationships. Examples from practice show that teachers are able to engage in critical thinking about their values and beliefs and to hold their practice up to scrutiny. In these ways they began to construct democratic principles and social practices through debate, dialogue and exchange of opinion. Yet, take-up of these supports was at the discretion of managers and not available to all practitioners.

These were powerful supports for participation and contribution of children, parents and community in their ECE setting and towards more open and democratic ECE provision.

References

Cabinet Policy Committee. (2004, March 31). *Minute of decision, Early childhood funding: proposed new system*: Cabinet Office. Released under the Official Information Act.
Carr, M. (2000). Technological affordance, social practice and learning narratives in an early childhood setting. *International Journal of Technology and Design Education, 10*, 61–79.

Cleveland, G., Krashinsky, M., Colley, S., & Avery-Nunez, C. (2016). *City of Toronto: Licensed childcare demand and affordability study*. Toronto, Canada: City of Toronto.

Dahlberg, G., & Moss, P. (2005). *Ethics and politics in early childhood education*. London: RoutledgeFalmer.

Dahlberg, G., Moss, P., & Pence, A. (1999). *Beyond quality in early childhood education and care. Post modern perspectives* (1st ed.). London: Falmer Press.

Davidson, E. J. (2005). *Evaluation methodology basics*. Thousand Oaks, CA: Sage Publications.

Davis, K., & McKenzie, R. (2016). Rainbows, sameness, and other working theories about identity, language and culture. *Early Childhood Folio, 20*(1), 9–14.

Dewey, J. (1915). *School and society*. Chicago: The University of Chicago Press.

Gibbs, R., & Poskitt, J. (2009). *Report on the evaluation of the early childhood Centres of Innovation programme* Retrieved from https://www.educationcounts.govt.nz/publications/ECE/22551/report-on-the-evaluation-of-the-early-childhood-centres-of-innovation-programme

Giroux, H. (1988). *Teachers as intellectuals: Towards a critical pedagogy of learning*. South Hadey, MA: Bergin & Garvey.

Giroux, H. (1992). *Border crossings. Cultural workers and the politics of education*. London, England: Routledge.

Hennessey, R., & Deaney, S. (2009). "Intermediate theory" building: Integrating multiple teacher and researcher perspectives through in-depth video analysis of pedagogic strategies. *Teachers College Record, 111*(7), 1753–1795.

Kelly, J., & White, E. J. (2011). *The Ngahere project: Teaching and learning possibilities in nature settings*. https://www.waikato.ac.nz/__data/assets/pdf_file/0007/146176/Ngahere-project_3-2013-03-14.pdf

King, J. (2008). *Evaluation of the sustainability of ECE services during the implementation of pathways to the future – Ngā Huarahi Arataki. Report to the Ministry of Education*. Wellington, New Zealand: Ministry of Education.

Kress, G. (2000). Design and transformation: New theories of meaning. In B. Cope & M. Kalantzis (Eds.), *Mulitiliteracies: Literacy learning and the design of social futures* (pp. 153–161). London: Routledge.

Lees, J. (2016). One centre's approach to supporting cross-cultural learning and contribution. *Early Childhood Folio, 20*(1), 15–19.

May, H. (2009). *Politics in the playground. The world of early childhood education in New Zealand* (2nd ed.). Dunedin, New Zealand: Otago University Press.

Meade, A. (Ed.). (2007). *Cresting the waves*. Wellington, New Zealand: NZCER Press.

Ministry of Education. (2002). *Pathways to the future: Ngā Huarahi Arataki*. Wellington, New Zealand: Ministry of Education.

Ministry of Education. (2005a). *Foundations for discovery: Supporting learning in early childhood education through information and communication technologies: A framework for development*. Wellington, New Zealand: Ministry of Education.

Ministry of Education. (2005b). *Kei Tua o te Pae. Assessment for learning: Early childhood exemplars. Books 1–10*. Wellington, New Zealand: Learning Media Limited.

Ministry of Education. (2006). *Ngā Arohaehae whai hua. Self review guidelines for early childhood education*. Wellington, New Zealand: Learning Media.

Ministry of Education. (2007). *Kei Tua o te Pae. Assessment for learning: Early childhood exemplars. Books 11–15*. Wellington, New Zealand: Learning Media.

Ministry of Education. (2009). *Kei Tua o te Pae. Assessment for learning: Early childhood exemplars. Books 16–20*. Wellington, New Zealand: Learning Media.

Ministry of Education. (2011). *Government expenditure on early childhood education* Retrieved from http://www.educationcounts.govt.nz/statistics/ece/55413/government-expenditure-on-early-childhood-education

Ministry of Education. (2014). *Public expenditure on early childhood education (ECE)* Retrieved from http://www.educationcounts.govt.nz/indicators/main/resource/public-expenditure-on-early-childhood-education-ece

Mitchell, L. (2007). A new debate about children and childhood. *Could it make a difference to early childhood pedagogy and policy?* PhD Doctor of Philosophy thesis. Victoria University of Wellington, Wellington. Retrieved from http://researcharchive.vuw.ac.nz/handle/10063/347

Mitchell, L. (2008). *Provision of ECE services and parental perceptions. Results of the 2007 NZCER national survey of ECE services.* Retrieved from http://www.nzcer.org.nz/default.php?products_id=2239

Mitchell, L. (2011). Enquiring teachers and democratic politics: Transformations in New Zealand's early childhood landscape. *Early Years. International Journal of Research and Development.* Retrieved from https://doi.org/10.1080/09575146.2011.588787

Mitchell, L., Bateman, A., Ouko, A., Gerrity, R., Lees, J., Matata, K., et al.. (2015). *Teaching and learning in culturally diverse early childhood settings.* Retrieved from http://www.waikato.ac.nz/__data/assets/pdf_file/0008/257246/Teachers-and-Learning-for-website_2015-03-05pm.compressed.pdf

Mitchell, L., & Hodgen, E. (2008). *Locality-based evaluation of Pathways to the Future: Ngā Huarahi Arataki. Stage 1 report.* Retrieved from http://www.educationcounts.govt.nz/publications/ece/28948/28949

Mitchell, L., Meagher Lundberg, P., Mara, D., Cubey, P., & Whitford, M. (2011). *Locality-based evaluation of Pathways to the Future – Nga Huarahi Arataki. Integrated report 2004, 2006 and 2009.* Retrieved from http://www.educationcounts.govt.nz/publications/ece/locality-based-evaluation-of-pathways-to-the-future-ng-huarahi-arataki

Mitchell, L., Meagher-Lundberg, P., Arndt, S., & Kara, H. (2016a). *ECE participation programme evaluation. Stage 4.* Retrieved from https://www.educationcounts.govt.nz/publications/ECE/ece-participation-programme-evaluation-stage-4

Mitchell, L., Meagher-Lundberg, P., Davison, C., Kara, H., & Kalavite, T. (2016b). *ECE participation programme evaluation. Stage 3.* Retrieved from https://www.educationcounts.govt.nz/publications/ECE/ece-participation-programme-evaluation-delivery-of-ece-participation-initiatives-stage-3

Mitchell, L., Royal Tangaere, A., Mara, D., & Wylie, C. (2008a). *Locality-based evaluation of pathways to the future – Ngā Huarahi Arataki. Baseline report.* Wellington, New Zealand: Ministry of Education.

Mitchell, L., Wylie, C., & Carr, M. (2008b). *Outcomes of early childhood education: Literature review.* Report to the Ministry of Education Retrieved from http://www.educationcounts.govt.nz/publications/ece/25158/48867

Moss, P. (2009). There are alternatives! Markets and democratic experimentalism in early childhood education and care. In *Working paper no 53.* The Netherlands: Bernard Van Leer Foundation and the Bertelsmann Stiftung.

Noonan, R. (2001). Early childhood education-A child's right? In B. Webber & L. Mitchell (Eds.), *Early childhood education for a democratic society. New Zealand Council for Educational Research Annual Conference October 2001* (pp. 61–68). Wellington, New Zealand: New Zealand Council for Educational Research.

Oberhuemer, P., Schreyer, I., & Neuman, M. J. (2010). *Professionals in early childhood education and care systems.* Opladen and Farmington Hills, MI: Barbara Budrich Publishers.

OECD. (2015). *Starting Strong IV: Monitoring quality in early childhood education and care.* https://doi.org/10.1787/9789264233515-en

Prout, A. (2005). *The future of childhood.* London/New York: RoutledgeFalmer.

Robertson, J. (2007). *Parental decision making in relation to the use of early childhood education services.* Wellington, New Zealand: Ministry of Education.

Simonsen, Y., Blake, M., LaHood, A., Haggerty, M., Mitchell, L., & Wray, L. (2010). *A curriculum whāriki of multimodal literacies.* Retrieved from http://www.educationcounts.govt.nz/publications/ece/22551/70769/71393

Timperley, H., & Robinson, V. (2001). Achieving school improvement through challenging and changing teachers' schema. *Journal of Educational Change, 22,* 281–300.

Tolley, A. (2009, January 31). *Changes in early childhood education.* Retrieved from http://www.beehive.govt.nz/release/changes-early-childhood-education.

Working Group for the Development of the Strategic Plan for Early Childhood Education. (2001). *Final report of the Working Group for the Development of the Strategic Plan for early Childhood Education.* Retrieved February 13, 2006, from www.minedu.govt.nz

Conclusion

Principles of democratic education that frame this book are summarised in this conclusion. These go back to Athenian times and are extended by consideration of contemporary models of democracy in education that are capable of both generating "a good life" for persons and being "good for society". The meaning of these values is itself a matter for democratic debate. Democracy in education is considered in relation to the interactions within ECEC settings amongst teachers and participants, in relation to the nature of ECEC provision and in relation to the policy settings that frame ECEC. Tensions that have arisen in New Zealand between aspirations for a democratic and public ECEC and oppositional influences of marketisation and privatisation are common to many countries, yet with sound analysis and concerted advocacy, these influences can be challenged and pushed back. In this conclusion, I bring together findings from the chapters to examine what conditions might be needed for integrated and democratic early childhood education provision in Aotearoa New Zealand, the progress made to date and what changes are needed for the future. This book was finalised in early 2018, only 4 months after a new left-leaning Labour-led government came into power in Aotearoa New Zealand. Its election and immediate actions during its first 100 days of office have raised hope that the decades of neoliberalism and marketisation may be ousted and replaced with a more humane and socially just approach to children, families, workers and education.

1 Democratic Ideals

Principles of democratic education are the framing for this book. I return to these principles in this conclusion to consider the Aotearoa New Zealand system of education, at levels of government policy, management and governance and grassroots practice, within the context of some global challenges. In Aotearoa New Zealand,

© Springer Nature Singapore Pte Ltd. 2019   145
L. Mitchell, *Democratic Policies and Practices in Early Childhood Education*,
International Perspectives on Early Childhood Education and Development 24,
https://doi.org/10.1007/978-981-13-1793-4_8

challenges arise from poverty, inequities in wealth distribution, an increasingly culturally and ethnically diverse population and inequitable access to good education, housing and health care. Climate change is an urgent problem. Neoliberalism and marketisation have deepened inequities in Aotearoa New Zealand society.

Principles for democracy in education began to emerge in Athenian times. Through combining expertise and knowledge, citizens were able to articulate and progress a common good; there was also an openness to diverse cultural groups that enriched ideas and their enactment (Ober, 2008). Yet appalling injustices in Athenian times lay in the non-recognition of women, children and slaves as citizens and in their treatment. In modern democracies, after Marshall (1950), citizenship entails human equality and full membership of a community, with all citizens having civil, social and political rights and responsibilities. Carr and Harnett (1996) make distinctions between different models of democracy: a "moral model", based on fundamental human values and emphasising equality and participation, and a "market model", based on ideas that people are self-interested, private individuals. These distinctions are similar to those made by Apple (2005) between "thick" collective forms of democracy and "thin" individualist forms of democracy that are associated with marketisation and consumerism. Principles for democracy in education are taken from the "moral" model and ideas about collective forms of democracy.

My framing takes from Dewey's consideration of democracy that education needs to operate as a democratic community and create the conditions for formulating and addressing shared concerns – and that education leads the way in developing democracy in society. It is through participation and interaction with others within educational settings that new thinking is produced. Critical thought and action are emphasised by Dewey (1916, 1944, 1939) and Giroux (1988, 1992), with "teachers as intellectuals" questioning what forms of knowledge count, producing curricula that are locally relevant and acting critically about individuals, groups and society (Giroux, 1988). Such approaches have been adopted in Aotearoa New Zealand ECEC centres where government policy initiatives have enabled teachers to research, analyse and develop their own practice in collaboration with academic researchers.

However, democracy in education goes beyond the teachers and children at the centre of an education system. In countries like Aotearoa New Zealand, which share a neoliberal and market philosophy, ECEC provision has become increasingly determined by external entrepreneurs. In a democratic society, the shape of education provision must be a public concern. Drawing from Aristotle's theory of education, Australian writers, Kemmis and Edward-Groves (2018), take the position that "the good life for each person cannot be enacted without some notion of good for humankind, and the good for humankind cannot be conceived or enacted without some notion of the good life for the person" (p. 14). Writing from England, Moss (2009, 2012, 2013; Moss & Petrie, 2002) has been a long-standing advocate for rejecting neoliberalism and marketisation and for public debate about aspirations for children, values about childhood and the place of children and childhood in society. Likewise, Penn (2012, 2013) is highly critical of for-profit provision, which she argues is able to be reversed if there is political will to do so. Democracy in education holds out new possibilities for reimagining education as a participative process in which all parties exercise agency.

In addition to this framing of democracy, the Aotearoa New Zealand system of ECEC is analysed as to whether it exemplifies the characteristics of strong ECEC systems as synthesised for the European *Competence Requirements in Early Childhood Education and Care* (CoRe) project by Urban, Vandenbroeck, Lazzari, Van Laere and Peeters (2012) – or whether in fact the Aotearoa New Zealand "system" looks quite different – and therefore sits beyond the framework devised in the CoRe project.

The CoRe project explored conceptualisations of "competence" and professionalism in early childhood practice through literature review, case studies, a survey of experts and discussion with key players. A main finding was that rather than competence being an individual characteristic, systemic conditions for developing, supporting and maintaining competence are necessary at all layers of the early childhood system (Urban, Vandenbroeck, Lazzari, et al., 2012; Urban, Vandenbroeck, Van Laere, et al., 2012). Likewise, the New Zealand Ministry of Education commissioned literature review on outcomes of early childhood education (Mitchell, Wylie, & Carr, 2008) found that "facilitating conditions" at levels of early childhood setting, management, government policy and societal conditions were interrelated and influential. This chapter considers each of these levels.

2 What Conditions Supported Democratic Practices?

In the Aotearoa New Zealand context, the foundation in enabling all parties within the ECEC setting to develop and sustain democratic values and practices is the early childhood curriculum, *Te Whāriki* (Ministry of Education, 1996). Values within *Te Whāriki* have stood the test of time. In the 2017 update (Ministry of Education, 2017), the aspiration statement for children; the principles of empowerment, holistic development, family and community and responsive and reciprocal relationships; and the goals that are each based on domains of mana (being strong) were all retained. The value base in biculturalism appears to have been strengthened and greater attention placed on transition to school and continuity across ECEC and school curricula.

Te Whāriki sets a framing for co-construction of democratic learning communities. Encapsulated in the metaphor of a "whāriki" (weaving), this framework "provides a basis for each setting to weave a local curriculum that reflects its own distinctive character and values" (Ministry of Education, 2017, p. 9). Examples from Aotearoa New Zealand settings (Chapter "Influencing Policy Change Through Collective Action") of curriculum weaving with local participants, including children and families and iwi (tribe), have illustrated that co-production of the curriculum democratises education by enabling participants to create the world in which they live. There is a shared responsibility. Children are encouraged to be "socially responsible, critically engaged citizens in a democratic society" (Giroux, 1992,

p. 11). This is democracy as "a way of personal life controlled not merely by faith in human nature in general but by faith in the capacity of human beings for intelligent judgment and action if proper conditions are furnished." (Dewey, 1976, p. 227).

Documenting pedagogy through narrative assessment is a process commonly used in Aotearoa New Zealand in assessment, planning and evaluation that lends itself to supporting and sustaining democratic practices. Assessment approaches founded on democratic values respond to the locally constructed curriculum, emphasise valued and socially just outcomes and afford opportunity for participation by children, families and practitioners. The assessment documentation is the subject of critical reflection and interpretation, undertaken alone and with others.

The examples in Aotearoa New Zealand where teachers worked in partnership with academic researchers (Chapter "Policy Frameworks and Democratic Participation") to research their own practice illustrate how such processes, through critical analysis and inclusion of perspectives of others, supported the construction of democratic practices. This is difficult pedagogical work. In a systematic literature review of characteristics of effective professional development, Mitchell and Cubey (2003) found the most valuable professional development involved participants in investigating pedagogy within their own ECEC settings, gathering and analysing data using a range of tools and with the engagement of a researcher or professional development facilitator. In particular, these processes had positive effects when practitioners gained insights that challenged taken-for-granted assumptions and practices. Through these processes, participants can become aware of ways in which they disempower or limit people. Participants in the ECEC settings exemplified in chapter "Policy Frameworks and Democratic Participation" collaborated with researchers, families, children and communities. Tools for analysis included video recordings, focus group discussions, family interviews, children's drawings and pedagogical documentation. Two ECEC settings, a full immersion Samoan setting and an English-medium setting, formed a "sister" relationship, exposing the teachers and researchers to both Samoan and Western world views. This interchange enabled them to engage in cross-cultural analysis of data concerning children's working theories about identity, language and culture. In another ECEC setting, theoretical ideas were introduced and discussed between teachers and researchers.

These examples of teachers being supported in their pedagogical work illustrate in action the characteristics of competent systems discussed in the CoRe project report (Urban, Vandenbroeck, Lazzari, et al., 2012, p. 27).

> Although the term 'competence' may often be associated with qualities of an individual, in fact the quality of the workforce is determined by the interaction between competent individuals in what we refer to as a 'competent system'. Among the more salient aspects of systemic conditions that allow for competence systems to flourish are good working conditions that reduce turnover of staff and continuous pedagogical support, aiming at documenting practice, critically reflecting upon it, and co-constructing pedagogy as an alternation between theory and practice. This requires time, team collaboration and continuous pedagogical support.

Oberhuemer (2005), writing of professionalism in Europe and beyond, suggested that "the concept of 'democratic professionalism' may help us to situate the role of early childhood pedagogues within ever changing societal, economic and knowledge contexts" (pp. 6–7). She explained that "Democratic professionalism is a concept based on participatory relationships and alliances. It foregrounds collaborative, cooperative action between professional colleagues and other stakeholders. It emphasises engaging and networking with the local community" (p. 13).

While Oberhuemer was writing of professionals within their local education setting, a similar analysis can be applied to collective organisations. The early childhood teachers' union in Aotearoa New Zealand, NZEI Te Riu Roa, describes itself as the professional and industrial voice of educators, "the collective voice of the profession" (NZEI Te Riu Roa, 2017). The union examples of the campaigns for pay parity and for a strategic plan for early childhood education in Aotearoa New Zealand (Chapter "Influencing Policy Change Through Collective Action") exemplify participatory processes and alliances operating collectively at local, regional and national levels. In each of these examples, policy goals and actions to achieve these were negotiated with the participating parties.

This strong union organisation representing kindergarten teachers formed alliances with organisations that may seem to be unlikely partners in the campaign for pay parity: the national employers' organisation and representatives of the regional kindergarten associations that employed kindergarten teachers. This alliance was made possible by a united union and employer belief in the fairness of the case for pay parity and of the need for state commitment to funding pay increases. By contrast, a low level of collective organisation of teachers in the education and care sector, combined with fractured and privatised employer groups, who held competing and contrary agendas, made a campaign for pay parity in this sector much more difficult and only partially successful.

The union-initiated establishment of the Early Childhood Education Group that developed *Future Directions*, which was then influential in shaping the early childhood long-term strategic plan policy development, further exemplified the value of building alliances and use of participatory decision-making processes, this time across a range of national early childhood organisations. I have argued that the involvement of different influential players enabled widespread dissemination and solutions that were both useful and innovative.

Competent systems, with Croatia as an example, were described in the CoRe project research report (Urban, Lazzari, Vandenbroeck, Peeters, & Van Laere, 2011) as going beyond government, management and individuals.

Educational quality is not conceived to be determined by the individual interventions of practitioners, but rather as being determined by the entire context of the institution, of which practitioners are an integral part and which practitioners can change according to their degree of understanding. (p. 21).

In the Aotearoa New Zealand examples, practitioner understandings and analysis of the policy context were deepened through union support. Opportunities were opened for practitioners, with other stakeholders, to gain, co-produce and discuss relevant information, enabling them to analyse the institutional conditions for their work and for the lives of families, and act collectively towards aims that were transformative and in the interests of the public good. Helen Kelly, who was employed in NZEI Te Riu Roa (the union) and played a crucial role during the campaigns described in this book, went on to become National President of the New Zealand Council of Trade Unions. She argued that unions are public institutions that are essential to functioning democratic societies. The International Labour Organisation (ILO) holds that "Sound industrial relations and effective social dialogue are a means to promote better wages and working conditions as well as peace and social justice" (International Labour Organisation, 2017). Competent and democratic systems will be strengthened through recognition and inclusion of unions as collective and democratic institutions representing those working in education settings.

Findings from the locality-based evaluation of New Zealand's strategic plan for early childhood education (Mitchell, Meagher Lundberg, Mara, Cubey, & Whitford, 2011), discussed in chapter "Policy Frameworks and Democratic Participation", show the value of a set of policy measures to provide support for a qualified and professionally supported ECEC workforce. These supports were integrated; a conclusion is that it was through their combined impact that practitioner competencies were strengthened. The measures were (1) targets and incentives to incrementally increase the qualification levels of teachers so that by the year 2012, all teachers in teacher-led services were required to be ECEC-qualified and ECEC-registered teachers. Registration is a system intended to ensure the currency of teachers as competent practitioners. The end goal did not eventuate as the targets and incentives were removed or altered with a change in government in 2009, but good progress was made along the way; (2) publication of a range of professional resources linked to the curriculum, made available to all ECEC settings, and accompanied by funded professional development and (3) opportunities for teachers in designated ECEC settings to work with academic researchers to research their innovative practice and disseminate findings over a 3-year period. These measures were powerful supports for the competencies suggested by the CoRe project as being needed at an individual practitioner level. Reflective competences were supported by tools for self-review, tools for data gathering and opportunities for professional development and researcher-practitioner partnerships.

A literature review for the CoRe project (Urban et al., 2011, p. 22) summarised conclusions from the Council of the European Union:

> The Council conclusions of 26 November 2009, on the professional development of teachers and school leaders, strongly emphasise that initial teacher education, early career support and continuous professional education should be treated as a coherent whole. Continuing professional development programmes need to be of high quality, relevant to needs and based on a wellbalanced combination of academic research and extensive practical experience. Newly qualified and more experienced teachers are continuously encouraged to reflect on their work individually and collectively.

Aotearoa New Zealand's experiences show that at the time of the strategic plan, such coherence was starting to be achieved within the integrated policy framing focused on qualifications and professional development. However, a serious flaw found in the evaluation (Mitchell et al. 2011) was the uneven and inequitable take-up by practitioners of the opportunities and resources that were available. In some private for-profit full-day education and care centres that were also rated as low overall quality in each year of the evaluation, the professional resources were not immediately accessible for teachers' use, teacher qualification levels were at the regulated minimum and teachers did not participate in professional development because their employer did not allow them to do so. This finding brings home the message that management plays a crucial role in affording professional development opportunities and providing conducive working conditions.

Both the pay parity campaign example and the experience of uneven take-up of teacher education and professional development opportunities highlight inequities. These are occurring in the largely privatised education and care sector (centre-based and home-based) in Aotearoa New Zealand and are linked to the freedom of employers to determine teacher working conditions within a framework of minimal regulations. The motivation in private centres for business owners to make a profit for themselves and for absent shareholders in the case of publicly listed companies is certainly a reason why spending on staff is kept low.

3   What Conditions Supported Universal Access?

In keeping with democratic principles, sector groups and individuals have argued (May, 2008; May & Mitchell, 2009; Mitchell, 2006) that every child in Aotearoa New Zealand should be entitled to free ECEC within their local community, of a nature that suits their family needs and aspirations, recognises their cultural heritage and the bicultural basis of Aotearoa New Zealand society, and that realises the aspirations, principles and goals of the curriculum *Te Whāriki* (Ministry of Education, 1996, 2017).

The principle of every child having an entitlement to free ECEC has not been realised in Aotearoa New Zealand's ECEC policy. One of the initiatives of the strategic plan for ECEC was the development of a new funding formula linked loosely to costs and the provision of funding for "20 hours free ECE" for 3- and 4-year-olds. The "20 hours free ECE" significantly improved the affordability of ECEC and reduced a main barrier to participation of cost to families. Although the intentions of the policy were to make ECEC free or almost free, some mainly private providers "got around the policy" by requiring families to enrol for more than the 20 hours and requiring fees for extra time. Other provider policies were to charge rather exorbitant amounts if parents were late in collecting their child (Mitchell et al., 2011). In addition, providers could ask for "voluntary donations". These loop holes could very easily be closed through government regulation as a condition for receipt of funding.

Aotearoa New Zealand's diverse ECEC services have arisen from a mix of community groups who are responding to needs in their community and private providers, many of whom see provision of ECEC as a business opportunity. One needs only to read the real estate pages of national and local newspapers to see property investment in the "childcare sector" portrayed as highly profitable, as the following typical advertisement by real estate firm Bayleys conveys. Headed *Childcare investment returns $243,100 a year,* the agency states:

> The childcare sector in Auckland is experiencing record growth, and properties occupied by childcare businesses are proving popular with investors. Public funding for the sector is reliable and secure, rising from $860 million in 2008 to almost $1 billion now.. .. [Bayleys Sales agent] Ms. Weng says early childhood education (ECE) is an in-demand sector for commercial property investors. "It is viewed as more secure than other asset classes, because of not only the strength of the leases involved but also New Zealand's high child-care participation rate," she says. (Bayleys Real Estate, 2018).

Aotearoa New Zealand has never had a coherent system for planning community-based or public provision in local communities. Following a rigid adherence to free market principles, all recent New Zealand governments have been unwilling to make comprehensive plans for ECEC provision or provide ECEC directly. The underlying thinking is that a competitive market will stimulate businesses and communities to establish ECE services that meet community needs and that parents will "vote with their feet" if services are low quality or not meeting needs. This has not happened, and many ECEC sector groups have complained that a competitive market has led to duplication of ECEC, with consequent oversupply in some areas and services becoming unsustainable so that some have to close and undersupply in others (Early Childhood Education Project, 1996; May & Mitchell, 2009).

A reliance on the market approach to provision without necessity for planning continued the inequitable distribution of services throughout Aotearoa New Zealand. Despite progress in regard to affordability, children from low-income communities are more likely to miss out on attending early childhood education (Mitchell & Davison, 2010). Aotearoa New Zealand's for-profit sector is a thorn in the side, an Achilles heel, in policy that on the one hand asserts principles of the benefits and rights for children and families to access quality early childhood services but then largely allows the market to determine where and how early childhood is provided and at what cost to parents.

Aotearoa New Zealand has much to learn from other countries where city councils and municipalities take responsibility for planning and ensuring provision of ECEC that is affordable and where ECEC is an entitlement. Vandenbroeck and Lazzari (2014, p. 327) in their review of literature and practice reports conclude that "Public policies that address issues of availability, entitlement and childcare costs – within a general regulatory framework for quality – are the most effective in reducing inequalities in enrolment". In Canada, which like Aotearoa New Zealand has a mixed childcare market, the City of Toronto has contracted economist Gordon Cleveland and his team to construct a childcare demand and affordability model for its city (Cleveland, Krashinsky, Colley & Avery-Nunez, 2016).

4 What Changes Are Needed in Aotearoa New Zealand's System of ECEC?

4.1 Individual Practitioner Level

There is much evidence highlighting that structural features of qualifications, ratios of adults to children, group size, ongoing professional development and pay and working conditions provide facilitating conditions for how practitioners carry out their role. Through the policy developments in Aotearoa New Zealand's strategic plan for early childhood education, levels of practitioner qualification were raised at the same time as professional resources and professional development linked to the national curriculum were provided. Of crucial value were opportunities for researcher and practitioner partnerships that enabled a deeply critical and reflective analysis of pedagogical practice over a 3-year time period. In combination, uptake of opportunity offered by these policy developments contributed to enhancing teachers' understanding of the curriculum, assessment, planning and self-review practices and higher ratings of quality. A sensible change in Aotearoa New Zealand's system would be to return to these policies which have shown highly promising results and this time ensure that all practitioners can access the opportunities they provide within a conducive working environment. This would seem to be a condition for teachers to practice as "intellectuals" in the sense Giroux (1988) has described. Furthermore, it is consistent with ideas for a competent system at individual practitioner level within the CoRe framework:

> At the level of the individual practitioner, being and becoming 'competent' is a continuous process that comprises the capability and ability to build on a body of professional knowledge and practice and develop professional values. Although the 'knowledge' and 'practice' are critical, practitioners and teams also need reflective competences as they work in highly complex, unpredictable and diverse contexts. A competent system requires possibilities for all staff to engage in joint learning and critical reflection. This includes sufficient paid time for these activities. (Urban, Vandenbroeck, Lazzari, et al., 2012, p. 512).

The issue of pay parity and reasonable working conditions for all teachers in ECEC needs to be addressed. Within a system where private sector employers have profit-making agendas and are responsible for direct negotiation of employment agreements with employees, this is not at all likely to happen, as experience shows. A radical shift in state responsibility for the whole of the ECEC teaching workforce to parallel their role in regard to kindergarten teachers' employment negotiations, where the Secretary of Education is a party to the employment agreement, would take the issue of pay parity and appropriate working conditions forward.

4.2 Management Level

Urban et al. argue that "A *competent system* includes collaborations between individuals and teams, and institutions (pre-schools, schools, support services for children and families), and *competent* governance at policy level" (Urban et al., 2011, pp. 515–516). A democratic system of education will ensure that ECEC services are treated as public services, where true to the curriculum ideals, management supports community, families, practitioners and children to participate in decision-making. Democracy in education raises possibilities for debating and generating new thinking and understandings about the purpose of education, children and childhood and the roles and responsibilities of the state, community and participants in early childhood services. In a for-profit system of education, business owners can and do make decisions without any reference to others.

4.3 Policy Level

4.3.1 Funding Systems

There has been a significant growth in the proportion of private education and care and home-based ECEC services in Aotearoa New Zealand which now far outnumber community-based ECEC services of these types. The New Zealand Education Act 1989 Section 311 (5) (b) specifies that government funding for ECE (the ECE Funding Subsidy) "May be paid to be used for any purpose the service provider considers appropriate, or for only such purposes as the Minister specifies in writing when the grant is paid or earlier". Currently the government places few conditions on the receipt of funding, and there is no cap on fees charged to ensure ECEC is affordable. It is astonishing that the Aotearoa New Zealand government generously funds for-profit ECEC centres, with no direct accountability for how owners spend the funding. Moreover, private business owners are eligible for Targeted Assistance for Participation grants that are used for upgrading facilities or building new facilities, making Aotearoa New Zealand infamous for providing taxpayer funding for privately owned capital assets.

Private services in Aotearoa New Zealand include sole traders, companies, partnerships, private trusts and state-owned enterprises. Community-based services include incorporated societies, charitable trusts, statutory trusts, community trusts, government departments, health boards, city councils and public education institutions. While both private and community-based services may charge fees, a crucial difference is that private services are able to make financial gains and distribute these to their members. Profits and assets for private services can go into the pockets of individual owners or groups of owners if the service stops operating or changes ownership; community assets remain with the community. Financial reporting to the Ministry of Education is weaker for the for-profit private sector. Community-based services are required to provide a full general purpose financial report, including a statement of financial performance (profit and loss account) and balance sheet, while private centres are required to provide only a special purpose financial report detailing accounting policies, amounts received from the Ministry of Education and how these are spent. The profits made by private owners through, for example, fee charging and rentals for privately owned buildings escape consideration.

4.3.2   Provision

In Aotearoa New Zealand, the market approach to provision and burgeoning dominance of corporate private education and care and home-based ECEC services has been actively encouraged through funding policies. The result is a radically unequal patchwork of provision and cost structures that largely favour those with the social and cultural capital of the dominant class. These developments are highly problematic. Earlier research has shown quality differentials between privately owned and community-based ECE services favouring the community sector (Mitchell, 2002; Mitchell & Brooking, 2007) and that private centres are more likely to be in high-income areas where fees could be charged. The 2006 OECD study of 20 countries (OECD, 2006) suggested that a reliance on privatised provision of early childhood education will almost certainly lead to inequities in provision in poorer communities because commercial providers are reluctant to invest in such communities.

One question is whether privately owned ECEC settings can also be involved in pursuing democratic ideals. In Aotearoa New Zealand, there seem to be two distinct types of privately owned ECEC settings. On the one hand, a centre or group of centres has been set up by a private individual/s intent on offering "quality" ECEC and with an understanding of how that might be achieved. Owners may be qualified teachers wanting to provide a community service. Any "profits" go back into the centre operation. At another extreme are for-profit ECEC centres and home-based ECEC services that are run as corporate chains. An extreme example of this is Evolve, a corporate company that is publicly listed on the share market and that portrays ECEC as an economic investment with good returns to shareholders. The corporate world constructs early childhood services as places of commercial exchange, where the first duty of directors is to shareholders, who expect a financial return on their investment, and where parents are positioned as consumers purchasing a product. With a focus on business and profit, corporate childcare will necessarily limit the potential for "what an early childhood service might be". The private profit motive is directly oppositional to and incompatible with altruistic aims of generating and fully supporting aspirational goals for the common good that are hallmarks of a democratic institution.

5   A Way Forward

The stories of ECEC policy and the struggles of advocates in Aoteroa New Zealand have been stories of success and accomplishment and stories of setback and reversals. Helen May (2017, p.14) calls the last 30 years "a roller coaster of curtailment and gain" that can be linked to the political priorities of the two main parties in Aotearoa New Zealand: a left-leaning Labour government and a right-leaning National government. An enduring influence throughout has been collective advocacy by the mainly women unionists, academics, teachers, families and others who care deeply about children and early childhood education and care. Insiders within government circles have sometimes had political influence too.

The election of a left Labour-led government 2017–2020 offers exciting promise for affirming a vision and action for children as citizens and a democratic system of early childhood education and care. Jacinda Ardern as Prime Minister, the world's youngest female leader, has captivated hearts and minds worldwide as a radical liberal leader who can do what she sets her mind to. The Labour Party election slogan "Let's do this" set this tone. The first 100 days of action by the new government prioritised lifting children from poverty, pledged to address pay equity "because it's time to do better by all women" (LabourVoices, 2018, webpage), raised the minimum wage, extended paid parental leave to 26 weeks, promised housing reform and environmental safeguards and promised a tax working group with a fairer taxation system – these measures are a radical departure from the previous government policies. They signal a strong platform for social democratic government.

In conclusion, I argue for six policy areas that are required for the New Zealand government attention to shift to a public and democratic system of ECEC. Already in some of these areas, the Labour-led government has pledged to take action.

5.1   To Improve the Social Context of Childhood

In combination, Aotearoa New Zealand's newly announced government policies convey a depth of understanding of key health, social and economic contexts that affect children in Aotearoa New Zealand and set immediate priorities for improving them. They are a sound base for the development of ECEC policies. John Bennett, writing of the OECD's *Starting Strong* policy reviews in 20 countries summarised findings about contextual factors.

> As in the first report, the second evaluation report *Starting Strong 11* (OECD, 2006), also outlines some of the contextual factors influencing ECEC policy, in particular, the growing need to safeguard equality of opportunity for women when organising ECEC services and to conceive of these services as instruments of social justice and cohesion. (Bennett, 2006, p. 143).

The OECD study proposes the reduction of child and family poverty as essential for social equity and a necessary precondition for early childhood and public education systems. While ECEC can do much to alleviate disadvantage, "a continuing high level of child and family poverty in a country undermines these efforts and greatly impedes the task of raising health and educational levels" (p. 143). The *Child Poverty Reduction Bill* introduced on 31 January 2018 by the Labour-led government in Aotearoa New Zealand proposes to set targets to reduce child poverty and require governments to report on these. The measures of poverty focus on low incomes, both before and after housing costs, material hardship according to the European Union's standard and a persistence measure for either low income, material hardship or both. The extension of paid parental leave, although still not long enough compared with many countries (the OECD study recommends 12 months), further supports parents in the child's first year. Forward thinking, too, is the commitment to pay equity, which holds promise for all teachers in the ECEC sector to at last receive pay parity, and for the many women who use ECEC services while in paid employment themselves to be paid equitably.

5.2   To Develop a Democratic Vision for Children and the Aims of ECEC

Despite the promise of radical improvements to the context of childhood and measures to address some of the major ECEC cutbacks of the last decade, the "vision for ECEC" that the Minister of Education, Chris Hipkins, wants to create with the sector, as set out in his cabinet paper (Hipkins, 2018), is disappointingly limited to children's early learning and to settings to support early learning outcomes. After a bold statement in the cabinet paper of "Returning to the principle of free public education that is available to all New Zealanders throughout their lives", the statements in relation to ECEC policy are cautious, alluding only to examining "the nature of the education market along with the network which underpins it and the role of government in managing provision". What this book has illustrated is that the aim for a democratic and public education system cannot be realised in Aotearoa New Zealand's market-dominated ECEC culture, where motivations of for-profit providers to make a financial gain for business partners and even shareholders compete with altruistic aims to invest fully in the ECEC service. For-profit ECEC centres are not able to operate as a community facility, there is not opportunity for participants to take responsibility for their shape and direction and "they are situated in the economic sphere; they cannot also be forums within civic society" (Dahlberg, Moss, & Pence, 1999, pp. 74–75). Affirming a democratic system of ECEC will require a radical shift in policy thinking about the role of government in respect to provision of public and community ECEC services that empower children, families and communities, which are locally accessible to all families and where the ECEC workforce is professionally supported and well remunerated. It is not a matter only of trying to make existing provision more democratic, where institutional thinking may create a barrier to what might possibly be. It is primarily a matter of creating ideas about what ECEC might possibly look like in a democratic society and the structures needed to support that.

A first outstanding task is to create a vision for children and childhood and for the primary aim of ECEC. As in many of the advances made in early childhood policy in Aotearoa New Zealand (May, 2009), early childhood activists have united to start to chart possible ways forward. The *Quality Public Early Childhood Education* project (May & Mitchell, 2009), undertaken by a coalition of community-based services, has developed a vision and proposals to counterbalance the market approach and strengthen community-based provision in Aotearoa New Zealand. Its vision is that:

1. Every child has a right as a citizen to participate in free early childhood education.
2. Every child that wishes to can access high-quality, community-based early childhood education.

The tenets of community-based provision align with principles of democracy – emphasis placed on collectivity, partnership and participation in decision-making and the idea of educational institutions as a community forum and asset:

1. The service is seen as a community asset and the children, parents, families and community benefit from it.
2. Collectivity, partnership and participation are hallmarks of decision-making.
3. The full funding from government resources goes into educating the child and supporting their family (May & Mitchell, 2009, p. 4).

The vision sets out important principles; yet a more eloquent and encompassing statement needs to be crafted about the aims of ECEC that captures the hearts and minds of New Zealanders, much as Prime Minister Peter Fraser's statement, penned by Cecil Beeby, did in 1935. His statement puts children at the heart of government aims. Helen May's rewriting of the Beeby statement for today encapsulates a vision in contemporary society:

> The Government's objective, should broadly speaking be, that every child: whatever their family circumstances, whether their parents are solo, separated, married or defacto, at work or at home, whether they be rich or poor, whether they live in town or country, are Māori or Pākehā, should have a right as a citizen to a free early childhood education that meets their family needs, recognizes their cultural heritage and provides a rich learning environment in a community of learning that empowers both adults and children to learn and grow as equal participants in a democratic society. (May & Mitchell, 2009).

In Aotearoa New Zealand, principles for children and the aims of ECEC need to be founded in Te Tiriti o Waitangi. A vision for ECEC could be developed through a wider debate within the proposed strategic plan working group and ECEC sector and crafted by an exceptional writer who works with the Prime Minister outside the limitations of officialdom.

5.3 To Retain Te Whāriki and Sociocultural Assessment Approaches

The Aotearoa New Zealand curriculum, *Te Whāriki*, and sociocultural narrative assessment approaches have been adopted wholeheartedly by many practitioners who have taken on board the spirit of creating their own curriculum whāriki (weaving) with their children, families and communities from a basis of empowerment and responsive and reciprocal relationships. There is pride and belief in the value of the curriculum aspiration statement, principles and strands. The examples of curriculum in action and associated sociocultural assessment approaches highlight that the curriculum is open to contribution from all players and implicitly linked to democratic principles through its emphasis on whakamana – empowerment in its principles and strands. The retention of *Te Whāriki* is assured in the 2017 update.

The announcement that *Te Whāriki* can be used as the curriculum in the first 2 years of school tilts on its head the fear of "schoolification" that could impose more narrow learning achievement standards onto ECEC services. Potentially instead, Aotearoa New Zealand's early childhood curriculum can now more directly influence pedagogy in schools. Additionally, the dismissal of the assessment and reporting required by schools against National Standards in literacy and numeracy allays some fears of a testing regime being imposed in ECEC with subsequent distortion of a holistic curriculum and detrimental labelling of children. Internationally, many academics (e.g., Moss et al., 2016; Carr, Mitchell & Rameka, 2016) have been highly critical of the OECD's *International Early Learning and Child Well-being Study* (OECD, 2017) for its assumptions, practices and potential negative effects. In Aotearoa New Zealand, such a standardised approach would compromise valuable and democratic sociocultural assessment practices; it is immensely satisfying that the policies of Aotearoa New Zealand's Labour-led government would not support this testing approach.

Already this government is pledging to address some of the ECEC cutbacks that were a legacy of the previous government's term – to reinstate a goal of 100% qualified teachers in ECEC, to return funding levels to those that were available before the cuts of the past and to develop a second strategic plan for ECEC through a consultative working group.

5.4 To Shift from a Market Approach to a "Partnership Model" of ECEC Provision

The *Quality Public Early Childhood Education* project report proposed shifting from a market approach to what it termed "a partnership model" where ECEC services work with the government and community to build a coherent network of provision in every community. Planning provision within communities, from the basis of a shared vision based on democratic ideals, and attention to "competent systems" would be productive of a new way of thinking and an inspiration for positive change. Aotearoa New Zealand has much to learn from other countries and states where ECEC provision is mapped and needs are forecasted as a basis for planning provision; see, for example, the demand and affordability study in Toronto (Cleveland et al. 2016), planning for integrated ECEC Sure Start Children's Centres in UK communities and Sweden where all children 1–12 years have a legislated right to preschool education and most preschool provision is provided directly by municipalities in daycare centres (OECD, 2006). Forecasting and planning could be done by the New Zealand government, in collaboration with iwi (tribes), councils and relevant community organisations to ensure a coherent patchwork of community-based and public ECEC provision is established that is locally accessible and appropriate for all families.

As a model for ECEC, integrated and community-based ECE services need to be prioritised and funded to undertake wider roles of participating, enabling families to access family services and being part of social networks. Bennett (2006), writing about conclusions from the OECD *Starting Strong* study of ECEC in 20 countries, states:

> Community involvement in the pre-school is growing in importance, not only for providing expanded services and referrals where necessary, but also as a space for partnership and the democratic participation of parents. When opportune, communities and education authorities will also provide adult education, information, services and social activities for parents, if possible from the early childhood centre. (p.151).

The model of early childhood education as a "hub", in which early childhood education is provided alongside integrated access to interdisciplinary teams and services has been shown to be highly successful internationally and in Aotearoa New Zealand. Integrated early childhood services are able to offer wide opportunities for family support and possibilities for family and community participation. Integrated services are in keeping with *Te Whāriki* which looks beyond the immediate setting to the wider context of family, culture and society, particularly, in its four principles' emphasis: empowerment, whakamana; holistic development, kotahitanga; relationships, ngā hononga; and family and community, whānau tangata.

Highly problematic is the burgeoning growth in private business owners and companies setting up education and care and home-based services in Aotearoa New Zealand and receiving full government subsidies, and even funding for capital works, on the same basis as community-based services. In this book, I have argued that private businesses that operate for financial gain for business owners and shareholders are incongruent with ideals of ECEC as a public and community asset. Particularly unethical are the ECEC businesses that are listed on the share market, where making profits for absent shareholders is clearly at odds with investing fully in the service itself. There is no place in a democratic ECEC system for public funding to be used for the benefit of shareholders.

It will be challenging to move from a privatised education and care and home-based sector where over 70% of these services are privately owned to a public or community sector. The private sector constitutes a strong lobby group that has resisted policy initiatives to curtail its freedom in staff employment matters and business operation; a broad base of support is needed for such a policy, and a government that does not waver in the face of opposition. As a first step, the government could begin to privilege the public and community sector through its funding policies and in planning new services. Eligibility for capital works funding for for-profit ECEC centres needs to stop. Until 2009, private centres were not eligible for capital works funding – and a return to this policy would restore some balance.

As interim measures, the government could look to arrangements in Aotearoa New Zealand's school sector, where some private schools are integrated into the state system. Teachers in these schools are paid by the government on a nationally negotiated employment agreement and receive some government funding, but building and property maintenance, which are in private ownership, have limited funding, if any. Controls on fee charging and enrolment policies and refusal to fund publicly listed companies would curb potential for private profit and help weed out the worst profiteers as ECEC providers. There needs to be full financial accountability to the ECEC constituency for all monies received from all sources. Democratic participation in decision-making should also apply.

5.5   To Provide Free ECEC as an Entitlement for all Children

The policy for free ECEC for 3- and 4-year-olds in Aotearoa New Zealand implemented in 2007 has not lived up to its initial promise. Characterised in 2007 as offering "20 hours free ECE" for 3- and 4-year-olds, the ability for managers to make optional charges which then become binding on families and to write enrolment policies that require families to "buy" additional hours ECEC regardless of their needs has subverted intentions for ECEC to be free. The National government dropped the word "free" from its policy writing. Moreover, not all ECEC centres have opted into the "20 hours free ECE" scheme, and some families are not able to access ECEC in their community because of waiting lists or that suitable ECEC provision is not available for them. Consistent with UNCROC principles, high-quality early childhood education needs to be an entitlement for all children. This will require provision to be planned so it is accessible and available for every family who wants their child to attend and for this to be genuinely free. As in some OECD countries, the entitlement to a place could start from the date that parental leave ends. As Bennett (2006, p. 144) writes: "To link the end of parental leave to an entitled place in a publicly supported early childhood service seems to be a critical element in parental leave policy that adds considerably to the wellbeing of families and infants."

5.6   To Improve the Qualifications, Professional Support and Remuneration of All Staff

The ECEC workforce needs to be well qualified and professionally supported to enact Aotearoa New Zealand's curriculum *Te Whāriki* and congruent assessment approaches and work responsively with families. Staff qualifications have been found in many international studies to be closely linked to quality outcomes for children. Qualified staff are likely to use their knowledge of children and pedagogy to offer the kinds of cognitively challenging interactions that are associated with gains for children. Ratios are also crucial in enabling more interactions between adults and children. The Labour-led government in Aotearoa New Zealand is far-sighted in its policy to reinstate the target for 100% qualified teachers that was dropped in 2009 and to review ratios and group size for younger children. Other staffing aspects in need of policy development are around offering sound professional development opportunities for all teachers and addressing the inequitable pay and working conditions of many teachers in education and care centres.

Research highlighted in this book has shown the value of past initiatives where practitioners, working with academic researchers, have researched teaching and learning in their own settings in cycles of action research. This model of research and development supported teachers as critical thinkers and democratic practice. Through research and critique, teachers gained new understandings of their own practice and made changes to it. The willingness by practitioners to critically analyse, develop and make public their practice is an outstanding legacy of the policy approach in the years 2002–2009 to provide integrated support for extending professional capabilities. Oberhuemer (2005) describes "democratic professionalism" as involving four levels: interacting with children, centre management and leadership, partnerships with parents and the professional knowledge base. She regards perhaps the most challenging aspect of democratic professionalism to be

> ... an awareness of 'multiple ways of knowing', an understanding that knowledge is in fact contestable. It requires a willingness and ability to reflect on one's own taken for granted beliefs. It implicates the professional skill to sensitively discuss pedagogical and ethical viewpoints against a background of increasing cultural, social and economic diversity, to recognise and examine both personal and publicly endorsed assumptions. (p. 14).

Within the strategic plan development, policy commitment to supporting democratic professionalism across the entire early childhood workforce and leadership structures through education and professional development opportunities needs to be a priority.

Crucially, resolution needs to be made of the employment divides that exist between the pay and conditions of teachers in kindergartens and schools and of teachers in education and care centres. Pay parity for equivalent qualifications, responsibilities and experience needs to be negotiated across the education sector. History indicates this will not happen in the education and care sector under permissive employment legislation when individual business owners are responsible for employment negotiations. Legislation for all teachers to come into the state sector, a national collective employment agreement negotiated by the government with the teachers' union, and government payment of teacher salaries would achieve pay parity. These measures would uphold the international right that "Everyone, without any discrimination, has the right to equal pay for work of equal value", which was enshrined in international human rights instruments as long ago as the 1948 Universal Declaration of Human Rights (United Nations, 1948, Sect. 23). This is the founding document for subsequent human rights treaties and is a responsibility of the state.

6 Conclusion

Aotearoa New Zealand practitioners, early childhood organisations and academics have kept democratic ideals to the forefront of their work through collective advocacy that has promoted policy developments at a national level. Reclaiming a rights-based approach and asserting democratic values is a way towards radical alternatives in Aotearoa New Zealand's ECEC provision. My hope is that within the new thinking and values of Aotearoa New Zealand's Labour-led government, united advocacy will transcend the limitations of new right ideology and take the ECEC sector on a pathway to a democratic and public ECEC system.

References

Apple, M. (2005). Education, markets, and an audit culture. *Critical Quarterly, 47*(1–2), 11–29.
Bayleys Real Estate. (2018, 26 March). *Childcare investment returns $243,100 a year.* Bayleys News and articles. Retrieved from https://www.bayleys.co.nz/news/commercial/childcare-investment-returns-243100-a-year
Bennett, J. (2006). New policy conclusions from starting strong 11. An update on the OECD early childhood policy reviews. *European Early Childhood Education Research Journal, 14*(2), 141–156.
Carr, M., Mitchell, L., & Rameka, L. (2016). Some thoughts about the value of an OECD international assessment framework for early childhood services in Aotearoa New Zealand. *Contemporary Issues in Early Childhood, 17*(4), 450–454.
Carr, W., & Hartnett, A. (1996). *Education and the struggle for democracy.* Buckingham, UK/Bristol: Open University Press.
Cleveland, G., Krashinsky, M., Colley, S., & Avery-Nunez, C. (2016). *City of Toronto: Licensed childcare demand and affordability study.* Retrieved from https://www.toronto.ca/wp-content/uploads/2017/12/8d0a-Community-Services-and-Facilities-Toronto-Demand-Affordability-Study-2016.pdf
Dahlberg, G., Moss, P., & Pence, A. (1999). *Beyond quality in early childhood education and care. Post modern perspectives* (1st ed.). London: Falmer Press.
Dewey, J. (1916/1944). *Democracy and education.* New York: The Free Press, Macmillan Publishing.
Dewey, J. (1939). *Creative democracy. The task before us.* Retrieved January 6, 2016 http://www.beloit.edu/~pbk/dewey.html

Dewey, J. (1976). Creative democracy: The task before us. In J. Boydston (Ed.), *John Dewey: The later works, 1925–1953* (Vol. 14, pp. 224–230). Carbondale: Southern Illinois University Press (Original work published 1939).

Early Childhood Education Project. (1996). *Future directions: Early childhood education in New Zealand*. Wellington, New Zealand: Educational Institute Te Riu Roa.

Giroux, H. (1988). *Teachers as intellectuals: Towards a critical pedagogy of learning*. South Hadey, MA: Bergin & Garvey.

Giroux, H. (1992). *Border crossings. Cultural workers and the politics of education*. London: Routledge.

Hipkins, C. (2018). *Education portfolio workplan: Purpose, objectives and overview*. Wellington, New Zealand. Retrieved from http://www.education.govt.nz/assets/Documents/Ministry/Information-releases/R-Education-Portfolio-Work-Programme-Purpose-Objectives-and-Overview.pdf

International Labour Organisation. (2017). *Tripartism and social dialogue*. Retrieved November 10, 2017, from http://www.ilo.org/global/topics/workers-and-employers-organizations-tripartism-and-social-dialogue/lang%2D%2Den/index.htm

Kemmis, S., & Edwards-Groves, C. (2018). Understanding education. In *History, politics and practice*. Singapore, Singapore: Springer.

LabourVoices. (2018). *100 days: Here's what we've done*. Retrieved from http://www.labour.org.nz/100_days

Marshall, T. H. (1950). *Citzenship and social class and other essays*. Cambridge, UK: The Syndics of the Cambridge University Press.

May, H. (2008). Towards the right of New Zealand children for free early childhood education. *International Journal of Child care and Education Policy, 2*(1), 77–91.

May, H. (2009) *Politics in the playground. The world of early childhood education in New Zealand* (2nd ed.). Dunedin, New Zealand: Otago University Press.

May, H. (2017). Documenting early childhood policy in Aotearoa New Zealand: Political stories – personal journeys. In L. Miller, C. Cameron, C. Dalli, & N. Barbour (Eds.), *Sage handbook of early childhood policy* (pp. 151–164). London: Sage.

May, H., & Mitchell, L. (2009). *Strengthening community-based early childhood education in Aotearoa New Zealand*. Wellington, New Zealand: NZEI Te Riu Roa.

Ministry of Education. (1996). *Te Whāriki*. Wellington, New Zealand: Learning Media.

Ministry of Education. (2017). Te Whāriki. He Whāriki mātauranga mō ngā mokopuna o Aotearoa. *Early Childhood Curriculum*. Retrieved from https://www.education.govt.nz/assets/Documents/Early-Childhood/ELS-Te-Whariki-Early-Childhood-Curriculum-ENG-Web.pdf

Mitchell, L. (2002). *Differences between community owned and privately owned early childhood education and care centres: A review of evidence*. Wellington, New Zealand: Council for Educational Research. www.nzcer.org.nz

Mitchell, L. (2006). Why free early childhood education? A policy based on evidence and children's rights. *Itirearea, 1*(February), 1–5.

Mitchell, L., & Brooking, K. (2007). *First NZCER national survey of early childhood education services*. Retrieved from http://www.nzcer.org.nz/default.php?products_id=1858

Mitchell, L., & Cubey, P. (2003). *Characteristics of effective professional development linked to enhanced pedagogy and children's learning in early childhood settings. A best evidence synthesis*. Wellington, New Zealand: Ministry of Education.

Mitchell, L., & Davison, C. (2010). Early childhood education as sites for children's citizenship: Tensions, challenges and possibilities in New Zealand's policy framing. *International Journal of Equity and Innovation in Early Childhood, 8*(1), 12–23.

Mitchell, L., Meagher Lundberg, P., Mara, D., Cubey, P., & Whitford, M. (2011). *Locality-based evaluation of Pathways to the Future – Nga Huarahi Arataki. Integrated report 2004, 2006 and 2009*. Retrieved from http://www.educationcounts.govt.nz/publications/ece/locality-based-evaluation-of-pathways-to-the-future-ng-huarahi-arataki

Mitchell, L., Wylie, C., & Carr, M. (2008). *Outcomes of early childhood education: Literature review.* Report to the Ministry of Education. Retrieved from http://www.educationcounts.govt.nz/publications/ece/25158/48867

Moss, P. (2009). *There are alternatives! Markets and democratic experimentalism in early childhood education and care* (Working paper no 53). The Hague, The Netherlands: Bernard Van Leer Foundation and the Bertelsmann Stiftung.

Moss, P. (2012). Need markets be the only show in town? In E. LLoyd & H. Penn (Eds.), *Childcare markets. Can they deliver an equitable service?* Bristol, UK: The Policy Press.

Moss, P. (2013). Beyond the investment narrative. *Contemporary Issues in Early Childhood, 14*(4), 370–372.

Moss, P., Dahlberg, G., Grieshaber, S., Mantovani, S., May, H., Pence, A., et al. (2016). The organisation for economic cooperation and Development's international early learning study: Opening for debate and contestation. *Contemporary Issues in Early Childhood, 17*(3), 343–351.

Moss, P., & Petrie, P. (2002). *From children's services to children's spaces.* London: Routledge Falmer.

NZEI Te Riu Roa. (2017). About us. Retrieved November 10, 2017, from https://www.nzei.org.nz/NZEI/About-Us/Aboutus.aspx?About_Us=1

Ober, J. (2008). *Democracy and knowledge: Innovation and learning in classical Athens.* Princeton, NJ: Princeton University Press.

Oberhuemer, P. (2005). Conceptualising the early childhood pedagogue: Policy approaches and issues of professionalism. *European Early Childhood Education Research Journal, 13*(1), 5–16.

OECD. (2006). *Starting strong 11: Early childhood education and care.* Paris, France: Organisation for Economic Cooperation and Development.

OECD. (2017). *The international early learning and child well-being study – The study.* Retrieved from http://www.oecd.org/edu/school/the-international-early-learning-and-child-well-being-study-the-study.htm

Penn, H. (2012). Childcare markets. Do they work? In E. LLoyd & H. Penn (Eds.), *Childcare markets. Can they deliver an equitable service?* (pp. 18–42). Bristol, UK: Policy Press.

Penn, H. (2013). The business of childcare in Europe. *European Early Childhood Education Research Journal, 22*(4), 432–456. https://doi.org/10.1080/1350293X.2013.7883300.

United Nations. (1948). .Universal Declaration of Human Rights Retrieved from http://www.un.org/en/universal-declaration-human-rights/

Urban, M., Lazzari, A., Vandenbroeck, M., Peeters, J., & Van Laere, K. (2011). *Competence requirements in early childhood education and care.* Research documents. Retrieved from https://download.ei-ie.org/Docs/WebDepot/CoReResearchDocuments2011.pdf

Urban, M., Vandenbroeck, M., Lazzari, A., Van Laere, K., & Peeters, J. (2012). *Competence requirements in early childhood education and care.* Research documents. Retrieved from http://files.eric.ed.gov/fulltext/ED534599.pdf

Urban, M., Vandenbroeck, M., Van Laere, K., Lazzari, A., & Peeters, J. (2012). Towards competent systems in early childhood education and care. Implications for policy and practice. *European Journal of Education, 47*(4), 508–526.

Vandenbroeck, M., & Lazzari, A. (2014). Accessibility of early childhood education and care: The state of affairs. *European Early Childhood Education Research Journal, 22*(3), 327–335.

Glossary of Māori Terms

Aotearoa used as the Māori name for New Zealand
**A muri kia mau ki tēnā, kia mau ki te kawau mārō, whanake ake, whanake
ake** Forever hold fast to the spearhead flight formation of the kawau
Anga whakamua Moving learners forward
hapū sub-tribe
harakeke flax
iwi tribe
kaiako teacher/educator – conveys reciprocal nature of teaching
kaitiaki guardian, protector
kanohi ora incarnation of the ancestors
kaumatua a Māori elder
kaupapa principles
kotahitanga unity, solidarity
mātauranga what counts as knowledge
mana prestige, power
mana aotūroa exploration
mana Māori what it means to be Māori
mana atua spirituality, wellbeing
mana whenua belonging
mana tangata contribution
mana reo communication
Maniapoto an iwi based in Waikato-Waitomo region of New Zealand
Manuwhiri visitors
marae the complex of buildings or land associated with a pan-tribal group, whanau,
hapū or iwi
moana sea
ngā hononga relationships
Ngāti Mahuta a sub-tribe (hapū) of Tainui iwi
oranga wellbeing

Pākehā white New Zealander
powhiri a Māori welcome
Powhiri whakatau welcome ceremony
puna Māori immersion playgroup
tangata whenua people of the land
taonga tuku iho treasures from the past
taonga a highly prized object or possession; includes socially or culturally valued
    resources
tapu sacred, set apart, prohibited
te ao Māori the Māori world
Te Atiawa a Māori iwi based in Taranaki
oranga wellbeing
te reo Māori me ona tikanga Māori language and culture
te taiao the natural world/environment
te taura here tangata living link with yesterday and the bridge to tomorrow
te ukaipō the favoured, the special
te uri o Papa-tū-ā-nuku child belongs to the land
tūpuna ancestors, forebears
tūrangawaewae tribal links
whakakoranga what counts as pedagogy
whakamana empowerment
whakapapa lineage, genealogy, ancestry
wananga educational forum
whānau extended family
whanaungatanga relationships
whānau ora health and wellbeing of whānau
whānau tangata family and community
whāriki a woven mat

Name Index

A
Alcock, S., 92
Alderson, P., 50
Anderson, G., 118
Anderson, M., 101
Apple, M., 3, 11, 45–47, 58, 146
Arndt, S., 12, 131
Asen, G., 82
Avery-Nunez, C., 130, 152, 160

B
Barsotti, A., 82
Bateman, A., 96, 97
Bender, N, 48
Bennett, J., 156, 160, 161
Biesta, G., 55
Boag-Munroe, G., 5
Bolger, J., 114
Borman, K.M., 123
Brennan, D., 6, 46
Bronfenbrenner, U., 49
Brooking, K., 36, 155
Brostrom, S., 12, 70, 75
Bruner, J., 12, 76, 101
Burns, J., 116, 117

C
Callan, E., 123
Carr, M., 6, 20, 28, 29, 48, 49, 66, 68, 87–89,
    92–95, 98, 100, 101, 110, 126, 134,
    147, 159

Carr, W., 45, 53–55, 146
Cavanagh, T., 80
Cheung, M., 79
Clarkin-Phillips, J., 100, 101
Cleveland, G., 6, 47, 130, 152, 160
Cohen, B., 25
Colley, S., 130, 152, 160
Cowie, B., 6, 48, 49, 90, 91, 95, 96, 99, 100,
    102, 103
Cubey, P., 13, 125, 148
Cullen, J., 70, 71

D
Dahlberg, G., 4, 8, 45, 59, 82, 91–93, 133,
    137, 139, 157
Dalli, C., 25, 29
Danzig, A.B., 123
Davidson, E. J., 128
Davis, K., 6, 48, 49, 95, 98, 135
Davison, C., 5, 6, 22, 33, 34, 77, 113, 129, 152
Deaney, S., 139
Dencik, L., 7
De Vocht, L., 87
Dewey, J., 11, 45, 55–57, 133, 146, 148
Durie, M., 77
Dweck, C., 88, 94

E
Edwards, C., 73
Einarsdottir, J., 51
Evangelou, M., 5

© Springer Nature Singapore Pte Ltd. 2019
L. Mitchell, *Democratic Policies and Practices in Early Childhood Education*,
International Perspectives on Early Childhood Education and Development 24,
https://doi.org/10.1007/978-981-13-1793-4

F
Farrar, C., 52
Fielding, M., 2, 3, 92
Fisher, D., 116
Fleer, M., 68
Ford, V.E., 111
Forman, G., 73
Freire, P., 73

G
Gandini, L., 73
Garcia, D.R., 123
Gibbs, R., 135
Giddens, A., 8
Giroux, H., 11, 45, 56, 57, 92, 123, 126, 133,
   146, 147, 153
Glynn, 80
Goller, M., 48
Göthson, H., 82
Grout, P., 6
Gundara, J. S., 53

H
Haggerty, M., 92
Hammarberg, A., 95
Hanna, P., 32
Hartley, C., 99–101
Hartnett, A., 45, 54, 55
Hattie, J., 89
Heise, N., 48
Hennessey, R., 139
Hill, D., 22, 87
Hipkins, C., 37, 92, 157
Hocke, N., 48
Hodgen, E., 127
Hubbard, P.M., 111
Hughes, P., 56

J
Jack, T., 101
James, A., 4
Jay, E., 94
Jenks, C., 4
Jensen, A., 7

K
Kalavite, T., 34, 77, 129
Kara, H., 12, 34, 77, 129, 131
Karmenerac, O., 46

Keane, B., 26
Kelly, H., 122
Kelly, J., 136, 137
Kelsey, J., 30
Kemmis, S., 146
King, J., 127, 130
King, M., 19
Krashinsky, M., 6, 47, 130, 152, 160
Kress, G., 6, 139

L
Lange, D., 31, 113
Langsted, O., 76
Lansdown, G., 50
Lawy, R., 55
Lazzari, A., 147–149, 152, 153
Lees, J., 137, 138
Lee, W., 20, 26, 28, 39, 68, 93, 110
Leggett, E., 94
Liljestrand, J., 95
Lingard, B., 91
Lloyd, E., 3, 5, 47
Lord, H., 6

M
Macfarlane, A., 80
Macfarlane, A. H., 26
Mackey, G., 87
MacNaughton, G., 56
Mara, D., 13, 22, 125, 127, 150
Marshall, T.H., 54, 146
Mayall, B., 7
May Cook, H., 25
Mayer, S., 7
May, H., 18, 22–26, 28, 29, 39, 48, 58, 65, 66,
   69, 93, 110, 111, 117, 118, 132, 151,
   152, 156, 158
McDonald, D., 8
McDonald, G., 23, 24, 58, 120
McKenzie, R., 135
McNatty, W., 80
Meade, A., 24, 31, 109, 127, 132
Mead, H., 79, 81
Meagher-Lundberg, P., 12, 13, 34, 77, 125,
   129, 131, 150
Metge, J., 79
Mitchell, L., 5, 6, 12, 13, 20, 22, 27, 32–34,
   36, 48, 49, 57, 59, 68, 71, 72, 77, 80,
   81, 87–91, 93, 96, 97, 99–103,
   109–111, 125–129, 131–133, 137, 147,
   148, 150–152, 155, 158, 159

Moll, L., 76
Moss, P., 2–4, 8, 12, 25, 31, 38, 45, 48, 50, 51,
    57, 59, 82, 87, 91–93, 133, 137, 146,
    157, 159

N
Neuman, M. J., 13, 49, 125
Noble, K., 5
Noially, J., 6
Noonan, R., 60, 128, 129
Nusche, D., 90, 100, 101
Nuttall, J., 81

O
Ober, J., 51, 52, 110, 120, 146
Oberhuemer, P., 9, 13, 125, 148, 162

P
Peeters, J., 147, 149
Pence, A., 4, 8, 45, 59, 82, 92, 133, 157
Penetito, W., 67, 68, 78, 82
Penn, H., 3, 5, 6, 39, 45, 46, 59, 146
Pere, R., 79
Perkins, D. N., 94
Peter, M., 22
Peters, S., 100
Petrie, P., 4, 12, 25, 31, 38, 45, 57, 82, 146
Pickett, K., 8, 30, 31
Podmore, V., 24, 29, 93
Poskit, J., 135
Press, F., 5, 6, 46
Prout, A., 4, 7, 8, 12, 45, 57, 134

R
Raaflaub, K., 51, 52
Rameka, L., 48, 87, 103, 104, 159
Randall, J., 35
Rau, C., 71
Reedy, T., 22, 66, 67, 79, 81, 83
Reid, R., 22
Renwick, W., 58
Resink, C., 101
Rigby, E., 49
Rinaldi, C., 92
Ritchie, J., 71
Roa, T., 80
Robertson, J., 129
Robinson, V., 134
Rogers, P., 99, 100
Royal-Tangaere, A., 22, 23, 27, 127
Rush, E., 6

S
Saporiti, A., 7
Schreyer, I., 13, 125
Shipley, J., 115, 116
Simonsen, Y., 138, 139
Siraj-Blatchford, I., 89, 94, 97
Smith, A.B., 4, 22, 24, 49, 111
Smith, J., 99, 100
Sosinsky, L., 6
Soutar, B., 20, 68, 72, 73, 93, 110
Stobart, G., 88, 91, 100
Stover, S., 20, 22
Sumsion, J., 6, 46
Swadener, B.B., 87

T
Tarrant, K., 49
Te One, S., 29, 110
Thrupp, M., 90, 91
Timperley, H., 134
Tisdall, K., 50
Tishman, S., 94
Tolley, A., 130

U
Urban, M., 87, 147–150, 153, 154

V
Vandenbroeck, M., 147–149, 152, 153
Van Laere, K., 147, 149
Van Wijk, N., 103
Visser, S., 6

W
Wagner, P., 48
Wallace, J., 25
Wells, C., 13, 32, 109, 115, 120
White, E.J., 111, 136, 137
White, M., 90, 91
Whitford, M., 13, 125, 150
Wikinson, R., 8, 30, 31
Wilson, M., 20
Wilson-Tukaki, A., 98
Woodhams, M., 20
Woodrow, C., 5, 6, 46
Wylie, C., 22, 31, 113, 126,
    127, 147

Z
Zigler, E., 6

Subject Index

A

Access, 2, 4, 6, 8, 9, 17, 19, 30, 32–34, 39, 47, 50, 57, 59, 60, 66–68, 73, 77, 103, 104, 117, 119–121, 126–131, 140, 146, 151–153, 158, 160, 161

Accountability, 1, 6, 19, 26, 31, 34, 39, 90, 91, 96, 122, 154, 161

Advocacy, 2, 3, 12, 17, 18, 20, 23–28, 31, 33, 39, 53, 91, 120, 156, 163

Affordability, 33, 127, 130, 131, 151, 152, 160

Agency, 1, 4, 49, 57, 60, 65, 66, 76, 81, 92, 93, 100, 120, 123, 126, 147, 152

Amalgamations, 10, 25, 110

Aspiration, 4, 5, 13, 58, 60, 65, 67, 68, 71, 73, 80, 82, 89, 96, 100, 127, 134, 146, 147, 151, 155, 159

Assessment, 3, 6, 9, 11, 12, 18, 19, 29, 37, 39, 48, 49, 73, 74, 88–104, 126, 131, 132, 136, 148, 153, 159, 162

B

Bicultural, 1, 10, 19, 20, 28, 30, 39, 65, 66, 71, 72, 83, 93, 96, 103, 147, 151

Bulk funding, 31, 113, 114

C

Childcare, 5, 9, 10, 12, 18, 21, 23–25, 32, 46, 47, 59, 65, 111, 114, 117–119, 122, 129, 130, 152, 155

Childhood as socially constructed, 1, 4

Child poverty, 7, 37, 156, 157

Children as citizens, 2, 4, 5, 49, 50, 69, 71, 81, 146, 156

Choice, 2, 5, 18, 28, 30, 36, 38, 47, 48, 101, 120, 129, 140

Citizenry, 12, 49, 52, 54, 55, 58

Citizenry rights, 12, 49, 58

Citizenship, 2, 4, 20, 51–56, 77, 89, 92, 134, 146

Collective, 2, 4, 11–13, 19, 23–25, 30, 33, 39, 46, 47, 52, 53, 56, 57, 76, 77, 79, 81, 82, 92, 95, 110–123, 133, 137, 146, 147, 149, 150, 156, 163

Collective bargaining, 30, 112, 118

Collective deliberations, 47

Collective vision, 52

Colonization, 20, 22

Combined Early Childhood Union of Aotearoa (CECUA), 65, 110, 112–114

Community-based, 5, 29, 35, 36, 98, 114, 129, 152, 154, 155, 158, 160

Competition, 1, 3–6, 8, 30

Conditions of employment, 13, 25, 31, 32, 125

Consultation, 13, 24, 25, 29, 32, 39, 52, 65, 66, 82, 110, 120–122, 127

Contexts for childhood, 3, 25, 99, 100

Corporate businesses, 5, 131

Critical, 2, 3, 10, 11, 13, 23, 34, 35, 45, 54, 57, 60, 70, 71, 75, 81, 91, 95, 104, 123, 133–140, 146, 148, 153, 159, 161, 162

Critical thinkers, 133–140, 162

Criticism, 11, 35, 45, 57

Curriculum, 1, 3, 4, 9–12, 18–20, 22, 25, 28–30, 38, 39, 48, 49, 54, 65–83, 88, 90–96, 98, 101, 102, 110, 126, 132, 134, 136–138, 140, 147, 148, 150, 151, 153, 154, 159, 162

© Springer Nature Singapore Pte Ltd. 2019
L. Mitchell, *Democratic Policies and Practices in Early Childhood Education*,
International Perspectives on Early Childhood Education and Development 24,
https://doi.org/10.1007/978-981-13-1793-4

D

Democracy, 1, 2, 4, 9, 11, 12, 19, 20, 28–30, 46–60, 67, 70, 76, 81–83, 92–95, 103, 110, 112, 120–122, 126, 145–148, 154, 158

Democratic, 1–3, 5, 7, 9–13, 18–20, 25, 30, 33, 37, 48, 49, 51–60, 66–68, 70–72, 76, 77, 81–83, 88, 89, 92–94, 98, 101–104, 110, 112, 125–140, 147–151, 154–163

Democratic education, 1, 12, 57, 87, 104, 145

Democratic institutions, 52, 110, 150, 155

Democratic participation, 12, 13, 18, 19, 25, 30, 33, 55, 57, 58, 66, 70, 125–140, 148, 150, 160, 161

Democratic practice and policy, 7, 9, 55

Deregulated labour market, 30, 111, 112

Disadvantage, 2, 23, 27, 117, 157

Diversity, 4, 8, 19, 21–23, 28, 29, 48, 52, 53, 56, 66, 71, 121, 137, 162

E

Early Childhood Workers Union (ECWU), 25, 111, 112, 114

ECEC as a public good, 2, 18, 33

Economic theory, 30, 31

Education and care centres, 21, 25, 32, 36, 98, 111–114, 117–119, 128, 135, 151, 162

Employment Contracts Act, 30, 32, 112, 117, 118

Empowerment, 1, 20, 57, 68–70, 72, 83, 93, 98, 131–134, 140, 147, 159, 160

Entitlement to a free place, 131

Entitlement to a place, 131, 161

Equal employment opportunities, 111

Equal pay, 37, 111, 112, 163

Equity, 25, 28, 30, 31, 35, 47, 52, 103, 109, 110, 112, 115–117, 119, 129, 156, 157

F

Family and community, 59, 68, 96, 101–104, 115, 134, 147, 160

Fees, 36, 46, 113, 129–131, 151, 154, 155, 161

Feminist, 20, 23

For-profit, 3, 5, 6, 9, 31, 36, 38, 47, 59, 117, 118, 146, 151, 152, 154, 155, 157, 161

Free early childhood education, 58, 59, 127, 131, 158

Free ECEC, 131, 140, 151, 161

Funding, 3, 5, 9, 10, 21, 22, 24–26, 31–37, 46, 47, 59, 77, 113–116, 119–121, 127, 129–132, 136, 140, 149, 151, 152, 154, 155, 158–161

Future Directions:Early childhood Education in New Zealand, 13, 33

G

Globalization, 3, 7–9, 47, 89

Good faith bargaining, 30, 118

H

Holistic, 39, 47, 59, 67, 68, 70, 90, 93, 121, 134, 140, 147, 159, 160

Holistic development, 68, 134, 140, 147, 160

I

Income inequality, 7

Indigenous rights, 26–28, 77, 82

Inequalities, 7, 8, 25, 30, 31, 48, 57, 130, 152

Integrate, 9, 23, 50

Integrations, 9, 10, 20, 23–26, 35, 38, 111

Intercultural, 53, 60

J

Job evaluation, 115, 116

K

Kindergartens, 10, 12, 18, 21, 23–25, 32, 66, 71–76, 81, 83, 96, 97, 99–102, 109–119, 128, 134, 137–139, 149, 153, 162

Kindergarten Teachers Association, 25, 114

Kōhanga reo, 20, 22, 23, 26–29, 39, 128, 132

L

Labour force participation, 2, 5

Learning dispositions, 6, 12, 87, 94, 126
Learning outcomes, 6, 7, 12, 48, 69, 70, 87,
    94, 157

M
Marketization, 1–4, 6–9, 11, 13, 21, 47,
    89, 146
Mixed market economy, 3, 5–7

N
Neoliberal, 1, 2, 46, 47, 57, 60, 146
Neoliberal ideology, 46, 57, 60
New right economic theories, 18, 25,
    30–32, 38

O
Outcomes, 2, 3, 6–8, 12, 18, 19, 34, 38, 39,
    46–49, 69, 70, 81, 88–91, 94–97, 120,
    126, 128, 132, 135, 147, 148, 157, 162

P
Pacific early childhood groups, 22, 128
Parent-/whānau-led services, 21, 22, 26
Participation, 2, 4–6, 12, 13, 18–20, 23–28,
    30, 32–35, 39, 48–55, 57–59, 66, 68,
    70, 71, 77, 82, 89, 93, 99, 100,
    102–104, 110, 123, 125–140, 146, 148,
    150–152, 154, 158, 160, 161
Participatory decision-making, 54, 109, 110,
    149, 154, 158, 161
Participatory democracy, 112, 121
Pay, 1, 10, 12, 13, 21, 26, 32, 33, 36, 37, 39,
    109, 111–115, 117–120, 125, 129, 133,
    149, 151, 153, 156, 157, 162, 163
Pay parity, 10, 12, 109, 111–115, 117–120,
    149, 151, 153, 157, 162, 163
Pedagogical documentation, 12, 37, 50, 71,
    81, 88–104, 133, 134, 139, 148
Pedagogical practice, 2, 3, 49, 71, 73, 92, 128,
    133, 134, 153
Pedagogy, 3, 5, 11–13, 18, 25, 39, 46, 48–50,
    53, 54, 67, 72, 73, 87, 93, 125, 126,
    133, 136–138, 148, 159, 162
Planned approach to provision, 38
Playcentres, 10, 20, 22–25, 102, 103, 128, 132

Playgroups, 22, 77, 80
Policy, 1–3, 5, 7–13, 18–39, 45, 47, 49, 53, 55,
    57, 59, 66, 67, 77, 80, 87, 89, 90, 92,
    93, 95, 102, 104, 110–123, 125–140,
    145–158, 161–163
Political, 1–3, 10, 17, 18, 20, 24, 26, 34, 47,
    48, 50–55, 57, 58, 79, 82, 91, 110, 112,
    116, 122, 132, 146, 156
Political advocacy, 2
Poverty, 7, 8, 17, 19, 30, 35, 37, 120, 146,
    156, 157
Private owners, 1, 32, 114, 118, 119, 155, 161
Professional development, 13, 33, 71, 81, 93,
    125, 131, 136, 140, 148, 150, 151,
    153, 162
Profits, 1, 6, 21, 31, 32, 36, 45–47, 59, 114,
    118, 119, 131, 151, 154, 155,
    160, 161
Public education, 13, 17, 37, 58, 140, 154, 157
Public good, 2, 11, 17, 18, 33, 45, 58, 123, 150
Public institutions, 2, 45, 58, 150
Purpose of education, 46, 56, 71, 154
Purposes of ECEC, 1, 2, 18

Q
Qualification levels, 13, 125, 150, 151
Qualifications, 3, 10, 13, 21, 22, 26, 31, 33,
    111, 112, 115–117, 120, 125, 127, 132,
    140, 150, 151, 153, 162–163
Quality, 5, 6, 8, 9, 13, 19, 26, 27, 29, 30,
    32–34, 36, 38, 39, 46, 47, 49, 59, 69,
    88, 111, 120–122, 127, 128, 131–133,
    135, 136, 140, 148–153, 155, 158, 159,
    161, 162

R
Responsive and reciprocal relationships,
    69, 147, 159
Rights movements, 3, 11, 18, 19, 54, 56

S
Schoolification, 12, 87, 159
Self-determination, 22, 26–28, 54, 77, 82
Social interventionist, 39
Social justice, 1, 2, 8, 9, 17, 20, 28–30, 39, 56,
    59, 98, 103, 150, 156

Sociocultural theoretical frame, 65
Staff:child ratios, 31, 38
State responsibility, 113, 153
State sector, 32, 111–113, 115–117, 119, 162
Strategic Plan for ECE: Ngā Haurahi
    Arataki, 13

T

Targeting, 34, 120
Teacher-led services, 21–22, 33, 37,
    129–132, 150
Teachers as intellectuals, 126, 146
Te Kōhanga Reo National Trust, 27, 29, 65
Te reo Māori, 26, 27, 80
Te Tiriti o Waitangi, 10, 19, 20, 26, 27, 71,
    77, 158
Te Whāriki, 1, 4, 9, 11, 19, 20, 27–30, 32, 38,
    39, 49, 65–71, 73, 77, 79, 81, 83,
    92–95, 97, 98, 100, 102, 110, 131, 132,
    136, 137, 147, 151, 159,
    160, 162
Tikanga Māori, 20, 26, 27, 136

U

Unionism, 25
Unionists, 10, 12, 109, 120, 156
Unions, 3, 7, 10, 12, 13, 25, 30, 33, 65, 91,
    109–120, 122, 123, 149, 150, 156, 157,
    163
United Nations Convention on the Rights of
    the Child (UNCROC), 3, 4, 18, 24, 49,
    50, 60, 128, 161
United Nations Declaration on the Rights
    of Indigenous Peoples
    (UNDRIP), 77
Universal, 13, 17, 34, 38, 39, 50, 68, 120,
    129–131, 151–152, 163

V

Vulnerable child, 5, 34–36, 38, 39

W

Whakamana, 1, 68, 96, 159, 160
Working theories, 12, 69, 87, 94, 135, 148

Printed by Printforce, the Netherlands